MW01177959

Inland Shores

MĀNOA 10:2   UNIVERSITY OF HAWAI'I PRESS   HONOLULU

Inland Shores

Frank Stewart

EDITOR

Charlene Gilmore

FEATURE EDITOR

Editor   Frank Stewart

Managing Editor   Pat Matsueda

Associate Editor   Charlene Gilmore

Designer and Art Editor   Barbara Pope

Fiction Editor   Ian MacMillan

Poetry and Nonfiction Editor   Frank Stewart

Reviews Editor   Lisa Ottiger

Associate Fiction Editor   Susan Bates

Staff   Kathleen Matsueda, June McKemy, Ritu Nagpaul, Lisa Ottiger,
Ellen Repalda, Rob Schulz, Michelle Tyau, Phyllis Young

Corresponding Editors for North America
Fred Chappell, T. R. Hummer, Charles Johnson, Maxine Hong Kingston,
Michael Ondaatje, Alberto Ríos, Arthur Sze, Tobias Wolff; Robert Shapard,
Josip Novakovich (Writing in the Stepmother Tongue)

Corresponding Editors for Asia and the Pacific
CHINA   Howard Goldblatt, Ding Zuxin
INDONESIA   John H. McGlynn
JAPAN   Masao Miyoshi, Leza Lowitz
KOREA   Kim Uchang
NEW ZEALAND AND SOUTH PACIFIC   Vilsoni Hereniko
PACIFIC LATIN AMERICA   H. E. Francis
PHILIPPINES   Alfred A. Yuson
SOUTH ASIA   Wimal Dissanayake

Advisory Group   Esther K. Arinaga, William H. Hamilton, Joseph Kau, Glenn Man,
Cornelia N. Moore, Franklin S. Odo, Robert Shapard, Marjorie Sinclair

Founded in 1988 by Robert Shapard and Frank Stewart.

"Bragg Creek, Alberta" is reprinted with permission from *The Wheatgrass Mechanism* by Don
Gayton, copyright © 1990 by Don Gayton (ISBN 1–895618–09–6), published by Fifth House
Publishers of Calgary, Canada. "Where the Deer and Antelope Play" originally appeared in *Canadian Geographic* (March/April 1993) and is excerpted from *Leaning in the Wind* (HarperCollins,
1995). Copyright © 1995 by Sid Marty. Used with permission from HarperCollins Publishers Ltd.,
1995. "Whoopers" originally appeared in *Coming West: A Natural History of Home* by Kevin Van
Tighem, published by Altitude Publishing of Vancouver, Canada, and is reprinted by permission
of the author.

Mānoa is published twice a year. Subscriptions: U.S.A. and Canada—individuals $22 one year,
$40 two years; institutions $28 one year, $50 two years; single copy $15. Other countries—
individuals $25 one year, $45 two years; institutions $33 one year, $59 two years; single copy $17.
For air mail add $12 per year. We accept checks, money orders, VISA, or MasterCard, payable
to University of Hawai'i Press, 2840 Kolowalu Street, Honolulu, HI 96822, U.S.A. Claims for
issues not received will be honored until 180 days past the date of publication; thereafter,
the single-copy rate will be charged.

Manuscripts may be sent to *Mānoa*, English Department, University of Hawai'i, Honolulu, HI
96822. Please include self-addressed, stamped envelope for return of manuscript or for our reply.

www2.hawaii.edu/mjournal
www2.hawaii.edu/uhpress/journals/manoa/

CONTENTS

Special Focus   **Nature Writing from Western Canada**

Editor's Note

Inland Shores is the latest collection of Asian and Pacific writing compiled by the editors of *Mānoa*. Twice a year, *Mānoa* gathers new work from a country or region in Asia and the Pacific and presents it alongside contemporary work from the United States. Over the past ten years, these collections have introduced readers to the work of authors from the Russian Far East, Japan, Korea, China, Australia, New Zealand, Indonesia, Papua New Guinea, the Philippines, and the Pacific islands. We have also featured works from places in the eastern Pacific—Mexico, Colombia, Chile, and Peru. In that spirit of exploring both west and east, *Inland Shores* presents contemporary writing from Western Canada, particularly nature writing in several forms.

Some of the most dramatically beautiful landscapes in North America are found across the 1.1 million square miles that comprise the western Canadian provinces—British Columbia with its sea coast and spectacular mountain ranges; the wheatgrass plains and cattle ranges of Alberta and Saskatchewan; the wetlands of Manitoba. In his book *Landscapes of the Interior,* author and scientist Don Gayton, who is represented in this volume of *Mānoa,* recalls the Irish Canadian artist Paul Kane, who sketched the basalt landscapes of the Columbia River in 1847. "In his journals," Gayton says, "Kane talks of being careful not to dramatize the sketches in any way, for fear that he would be accused of fabricating fantastic landscapes to sell to a gullible European audience, eager for images of the wild Western Interior." Literary nature writing helps us see clearly those fierce and even fantastic territories of inner and outer landscape, the combination of which forms us as individuals and nations; and the best authors are careful not to exaggerate, but to tell stories that bring us to our senses—all of our senses —and bond us to the real.

The Western Canadian feature in this volume was guest-edited by Charlene Gilmore, a nature writer whose home is a small town in southern Alberta but who has been living in Honolulu. As she states in her overview essay, "Passages Home," the works she chose "are by no means a complete representation of Western Canada's literature," but they do present "some of the directions writers [in this region] are taking as they turn a careful eye to the places where they live." In essays, fiction, and poetry, these authors explore not only what it's like to be *on* the land, but also *of* the land: perhaps even more than their southern neighbors, Western Canadians struggle with issues of national identity, immigrant histories, displacement of Native peoples, and preservation of the natural landscape. While addressing such serious concerns, these authors also display a distinctive humor that sets Canadians apart: wry, self-effacing, laconic, sometimes off-beat. And finally the writing here communicates a sense of the importance of individual and communal memory—a concern of authors from many regions in the Pacific who are helping us to negotiate the critical territory between the end of this tumultuous millennium and the beginning of the next.

Among the most remarkable writings to address the importance of this kind of memory is "Revenge of the Pebble Town People," a reconstruction in poetic lines of an oral history told by a Haida warrior. The warrior's account of a Haida raid on the Tlingit of Canada's northwest coast was written down and published in 1905 by John R. Swanton, an American ethnographer. This reconstruction by Canadian poet and historian Charles Lillard transforms Swanton's rough rendering into an epic of Homeric intensity. Lillard sent "Revenge of the Pebble Town People" to *Mānoa* in 1996, the year before he died. The poem was subsequently published in "Native Peoples and Colonialism," a double issue of the journal *BC Studies,* and is reprinted here with the permission of Lillard's wife, the poet Rhonda Batchelor.

Another group of authors concerned with memory is featured in a section we call "Brief Lives." These writings include a sketch from the unpublished memoirs of the distinguished biographer Leon Edel. Raised in rural Saskatchewan in the 1920s, Edel became one of the century's preeminent men of letters. Before he died in Honolulu in September 1997 four days short of his ninetieth birthday, his wife, the author Marjorie Sinclair, wrote a birthday poem for him. As a memoir and tribute, that work is also here. Other works in "Brief Lives" include recollections of an Irish family funeral in New York by M. G. Stephens; of growing up in a Cuban family in Florida by Virgil Suarez; of marriage and friendship by Kimiko Hahn; of a Tibetan monastery by Colleen Morton; and of a family's prized possessions during tremendous social upheaval in the People's Republic of China by Gao Da.

We are also pleased to present "A Usable Past," an interview in which fiction writer Bharati Mukherjee talks with Shefali Desai and Tony Barnstone about growing up in India, living in Canada and the United States, and portraying in her work the lives of women in transition between cultures.

Other prose in *Inland Shores* includes a story by Korean Russian novelist Anatoly Kim (whose work was first published in *Mānoa* in 1994) about a family devastated by a curse; a haunting essay on the Nicaraguan lionbird by Dorie Bargmann; and an essay by Ken Lamberton on the redemptive power of a flock of swallows for a man serving time in an Arizona prison. Poetry in this volume includes work by American poet Carol Moldaw and new translations of Japanese poet Ayukawa Nobuo, whose resistance to World War II made him the conscience of his generation. These translations come to us from Leza Lowitz and Shogo Oketani, who received a National Endowment for the Arts translation fellowship to work on Ayukawa's poetry.

The art in *Inland Shores* gives yet another perspective on Western Canada and on memory. The cover art is by Native artist Joe Peters Jr. "The painting on this drum represents part of the story of the Undersea World," Peters said of this work. "Tahkwa, the Octopus, is the collector of food, and Me-kwat, the Sea Lion, protects Komogwey's house. During our ceremonies, the sound of the drum brought us the heartbeat of mother nature. Our drums were traditionally carved from the red cedar tree into the shape of the sea lion. My grandmother, Lydia Peters, told me that our ancient words and songs came from the sounds of the sea lion."

The interior art is by John Webber, who accompanied Captain James Cook on the voyage of discovery that included a landing in British Columbia in 1778. Webber made hundreds of drawings, sketches, and watercolors, many of them of the Native peoples that the European explorers met. The engravings here, originally reproduced from Webber's drawings to illustrate the 1784 published account of Cook's voyage, render some of the animals and objects that he encountered, but more important, they portray some of the faces he saw. They are as close as we can come to looking into the eyes of Canada's coastal aboriginal people at the moment of early European contact.

Inland Shores is the second of two issues that mark *Mānoa*'s tenth anniversary. We have many people to thank for making this decade possible, including the eight hundred authors, translators, and artists from around the world who have appeared in our pages; our readers and subscribers, who live in every state and in thirty-four foreign countries; the grant agencies and institutions who have had faith in us; and the staff members who have put their hearts into their work. We'd especially like to thank Wayne Levin, one of the many artists who have given our pages a dignity and beauty that words alone cannot achieve. Levin's stunning underwater photography appeared in our inaugural issue and two subsequent ones and has been representative of the goals of *Mānoa* as a project, because it allows us to experience more than one world at a time. This year, Levin published his first book of photographs, *Through a Liquid Mirror* (Honolulu: Editions Limited), with text by Thomas Farber. Our congratulations to Wayne Levin, our thanks to him for his inspiration, and our aloha to all who have helped make *Mānoa* a reality.

The Day Mr. Kaahunui Rebuilt
My Old Man's Fence

Every time it rains, I think about the place.

Overlooking my backyard there was a house—much larger than mine —with dirty white walls and a green roof with peeling tarp. The plumbing hummed loudly in the middle of the night, and the screens were torn, as if by large, angry cats. When planes flew over the house, the chipped paint fell to the ground and collected in the patches of mondo grass that sprouted through the cracks in the concrete driveway. If you had seen the house, you might have told yourself that it looked a little run down but was a steal anyhow at sixty dollars a month. But let me tell you, bad things—terrible things—happened in it. My grandmother kept asking us how we could live next door to an evil, unhappy house like that. She wanted us to move to Liliha, near the bakery, and live with her.

Many years ago on a winter day near Christmas, Dad started building a fence between that house and ours. I had just turned seven. Three days later, Dad got a call from the merchant marine, and the next thing I knew, he was packing his bags and leaving on an evening plane for Singapore. I never saw him again. He left Mom, my older brother, Kirk, and me out in the cold, scrounging for rent money. Mom worked twelve-hour days at minimum wage just to put food on the table. The unfinished fence grew soft and moldy, an eyesore that no one had time to finish up or take down. But Mom seemed to want it there. I guess she thought that as long as the fence was there, it was like Dad was home. Or coming home.

Bad things kept happening in the house in back, but a funny thing happened as I grew older. It was like I got numb—immune—to the questions from the ladies in the grocery lines, the visits from the priests, the newspaper write-ups, the people moving in and then quickly moving out. Even the damned violence. This is not a ghost story. But I gotta tell you. It was only after living next to the house for almost twenty years that I finally learned my lesson. It was a bad place, just like the old ladies said—an evil place.

Mr. Kaahunui had no telephone, so I caught the number one bus to his place in Kaimuki. I hadn't seen him in years. Everyone on the bus seemed to be reading the newspaper. Kelly's picture, the one she had taken for her high-school graduation, was on the front page. Mr. Kaahunui lived above Pak's Groceries, where children were eating shave ice and ice cream and sitting on stained wooden benches when I arrived. I knocked on the screen door of his apartment, and Mr. Kaahunui pulled back a thin white curtain and unlatched the door.

A big man, about six-four and maybe three hundred pounds, Mr. Kaahunui looked bigger in person than in the pictures I had seen of him in Dad's programs and magazines. Mr. Kaahunui used to be a professional wrestler. He and my old man went back a long way. He was the best man at Dad's wedding. Mr. Kaahunui was nearly bald now and shaved his head very close to the scalp. Dad had said he was blind in one eye. One ear was almost closed with cauliflower, and there were triangular scars on his cheeks and forehead. Those came from the screwdrivers and broken-necked beer bottles that wrestlers used to hide in their trunks and boots. Dad was always talking about a match Mr. Kaahunui had in the Civic Auditorium with a guy named the Hollywood Sheikh or something. They were locked in an enormous steel cage, and a chain bound one of Mr. Kaahunui's wrists to one of the Sheikh's. Dad said that there was blood all over the place and that Mr. Kaahunui won when he grabbed the Sheikh by the hair and began rubbing his face back and forth, back and forth against the iron bars of the cage. Dad said the Sheikh's nose was hanging from his face like tinsel from a Christmas tree.

"Long time no see," said Mr. Kaahunui. "Whoo, you big boy now." His voice was soft and very hoarse. A wrestler named Mad Man Kobayashi broke his windpipe by jumping off the top rope of the ring and landing with his knee on Mr. Kaahunui's throat.

"You looking like yoah old man now," he said as I walked in. There was a smell of burnt cooking oil. "Foah a second deah, I thought was yoah daddy standing outside."

I was a bit flattered because from what I remembered, my old man was a pretty good-looking guy.

Mr. Kaahunui sat down at the kitchen table and fed the Siamese fighting fish he kept in an old jelly jar. I told him I hoped I wasn't bothering him, and he said no, no, he always welcomed guests. We talked for a while, mostly about my dad, and then I asked him if he'd help me finish Dad's fence. He looked at me funny and glanced through the television guide, then shrugged and accompanied me home.

When we got to my house, Mr. Kaahunui looked at the fence and shook his head. The fence—speckled with brown gecko crap the size of rice grains—was crooked and covered with brittle patches of lichen. He ran his thick fingers over the wood, and it splintered under his touch, like rust on the sides of an old automobile.

"How long dis buggah been here?" he asked.

"Ten years, come Christmas."

Mr. Kaahunui let out a whistle and smiled, dimples in his cheeks as big as cherries. "Ten years, ah?" Dad always called Mr. Kaahunui "Smiley" because Mr. Kaahunui was always smiling and had the nicest, straightest white teeth. "Seem like only yesterday yoah old man and me was shooting pool and raising hell down on Hotel Street."

"Dad started dis fence when I was seven years old," I said. "Da year he went away . . ."

"Jeez, da last time I seen you, you was dragging one blanket around with you every place you went. Like da kid in da comics—what da buggah's name?"

"Linus."

"Deah you go. Das it. Linus. Eh, you big boy now. How many years school you get left?"

"Me, I one senior now."

Mr. Kaahunui grabbed the top of the fence and shook it. The ground beneath the fence caked and gave under the movement. "Gotta tear da whole ting down and start all over again," he said, shaking his head.

"But we can finish 'em, right?" I said. "You and me?"

"Oh yeah. Too bad yoah father no stay around, though. He was one damn good carpenter. Me, all I know how foah do is eat and sleep."

"And wrassle."

"No, no. Mr. Kaahunui forget how wrassle."

"Screw."

"Mr. Kaahunui forget dat, too." He smiled, and I wondered how a guy who used to fight in iron cages could have such straight, white teeth. "Yes suh, too bad yoah pop no stay. Singapore, hell. He could rebuild dis fence in one day. I don't know how fix stuff. Only know how break. Brokanic."

"Make da fence high. I no evah like see da damn house again."

Mr. Kaahunui squinted at the sky. "As long as no rain."

"We gotta build da fence," I said, also looking up at the sky. Thick, dark clouds covered the sun, making it look like a dust ball. "Dat house is no good."

"Always I heard stuffs about dis place," said Mr. Kaahunui. "But you know me, I no believe nothing. Not unless I see 'em." He took out a crushed pack of Kools from his back pocket and lit a cigarette. He started to cough, sounding like an old man with bad lungs.

"I finally learned mah lesson," I said.

"No worry," Mr. Kaahunui said, smiling. "We get da job done . . ."

"Mr. Kaahunui," I said after a while, "I should have told Kelly."

"Wha?"

"Long time ago, I killed one guy in deah." I said it real quick and real quiet.

"Huh?" said Mr. Kaahunui, smiling. "No mumble, pal. Us old men, we no hear too good. Whatchoo said?"

"Nothing," I said, relieved. "Nothing."

I remember the day Dad started the fence. We collected all the wood he had lying around the yard and underneath the house.

"Are we gonna make da fence high?" I asked. "Like at Honolulu Stadium?"

"Not dat high, boy."

"What da fence foah, Dad?"

"Keep da stray cats out of da yard."

"Kirk says dat house is no good. Is da house haunted like Kirk says?"

"Whatchoo going be, kid, when you grow up? One professah?"

"Somebody wen go die in deah?"

Dad smiled and rubbed his fingers on his chin. "It's yoah mom. She no like da house. She all da time complaining dat when she do da laundry and she gotta look at da place, she get all nervous. It's either build da fence or move da laundry lines." The lines swayed over my head, and the shadows scratched the yard, marking mango trees and ceramic pots and fertilizer bags.

"Do you hate da house, Dad?"

"House is house. How can you hate one house?"

Mr. Kamitaki walked up the driveway carrying a mop and bucket. He was the owner of the house, an old Japanese man who stooped over when he walked and who filled the air with the smell of Wildroot hair cream. He smiled at me and I smiled back, and Dad asked about his fishing and Mr. Kamitaki said the ulua were biting like hell past Portlock. Then he took a key from his pocket and opened the screen door of the house. It was the only time I would ever see the inside of the place. Everything was still. There were just the wall and the hardwood floors. The house was empty.

"How come people always move out of yoah house, Mr. Kamitaki?" I asked.

He smiled and ran his hand through his hair, which was dark but had long streaks of gray curling like corkscrews across the top.

"I don't know, boy," he said. "People always moving . . ."

"Maybe get ghosts," I said. "Mah brother, Kirk, says people die in yoah house—"

"Boy!" said Dad sternly. "Shut up awready. Let Mr. Kamitaki do his work."

"Kirk said da house get ghosts dat make da walls bleed."

"No," said Mr. Kamitaki, smiling. "No moah ghosts." He put his hand on my head. "If I thought people could get hurt in mah house, I would burn dis baby down with mah own two hands." He snapped his fingers. "Just like dat."

"No moah ghosts?" I said.

"No moah ghosts, boy," he said. "Only get cockroach."

Dad laughed. Mr. Kamitaki walked into the house, and I could hear him laughing in the kitchen, complaining about the cockroaches.

There was an old man I used to see every day. He had a dark face and white hair coming down to his shoulders, and he slept under overpasses and coconut trees, or stood alongside traffic lights and watched the signals change. He wore either a baggy gray shirt or a black polyester aloha shirt. On hot days, if he wore the polyester shirt, you could smell him a block away. No one knew his name or where he came from, but he waved every time he saw me.

One day, the old man was sitting on the steps of my house. I was in the seventh grade at Kalakaua Intermediate School and coming home from after-school practice with my Polynesian-music class. I played the vibes and acoustic bass. The corners of the old man's left eye were twitching, and a small vein pulsed through one thick, gray eyebrow. "Going rain tonight," he said.

I looked at the sky. It was clear.

"Tonight," he said. "Big rain."

"So?" I said.

"I sick." He coughed softly, then harder and harder, until he cleared his throat loudly and spit out a dark, hard ball of mucous and blood. It seemed to beat like a heart on the surface of the hot sidewalk. "Lemme sleep in yoah house," he said. "Just foah tonight. Till da rain pass."

"Ain't going rain tonight." I looked up at the clear sky once more.

"Please . . ." He began to cry. He fell on his knees and wrapped his arms around my legs. I could feel the stubble of his chin through my pants. "Da rain going kill me, boy . . ."

"Ain't going rain, old man."

It rained hard that night, but I forgot about the old man. I sat in bed reading a Batman comic book and listening to the rain pound the corrugated metal over the garage. Kirk had invited over some of his friends on the football team, and they sat on the lanai drinking wine and blasting Hawaiian music on their portable radio. I got out of bed and went outside.

The four of them wore long-sleeved sweatshirts and shorts and sat around a hibachi. The charcoal was still hot, and now and then, when the wind blew, it burned a dull orange. One of the boys, Jeff, sat on a big plastic cooler and played his guitar, trying to keep up with the Sunday Manoa.

"So I was in da back seat with Leesa," said another guy. Ben was a defensive back. "And I wen tell her . . ."

"Eh!" said Jeff, smiling and winking at me. "Da kid! Give da man a seat!"

"So what about dis Leesa?" said Kirk.

"Nah, not in front da kid, brah," said Ben. "X-rated. No one undah eighteen admitted . . ."

Kirk pulled up an old Wesson oil can for me to sit on. Jeff was still trying to play along with the Sunday Manoa. The others had a large, three-dollar bottle of Burgundy. With the rain falling hard around us, the fire from the hibachi felt nice. The breeze began to pick up, so you could smell the acidic, faintly sweet smell of the insecticide from the house next door. The house was covered with a large, yellowish-brown plastic tent and a red sign with a skull and crossbones that read DANGER! POISON GAS. When the wind blew through the tent, it made a whipping sound. The rain made a *tap-tap-tap* noise against Dad's fence.

I fell asleep, and when I woke to the rain on my face, I thought Kirk or one of his friends was spilling wine on me or taking a leak on me or something. But Kirk and his friends were asleep on the floor of the lanai. It was morning, and the sparrows and mynah birds chirped loudly in the mango trees. The men from the exterminator company were removing the clothespins that held together the tent over the house next door. The smell of the insecticide was heavy in the air.

I was rinsing my face in the basin where Mom does the laundry when I heard the ambulance's tires crush the gravel in the driveway. There was no siren or flashing light. The two men in white did not hurry as they took out a stretcher. The ambulance driver asked the men removing the tent if it was all right to go into the house, and one of the men on the roof said yes. Kirk and his friends woke up. The dew on the mondo grass sparkled in the morning sun like diamonds.

The men in white came out of the house quickly. A white sheet covered the body on the stretcher.

"What da hell happened?" asked Kirk.

"Guy must've snuck inside last night," said the ambulance driver, shaking his head. "Clothes all wet. Nevah like get caught in da rain, I guess."

"No can read, or what?" said one of the exterminator guys as he took down the red warning sign.

"Happened befoah," said the ambulance driver, shrugging and spitting on the driveway just below Dad's fence. "Going happen again."

Mr. Kamitaki stood in the middle of a small crowd that had gathered. He pinched the skin between his eyes with his thumb and forefinger. The ambulance driver said something to him, then helped put the stretcher into the ambulance. Mr. Kamitaki looked at the house for a very long time. Then he closed his eyes, looked at the ground, and shook his head. His mouth was moving, as if he was trying to say something.

I stood with cold water running down my face. My knees were shaking, and I could hardly stand on my feet. I heard the old man's voice in my head, asking me if he could stay at our house for just that night. I had killed someone. Why the hell did it have to rain?

I heard Kirk call the house a bastard.

As we began pulling out the planks from Dad's old fence, Mr. Kaahunui said that he wasn't as young as he used to be. He used the back of the hammer to tear out the nails. Then he grabbed the old wood with both hands and yanked it out of the soil. Sweat spilled down his head and fell on the ground. It felt strange seeing Dad's fence lying scattered on the ground after it had stood in the yard for ten years—now nothing more than a bunch of old, termite-eaten boards. Mr. Kaahunui was breathing heavily, the sound of the air coming out of his nostrils like whistling.

"So how's yoah mom doing?" he asked. "Still one waitress? How's her back? She was always complaining about her back. Pretty lady like dat. I always thought she should've been one actress. *Hawaii Five-O* or someting."

"Mr. Kaahunui," I said, "I gotta thank you foah coming ovah and helping me with da fence . . ."

"Forget it, boy," said Mr. Kaahunui.

I put all of the planks in a neat pile. Then I looked at the porch of the house next door, and something caught my eye. Right where Kelly used to keep her slippers, umbrella, and sneakers, someone had left a single long-stemmed rose.

"Old bastard like me," said Mr. Kaahunui, scratching a mosquito bite on the inside of his forearm, "nothing bettah foah do anyway . . ."

"No scratch yoah arm like dat," I said. "Bumbye da buggah bleed."

"Good bleed," said Mr. Kaahunui. "Den no itchy."

Neither of us said anything for a while. Mr. Kaahunui coughed and covered his mouth with a fist.

"Mr. Kaahunui," I said, "you seen dis morning's paper? Kelly's pitchah made da front page. You seen 'em?"

"I seen 'em," Mr. Kaahunui said. "Pretty girl."

"If dis house was a man," I said, "I'd cut his fricking throat."

"I don't know," said Mr. Kaahunui. "Maybe dey should come dig up da house. See what get undahneath. Maybe get some unsettled bones undah deah."

I picked up a block of wood the size of a brick and threw it hard at the house. It hit the wall with a thud, right near the front steps, and fell to the ground.

"Boy," said Mr. Kaahunui, putting his hand on my arm, "dat ain't going solve nothing."

"She was a good girl."

"Tings happen, boy. Nowadays, everyting happen so fast. In one day, tings can change—*boom!*—just like dat. Even to nice people, bad tings happen . . ."

"Why?"

"Cannot always ask why," he said. "You ain't always going find answers."

I shook my head and looked at the house.

"Dat Ahuna girl," Mr. Kaahunui asked softly, "she, uh, went yoah school, I hear?"

"Yeah."

"Close friends?"

"Pretty much."

Kelly Ahuna was the most beautiful girl in the world. What made her seem even more beautiful to me was the fact that she didn't know it. She lived with her grandmother in a small apartment near Punchbowl because her father was in jail and her mother had died of a heart attack. She worked in a small beauty salon in Nuuanu, near Foster Gardens and all the mortuaries. I met her in a home-economics class in high school. We had baked a chicken, but I didn't know how to cut it, so she cut it for me. We started going to the library and then to dinners and movies. She was a year older than I was, and she took me to her senior prom.

One summer afternoon we were sitting on a park bench at Kapiolani Park, watching children play soccer and adults fly kites with long tails, when Kelly opened her purse and showed me a letter. She had gotten into the University of Hawaii.

"Congratulations," I said.

Kelly's cheeks turned red, and she smiled and said, "And that's not all." She took out a folded piece of newspaper. It was the real-estate section of the Sunday classified ads. She showed me two house listings circled in red. One was in Kapahulu, near Leonard's Bakery, and going for a hundred and twenty dollars a month. The other was the house next door to mine.

"Take da Kapahulu house," I said. "It sounds like a bettah deal."

"Why?" she said, pretending to pout. "Don't you want me living next to you? That house has three bedrooms for sixty dollars a month."

I had a hard time explaining about the house. I didn't want to scare her, so I watered down the facts, and the stories wound up sounding funny. All they did was make her laugh and play with her hair and call me names.

"I'm telling you, Kelly," I said, "I can't let you near dat place."

"Don't be silly," she said. "Listen to yourself. You sound like a seven-year-old . . ."

"I just don't want to see you get hurt," I said. "Kelly, jeez, I care a hell of a lot about you. You don't want to live in deah."

"But don't you see," she said, her brown eyes sparkling, "it'll be great.

We could get two cans and connect them with string and talk to each other all night. Just like in the movies."

I had to smile.

"Befoah Dad left foah Singapore and all, he worked his ass off trying foah finish da fence in da backyard—you know da one." I shifted on the bench. "Bad tings happen in dat house. Evah since I can remembah. Evil tings."

"You're scaring me."

"Don't be scared," I said, putting my hand on her smooth arm.

"The landlord hasn't said there's anything wrong with the house."

That hit me like a rock. "Mr. Kamitaki?" It occurred to me that I hadn't seen the old man in years.

"Kamitaki?" she said. "The landlord is a guy named Nishioka."

The air was getting so thick that even in the shade of the mango tree it was hot. I opened Dad's old mayonnaise jar of nails. I handed the nails to Mr. Kaahunui, and he bit down on each one, putting some in his pocket and throwing some on the ground.

"What evah happened to yoah brothah, Kirk?" he said.

"Kirk, he move out. Long time ago. Living Waianae now. Truck driver. Married and everyting. Nice girl from Kauai. Kid and all."

"I no can pitchah Kirk as one daddy," said Mr. Kaahunui. "What, boy or girl?"

"Girl. Tiffany."

"Remembah how he used to hate girls?" Mr. Kaahunui laughed and shook his head. "Seem like only yestahday I was rolling around with dat boy on da grass, teaching him how foah wrassle." Mr. Kaahunui smiled and wiped his forehead with the back of his hand. "Kirk married, I'll be damned. Next ting I know, you going get married."

I tried to smile.

"What da hell is dat?" asked Mr. Kaahunui suddenly.

"What?"

In the shade of one of our large ti-leaf plants was a white object, like a large egg, only bigger. It was half-buried in the grass and dirt. Near it was a silver trail that slugs had left behind. I walked to the plant and started digging. I felt the dirt collecting under my fingernails, which I hadn't cut in a long time. The object turned out to be an old baseball. I scraped off the dirt that had caked on the ball. If I looked hard enough, I could still see the signatures of Dad's former teammates.

Dad used to be a professional baseball player. He played Triple-A ball with the Hawaii Islanders. Two or three times a week, Kirk and I would watch him practice or go to the games at the Honolulu Stadium in Moiliili and watch him pitch. One day Kirk brought our baseball to practice, and Dad asked all his teammates to sign it. The threads of the ball were coming off and the skin was brown with dirt and mud, so the players had to press down hard on the ball-point pens.

Kirk and I used to throw the ball in the backyard after school. He had an old third-baseman's glove, and I used Dad's pitcher's glove. Kirk threw the ball hard, so it landed in my glove with a loud *pop* that rang in my ears. I had to catch the ball or else it would land in my face. Dad said that once he was hit by a line drive and it took seventeen stitches to close the hole in his mouth.

One day, we were throwing the ball while Dad worked on the fence. I asked Kirk why Dad was building the fence. Dad was cutting boards over two sawhorses.

"Because da house no good," said Kirk. "Haunted." I looked at the house. Someone was drying clothes on the windowsill. The air smelled like strong detergent and dog crap. "Blood come out of da walls. Every time da cops gotta come and mop da place and wipe da windows. Blood. I seen 'em."

"Not!"

"Yes!"

He threw the ball at me, but I turned my wrist the wrong way and it hit my arm and rolled to a stop at the legs of one of the sawhorses. Dad picked up the ball and tossed it to me, underhand.

"Everybody who live in deah, dey die," Kirk said. "Da place was built on one graveyahd. Ass why da walls bleed . . ."

"Mr. Kamitaki said no moah ghosts. Only get cockroach."

"You calling me one liar?" Kirk stopped throwing the ball.

"No."

"You bettah not," he said, "else I kick yoah ass!" He whipped the ball at me, and it bounced off my glove and hit a part of the fence Dad had just put up.

"Eh!" Dad said in a low voice. "Knock it off."

"You live in deah," Kirk whispered to me, "you one dead man."

I looked at the house and at the plants Dad had pulled out to make room for the fence. I wondered if he'd finish before nightfall.

It wasn't until she had spent about three or four months in the house that Kelly started getting upset because I always had something else to do when she invited me over—the yard or the plumbing or maybe even something stupid like homework.

Kelly made a lot of friends in college. She was going to be a psychology major, she said, and maybe go into social work. Once or twice she invited her friends over for a yard party. I remember listening from my bedroom window to the carefree laughter and the Hawaiian music. Once in a while, I'd peek outside and see her walking around with a tray full of grinds and wearing a pink dress and a yellow hibiscus behind her ear. I could smell the charcoal on the barbecue and the fresh beer. The moon made everyone's skin look pale and silver.

One Saturday, we sat in a small restaurant downtown, near Fort Street Mall. Kelly was buying me lunch because I had gone with her to Kress to buy curtains. She'd fallen in love with these orange ones with tiny embroidered flowers. When she asked me to help her put the curtains up, I told her I was sorry but I couldn't.

"What's wrong with you?" she said suddenly. "You won't visit me, you didn't help me move my furniture in. What's wrong with you?"

"I can't go in dat house," I said. "I just can't. I'm sorry."

"Are you trying to tell me the house is haunted?"

"No," I said. "It ain't haunted, not with ghosts and stuff. It's just dat, jeez, bad tings happen in deah. People get hurt. It's an evil place."

"Look," said Kelly, "I've been in that house for, what, four months now, and nothing strange has happened."

"But see, Kel," I said, "das how da house works." Because she was a student at the university now and was always talking facts and logic and all that other B.S., I wasn't going to get into any arguments about how short a time four months was. "All I know is people get hurt in deah."

"Who? Who gets hurt? Do you know of anyone who ever got hurt in there?"

"Yeah," I said quietly. "I do."

"Who?"

"Kelly," I said, "deah's so many stories I could tell you. One night, one rainy night, dey put up one termite tent. Had dis old dude—"

"I don't know why you're trying to scare me," she said, biting the fingernail of her pinky. "Do you know what it's like living in a one-room apartment with your eighty-four-year-old grandma?"

"I know what you're—"

"There aren't even any roaches or termites in the house," she said. "But it could use some repainting. We could go to City Mill and buy some paints and, *ooh,* brushes and overalls—"

"How's da locks?" I said. "Old house like dat, people can just come in da middle of da night, when you sleeping, open da lock easy—"

"Stop it!" said Kelly. "Stop talking like this!"

Kelly put her face in her hands, real quick-like, and I watched the light glance off the gold bracelet I had given her for Valentine's Day. I waited for her to look up, but she didn't. I hoped that she wasn't crying, but I knew she was. The restaurant was dark and there were ferns hanging in plastic pots from the ceiling and I heard the rattle of dishes and the running of water from the kitchen. I didn't know what to say, so I was quiet for the rest of the afternoon.

With nails between his teeth, Mr. Kaahunui made a sucking sound with his mouth, like people trying to clean their teeth with a toothpick. He was on one knee measuring wood with a tape measure. In his back pocket was a hammer. He wiped his nose with the back of his hand. A dog barked somewhere in the distance. Mr. Kaahunui smiled, and I hoped that when I got to be his age, I'd have teeth that white.

"You and mah dad went back a long ways, ah?" I said.

"I used to go to da stadium watch him pitch. He came down to da arena to watch me wrassle. Yoah fathah was always asking me, 'Eh, real or what, wrasslin'? Ass real blood, or what?' I would be bleeding from mah forehead aftah some stupid bastard bang mah head open with one chair, or I would show him da bite marks on mah arm, but still yoah old man would be drinking Seagram's with me and asking, 'Ass not real, ah? Ass bull, ah?' Yoah old man. Always asking questions."

Mr. Kaahunui laughed and his eyebrows sagged. He stuck a large finger in his curled-up ear and looked at the sun. His face was a bit red. "Lemme show you someting," he said, lifting up a pants leg. His calf was discolored. "I still no moah feeling ovah heah aftah Killah Kamana came aftah me with one ironing board one night at da Civic. He went knock da referee out cold with one crescent wrench. Dey had to take da referee out of da ring with one stretchah. Killah Kamana, dat bastard. He stay on TV making tire commercials now."

I looked at the leg. Mr. Kaahunui closed his eyes and told me to tap it. I put down the baseball we had found under the ti-leaf plant and tapped his leg, but he didn't open his eyes. When I told him I had tapped it, he didn't believe me, so he told me to do it again.

"I was tinking about donating mah body to science when I die, but I no tink dey going take 'em." Mr. Kaahunui laughed to himself. "Das da price you gotta pay foah living one violent history, I guess . . ."

"Wha?"

"Ass what some reporter guy wrote about me in da newspaper. About mah, whatchoo call, wrasslin' career. Had one pitchah of me. Werewolf Collins was rubbing rock salt in mah eyes and deah was blood all ovah da place—wasn't a good pitchah of me—and undahneath, da caption said, 'A Violent History.'"

I looked at Mr. Kaahunui's triangular scars and his dimples. His left eye twitched every now and then, and when he stopped to rub it, the eyeball got very red. He patted his stomach, and his belly shook.

"Yes suh," he said, "das me. One violent history."

Mr. Kaahunui picked up the baseball and turned it around slowly, smiling. The old ball looked tiny in his hands.

"Yoah old man could pitch," said Mr. Kaahunui. "Da slider. Da fork ball. Da curve. Ninety-five-mile-an-hour fast ball." He let out a whistle.

"One night he struck out twenty-two batters. I thought foah sure he was going to da majors. Just nevah work out, though. So he joined da merchant marine. Pissed yoah mothah off."

"Yeah?"

"Oh yeah," said Mr. Kaahunui, picking at his teeth with his ring finger. He wore a large jade ring with a gold band. "She took it hard. But yoah fathah, he one hard-headed bastard. No can stay one place. Da most hard-headed bastard I evah know."

I looked at the house. A large, green horsefly buzzed around the burned-out porch light, and a warm breeze rustled the bright-orange curtains that Kelly and I had bought at Kress. They were still hanging there in her bedroom window as if nothing had happened.

"Wish I'd met Kelly," said Mr. Kaahunui quietly. "Sounds like one nice girl."

I tried to laugh. "She would have loved you. All dose wrestling stories."

"Let's finish yoah old man's fence," he said, smiling, "befoah da rain comes."

The Dallas Cowboys were playing the Minnesota Vikings. It was a Monday-night game, and the Cowboys were behind by two touchdowns. I was in the ninth grade and had a big test the next day. Kirk and several of his friends were sitting around, drinking Millers and nibbling on tako poke. One of the guys, Ricardo, had speared the octopus off Swanzy Beach, on the windward side of the island. This other dude, Jerome, was supposed to bring over some sashimi and the poker chips, but he hadn't shown up yet. He was always like that. I had ten bucks on the Cowboys.

"Five moah says Dallas scores heah," I said.

Ricardo laughed. "Shoots!"

Loud voices came from the house in the back. A deep man's voice was calling someone a dirty bitch, and the other voice, a lady's, was crying.

"Radical, ah, yoah neighbors?" said another guy, Major.

"Always like dat," said Kirk. I was a bit embarrassed.

"Dey always fighting . . ." I stopped. It was first-and-ten on the Viking fifteen.

"Wheah da hell is dat bastard Jerome?" Kirk asked. "How we going play poker without chips?"

I heard the sound of pots banging the walls and glass being smashed. Major laughed and turned up the volume on the set. We heard a slap and then loud crying. The man and the woman swore at each other. Then we heard a loud noise, a *pop,* like a firecracker or a car backfiring.

"You heard dat?" said Major. "Sounded like one gunshot . . ."

"No ways," said Kirk.

"Maybe ass Jerome's Bug," I said. "You know his scrap-heap car."

"I heard 'em, too," said Ricardo. "Sounded like came from da house in back. Da haunted house. Maybe we should check 'em out."

"Shut up and watch da game," said Kirk. It was first-and-goal at the five.

"Eh," said Major. "Dat sounded like one gun."

"Gun, mah ass."

"Fricking Jerome. He bettah show . . ."

A knock came at the door.

I looked at Kirk and Kirk looked at me, and then he looked at the floor and I got up and opened the door. My heart was beating fast. An old Hawaiian lady, her white hair hanging over her eyes, stood in the doorway. The moon bathed her in a silvery light. A few strands of hair were caught between her pale, cracked lips. She was crying, and mascara ran down her cheeks like black tears. She wore a string of pearls and an orange muu-muu. She looked as though she was ready to go out. I swear I didn't notice anything extraordinary until Ricardo stood up and said, "Oh, God!"

Kirk rose and turned on the porch light. The woman fixed her hair, making a thin, red mark on her forehead. She was barefoot, and her feet were covered with blood. She was trying to say something, but her mouth shook and she made no sound. I saw her red footprints on the ground. There was a loud wind, and the night was very cold. Slowly, she raised her hand into the light, and I saw the silver nail polish on her sharp fingernails. Her fingers were covered with blood. Clenched in her left hand was a black pistol.

The air has a funny smell just before it rains.

"Stop daydreaming and hand me dat board ovah by da plant," said Mr. Kaahunui.

I picked up the heavy board and passed it to him.

Mom never talked about Dad and neither did Kirk, but every now and then, Dad wrote a letter and we knew where he was by the name of the country on the stamp. We never wrote to him because his return address was always changing. Sometimes he didn't even write one on the envelope. I remember the last time I talked with him. It was the morning of the day he left—three days after he had started the fence. He was clean-shaven and had cut his hair. He was working on the fence.

"Whatchoo going do when you go away?" I asked. Dad knelt on one leg, making marks on the wood with chalk. The smell of the wood was very sweet.

"Go on a boat and see different places," he said. Dad had a tattoo of a snake on his right forearm. When he wiggled his fingers, the lines in his forearm danced and made the snake dance, too. When I grew up, I wanted a tattoo like Dad's.

"Dad? What's wrong with da house?"

"I suppose you ain't evah going quit until you get one answer," he said, sighing. "All I know is evah since I can remembah, all kind stuffs happen in deah . . ."

"What kind stuffs?"

"I don't know," he said, putting his hand on my head. "I no can undahstand da place. But I tell you one ting. Dis house, da buggah is sharp, clevah. Someting bad happen, and everybody, dey start talking, 'Eh, stay away from dat place.' So da place stay empty couple months and tings stay quiet, but aftah a while, people forget and somebody move in and *bang*, someting happen again . . ."

A pair of sparrows sat on the telephone line above the house.

"You gonna come back and finish da fence, Dad?"

"Yeah," he said. "When I come back home, I finish it up."

He began pounding nails into the solid fence. I walked into the house and saw Mom packing Dad's bags. Next to the olive-colored duffle bag was a stack of blank envelopes.

The rain came very quickly.

The sound was loud, like the roll of marching drums, and the water splashed out of drain pipes and spilled down the narrow concrete stairways. Mr. Kaahunui put his large hand on the top of the fence and shook it, but the wood and the soil beneath did not budge. "Not bad foah one old man wrasslah, ah?" he said.

I smiled. "Maybe we should just do what Mom says," I said.

"What's dat?"

"Pour gasoline on da house and watch da bastard burn to da ground."

Mr. Kaahunui started hammering the nails into the fence. The rain began to fall harder and harder, and the cars on the road made tearing sounds on the slippery streets. "Let's go in mah house," I said, picking up Dad's old tool chest and his mayonnaise jar of nails. "Take a break."

"I almost finish," said Mr. Kaahunui, squinting because the rain was getting in his eyes.

"Let's wait foah da rain to settle down. Befoah you catch cold."

When we were inside, I made coffee, and Mr. Kaahunui drank it black.

"I haven't been in heah since da day yoah old man and yoah mom got married," said Mr. Kaahunui, sitting down on an old orange chair. "I was yoah dad's best man, you know."

"What was da wedding like?" I asked.

"Lot of baseball playahs and wrasslahs."

"I've seen Mom's pitchahs."

"Wasn't she da prettiest ting?"

"Yeah." The air in the room was warm and still.

"Yoah dad stood right heah, in da middle of da floor, and made one big speech about how deah was no way in da world he was evah gonna leave yoah mothah's side." Mr. Kaahunui smiled and shook his head.

"Mr. Kaahunui, you tink Dad'll evah come back home?"

"Das kinda hard to say," he said, smiling. "But you can nevah tell."

"You know what I no can undahstand?" I said after a while. "If dis kind terrible tings happen to nice people like Kelly—people who was always trying foah do good—what da hell kind world we living in?"

"I don't know, boy," he said. He ran a thick finger over one eyebrow, and his voice became soft. "If da world can make one big, strong, dumb bastard like Mr. Kaahunui stay awake at nights and start tinking, you know dat someting very wrong, someting very bad is going on . . ."

"Mom like move away from da house," I said. "She say she cannot take it anymoah. She cannot sleep. But hell, we no moah no place else foah go."

"You fellahs can always stay with Mr. Kaahunui."

"Nah, we'd get in yoah way."

"No be stupid," said Mr. Kaahunui. "Always get room foah friends."

"Tanks, Mr. Kaahunui," I said. "Tanks foah everyting."

Mr. Kaahunui smiled. I listened to the rain and thought about the termite man. I wondered if that old bastard was pissed off at me, wherever he was. Then I began thinking about the house in back and who was going to move in there next. A lot of people could forget the stories in the newspaper for a roof over their heads at sixty dollars a month. Then I started thinking about Kelly and that afternoon at Kapiolani Park when she said that we could attach a piece of string between two tin cans and talk to each other about silly things until night became morning. The grayish light from outside came through the window and fell upon the triangular scars on Mr. Kaahunui's cheeks and forehead. I thought the rain would never end.

Lucha Libre ———————————————————————————————

for Sebastian "Chevy" Lopez

When we lived in the Spanish Arms apartment building off Marbrisa Avenue, next to the McDonald's in Huntington Park, California, my parents decided they wanted to learn to speak English. "Learn to defend ourselves" was how my father put it. This was around 1974 to 1975. By then, he had already had a few showdowns with Mexican Americans, or *pochos,* who didn't want to speak Spanish. It drove my father into rages. "How could you not know Spanish?" he would ask, pointing at their name tags. "Look where you come from; look who you are." The young men and women merely stared at him as though he were mad. One day, my parents decided to go to night classes at the local elementary school and pick up a few words, enough to fend for themselves on the streets. These classes were offered between 6 and 8 P.M. from Monday through Thursday—a pretty tough schedule for my parents. This was before my mother worked in the same factory as my father, so he had to punch the clock out and then zoom over and pick her up. They made an arrangement with a couple they knew to keep an eye on me after I came home from school. So, for the first few weeks they went to night class, I sat in the living room of Hilda and Rey's house and watched television. Usually I would watch cartoons like *Johnny Quest* and *Speed Racer.* But then Rey would get home from work and want to watch *Lucha Libre* on KMEX, Channel 34. He was the one who got me hooked on watching wrestling. With every week that passed, I liked it more and more and came to look forward to it—so much so that on those days it was on, I couldn't wait to get home from school so I could watch it. A lot of people say that the midseventies were the Golden Age of *Lucha Libre.* I would agree. Those guys really knew how to put on a show. Rey and I would sit in the living room and watch the action being broadcast from the Los Angeles Olympic Auditorium, drinking sodas and munching on saltine crackers. "That's all true," Rey would often turn to me to say. I was caught in the magic of the violence. I sat there and stared, looking for ways that these men would give their craft away. I mean, how could they hit themselves so hard, coming off the ropes, then get up and continue to slug it out a few seconds later? Rey especially liked tag-team wrestling, when the guys losing got tossed out of the ring. I preferred it when the bad guys got cornered and then pinned, and the referee threw himself on the mat, slammed his hand down three times, and the bell signaled the end of the match. Rey and I sat transfixed by so much action. Once in a while, when he got up to get more drinks, more munchies, he would mention the cage: the infamous cage, which they put up only for stadium-going, stadium-paying audiences. His eyes wet with the gleam of the possibilities, Rey described the cage as a free-for-all. The last man standing won. There was also Mexican wrestling with El Santo and Mil Mascaras—those mysterious characters that the bad-guy wrestlers tried to unmask for the world to see. Mil Mascaras even made movies; El Santo did too, but his movies were hard to find on television. So, many months passed by with us watching *Lucha Libre.* Rey and I bet—not real money, of course—to see who could pick the winning teams. My favorite moments happened after the fights: when these sweaty, saliva-frothing, out-of-breath men approached Jaime Jarrin, one of the MCs, and tried to intimidate him. My favorite host, Luis Magaña, cowered and trembled with fear when guys like Andre the Giant stood next to him, and even though Andre was on the good-guys team, Luis tried to keep his distance. There was—and still is, of course—something regal about wrestling, but the old days of Johnny Chibuye, Andre the Giant, Greg Valentine, and John Toulous and his famous corkscrew were the best. When those guys charged into the ring, the crowd roared and Rey and I shifted in our seats. We got ready for the heavy-duty hitting action. Eventually, my parents stopped going to school to learn English, tired of the hectic schedules, the running around. At that time, my mother didn't know how to drive and had to rely on my father to pick her up and take her where she wanted to go. When they stopped going to school, my afternoons over at Rey and Hilda's came to an end. Lucky for me, *Lucha Libre* was moved to Saturday morning, and I could spend the entire Saturday morning watching it in my room, still in my pajamas. My mother made hot cakes by the half-dozen and brought them to me. She'd tease that I would get so big that instead of being on *Lucha Libre,* I'd have to move to Japan and become a *sumo* wrestler—another kind of wrestling altogether, no? Ah, those were glorious mornings. It didn't bother my parents that I watched television all day. What was an only son to do but find ways of entertaining himself, and there was no better entertainment than *Lucha Libre* for a boy of thirteen, filled with growing pains, on the verge of a major voice change, on the verge of hair, on the verge of muscles and manhood.

from *Mother Tongues and Other Untravellings: A Long Poem in Prose*

Fed on American beef and milk, *we* were supposed to grow tall, big-boned as the blond people my grandmother sees on TV. At four-foot-eleven I have betrayed them all, with my little-girl rib cage and feet too small for American shoes, my hip bones exactly like my mother's. I was always the shortest one in my class, the slightest. No one even bothered to shove me around. The only black boy in my fourth-grade class asked if I was a midget. I think he was disappointed. My mother said, *In Japan, you'd be average.* I imagined a land of small people, a country the size of my parents.

Still, every summer she signed me up for swimming lessons, drove me to the YMCA and back. On the way home I sat in the back, sticking to the seat in my wet bathing suit and shorts, and ate ice-cream sandwiches that tasted of chlorine. The trouble was that I could swim, but not very far. *An eager learner, but has no stamina,* my report cards said. At ten I loved only the rush of diving: the rough tile beneath my toes, where my whole body waited for the spring up my spine, the arc forward into air, where for a moment I was no one between spaces; the noiseless contact with water, familiar again, and moving through it without resistance as if returning. I never wanted to come up. When I did, the task became something else: breathing, breaching the surface, reaching the other side of the pool and starting out again, counting, keeping score. All summer I kicked and splashed across the distance, the taste of salt in my mouth, my seaweed hair.

When I went back to Japan, I was the second shortest.

English was my brother tongue, the sound of school and driveways, of summer camp, the backyard pool. At home we were forbidden to speak it, for fear of losing our mother tongue, though our mother, too, spoke it, her tongue not quite fitting around the *th,* the *v.* My brother taught me the words we couldn't say at school or in front of our friends' mothers, words our mother wouldn't know. She'd studied Faulkner and Brontë, said *often* with a British accent. Its secret music I shared with my brother, though secret to no one else; from the beginning, I shared it with my mother, later my sister. Like all my childhood secrets, my mother and I told it to each other, a story she knew only the ending of. *They lived happily ever after— mother, other, brother, voice.*

Excused from Sister Mary's English class at the missionary school in Japan, I sat alone in the unlit language lab, rehearsing my tongue's confessions. On Saturdays I spoke English with others like me, so as not to lose my brother tongue. People stared at us in stores. *Speak Japanese, children. Can't you speak Japanese?*

Very, listen, never, prom. The last time she lived here, my sister and I tried to correct our mother's pronunciation. *Bitter, early, rather, love.* In silence she suffered our impatience, our unforgiving daughterhood, the hard candy arrogance of smooth *l*s and *r*s.

When I returned to Hiroshima at ten, I found that I did not speak the language, though I recognized its fast clanging sound, like rough salt from the harbor. I spoke instead a Japanese without dialect or accent, as my parents and the teachers at Japanese School did. My mother grew up one prefecture west, in Yamaguchi, where the vowels were softer, the lilt slow and round as the oranges my grandmother fed me. My father's family was from Himeji, but he spent his childhood north, where the steel mills were. And although our parents had lived in Hiroshima for years before we were born, they never spoke the dialect while abroad.

More than my clothes, than that I'd spent seven years abroad, than that I spoke English, it was my mother tongue that separated me: even in this language we shared, we were different. The sounds bore no resemblance: *Hiroshima-ben* is notoriously combative, its vowels and word endings harsh, jagged in their upward notes, everything sounding like a command or an insult. The consonants, too, are the hard noises of *g*s and *d*s, *j*s and *k*s. It is the language of survivors, of those who have had to carve a city out of seven rivers, mountains on three sides and an inland sea, and later out of ash and rubble; who have seen battles over a moated castle, navy shipyards dominating the bay, where two *yakuza* groups spreading their turf north and south would meet. The tongue has become hard and rough as the oyster shells gleaming on the docks all winter. It is a hot, blunt language, honest and quick to forget. Although we did not understand one another at first, the children were kind to me, for I was a newcomer; I might as well have been blond and blue-eyed.

It wasn't until I'd moved to a new school in the suburbs that my speech was seen as a sign of snobbery. *You don't sound like us. You think you're better, you put on airs,* they said in the perfect standard Japanese they accused me of speaking, reserved for classroom manners. In their mouths, this was what you spoke to injure, to mark distance, to recognize some central authority. I'd moved to the suburbs from downtown Hiroshima, so they couldn't have guessed I couldn't speak the dialect.

Still, in three or four years I lost my mother tongue to a *Hiroshima-ben* as fierce as that of anyone who'd lived there all her life, and to my surprise, my mother did, too. The dialect was something we learned together, for the first time, like classmates, or sisters at the piano. It has become my sister tongue, what I speak with my sister, my mother, the dialect of my teenage years, of growing up, of leaving. It is the language of returning, of common knowledge, of fights and oranges and silver-green oysters.

And now when I call, it is the dialect I listen for, the hard, familiar ring in my mother's speech, the unmistakable music we learned together—immigrants in a foreign land.

A Man of Nootka Sound. 1778.
Nootka Sound (King George Sound),
Vancouver Island, S. W. British
Columbia, Canada. Engraving
by William Sharp after drawing
by John Webber.
PL. 38

Link of Tenderness

Great-grandmother didn't take off her white mourning clothes for the final twenty years of her life. She had long before prepared for death, and now peacefully awaited her departure. I don't really remember if the old woman talked; she was quiet and spent her days smoking a long copper pipe in a far-off room of the house. She stayed with us one summer, then they took her away somewhere. And I remember the thin, straight, gray hair at the nape of her neck, the dark, sorrowful eyebrows raised high above undisturbed eyes, and the snowy glow of her spotless garments: a white jacket and skirt, and white socks made from padded cloth.

And I still recall: the summer I was six, a hedgehog appeared—it's uncertain from where—to loll around on our porch. The few rows of soft feathers on its back were dark and would soon become sharp needles. The hedgehog could not see, and cheeped like a baby bird. I placed him on a cushion, poured a drop of warm milk in a teaspoon, and fed him. Every day after that I was busy with the hedgehog, and spent a great deal of time working on a cardboard box, building a nest inside. From the opening came the sweetest scent of milk and a baby animal.

Soon the hedgehog gained his sight and began to run around. His feathers turned into myriad needles sharp enough to prick a finger. At night I listened as he sneezed and panted in the box, and I dreamed that he would grow big and run behind me, like a trained dog.

The adults were at work during the day, leaving no one to disturb our life of endless dreams, or the old woman's. Silence filled our home, though in her far-off room Great-grandma would issue dry, light coughs that sounded like the clap of hands. Or we would hear the striking of a match as she relit her dying pipe. She was so old that nothing aroused her interest. In those days I heard a story about her from the grown-ups—a terrifying one that made me want to keep my distance from her.

The story was about the deaths of her husband and eldest son, which happened in the same year. At that time, they all lived in the far east of Russia, having migrated from Korea. The father of seven children, her thirty-four-year-old son (my uncle) all of a sudden took ill and died. Within a few months Great-grandfather fell ill with grief and also passed away. Then one of the children died. At that point they called for a fortune-teller, who performed her rituals and then said, They are dying in your family because some invisible but furious spirit is flying over your house. It will kill more yet, for it is very angry. It is the spirit of a relative who was not properly buried.

At that moment my great-grandmother remembered that in Korea her husband once had a brother—a happy bachelor peasant. One day while strolling through a neighboring forest, he realized that night was fast approaching. Wanting to shorten the way home, he went straight through the heart of the forest. He was walking along an animal path when he tripped the wire of a gun trap that had been set by a hunter. A shot sounded. The bullet blew away the peasant's side. In the morning the hunter appeared, saw the dead body, became frightened, and, after dragging the body from the path, buried it somewhere. Then the hunter, beset with fear and a troubled conscience, said goodbye to his family and fled. When he reached China, he sent a letter in which he confessed his crime and asked the dead man's relatives not to take their anger out on his innocent family. No one, of course, did such a thing, though the place of the dead man's grave remained unknown, causing his relatives great sorrow.

Soon after that the family migrated to Russia, the happy-go-lucky peasant's final winter resting place still unknown. For fifteen years the spirit of the forgotten brother and relative patiently waited. Then it flew into a rage. I imagined how he soared above the forest, his fiery eyes glowing. I feared that spirit and thought, Why did he have to kill his brother, his nephew, and a small girl? If he was reluctant to lie quietly in his forest grave, he should have flown to China to find that hunter and make him rebury the body.

My great-grandmother, sitting in the other room, may have been able to explain to me why the spirit did such brutal things, but I didn't talk to her. Death seemed much worse to me than life, and I had no desire to know about all those gloomy things of the distant past.

In those difficult days after the death of the master of the house and his eldest son, the old woman became the head of the large family. The daughter-in-law, with many children—the oldest of whom was fourteen—tried to fight off grief, but she could only shed tears and was hardly alive. Nothing remained but for her mother-in-law, then already sixty, to save the family herself.

Without a word to anyone, Great-grandmother left the house one day and crossed the Korean border. Twenty years had passed since the family migrated, and the border was blocked. By night the old woman swam across the border's river, holding on to an air bubble made out of her wet skirt. In the middle of the river, the air escaped and she almost drowned. Surfacing, she heard the voices of Japanese soldiers on the shore. They would have chopped off her head.

She reached the mountain village by foot and searched for the hunter's house. He had long ago returned from foreign soil and was now a farmer. The old woman asked, Would you really, having killed an innocent man, want the entire family to die as well? No, the hunter answered. And the two prayed together. Then the hunter went to look for the anonymous grave; after a week he found it. Unearthing the bones, he wrapped them in a clean linen sackcloth and carried them to a different place. A beautiful hill with a few young pines growing on it was selected. There, among the golden trunks, the hunter and my great-grandmother reburied the bones of the merry peasant.

The old woman returned home to sit, thirty years later, in the far room of our log cabin somewhere in Kazakhstan, where the whole family had been relocated in the 1930s. One of her granddaughters became my mother. My enormous uncle and fat aunt bowed before this small, shriveled old woman, who always held her body solemn and straight. Old and graying collective farmers would visit us, smoke cigarettes and pipes, and play their Japanese cards with pictures of flowers on them. But my great-grandmother would never enter into the conversation, nor pick up a single card. Aloof, almost sad, she sat apart, as though she considered herself to have performed the most important feat of her life and now had nothing left to do among people. These farmers, having not performed such a feat, could only watch her with reverence and guilt. Or so it seemed to me.

So how surprised I was one day when she left her far-off room in her padded cotton socks and without a word came up to me. I was sitting on the floor, bent over the hedgehog, urging him along with a straw. Her dark, sharply peaked eyebrows remained high and sorrowful above tearful eyes. Without a word, she began to attentively watch the hedgehog's movements. Ever so lightly, she sat close to me and put her tiny translucent hands together on her knees. With added zeal I took to prodding the hedgehog with the straw.

From that day on we were entertained by the hedgehog together. Now I boldly went to her, released the cub on the floor, and crawled around the whole room with him. The hedgehog was a very good learner. I trained him to pull a paper wagon, upon which I would load more and more cargo. When the weight finally exhausted him, he would angrily roll up into a lump and refuse to work. Great-grandmother, an old farming peasant, wanted to determine the towing capacity of the small animal. One day, with the end of her long pipe, she knocked one wooden cube from the overloaded wagon, and then a spool of thread. I wasn't at all surprised that the old woman, having long awaited death, played my games with me. Here was the essential secret of our existence, though at that time I didn't understand this.

I don't know when they took Great-grandma away from us. I don't remember where the hedgehog disappeared to. He might have run away from me to a mother who lived under the house. That year I started school, and there were many new concerns, joys, and games . . . and afterwards, a long silence, and then oblivion. Thirty years have passed since that time.

One day I found myself on business in Sakhalin, standing on a wet stone before a waterfall. It was a great, beautiful waterfall at the south end of the island. I was holding a camera, preparing to take a picture. The waterfall cascaded in a clear wide veil from a rock and, falling on a stone ledge below, bubbled and boiled into clean, white foam. A diaphanous seven-colored rainbow rose from the waterfall, the upper end soaring somewhere into the heavens.

I looked at this rainbow and the thick white froth as the water-sprite dust disintegrated against my face. Gradually beginning to comprehend the immaculate beauty before my eyes, I unwittingly lowered the camera. To hold this vision on film would be impossible.

So instead of a photograph, I took from this business trip the recollection of a seven-colored rainbow, a wet rock upon which bees nestled and drank, and the incredible white foam, boiling at the foot of the rainbow.

And now, trying to find something to compare with the sensation of white that surprised me so in this Sakhalin rainbow, I imagine first a white cloud in the clear sky, then a cap of snow on the rooftop of a log cabin in February, bursting bolls of cotton in Kyrgyzstan, white gladiolas in a field, and, inevitably, the mourning clothes of my great-grandmother. Then I recall the strange, storylike history of her life, a hedgehog well trained and then lost by me, and much more, and it seems like I can remember everything. Then comes the insistent desire to consider for a moment what exactly my immortality is in this world. It flows into all those lives before and after mine.

I must forge them with a precise link of tenderness.

Translation by Edward Bok Lee

Where the Deer and Antelope Play

The dryland prairie of Canadian Forces Base (CFB) Suffield is a land where even the wind gets lonely. This rolling terrain in southeastern Alberta was carved and shaped, mounded and flattened by the great glaciers thousands of years ago. Its sheltering coulees, spotted with white-rimmed alkali sloughs, began as drainage canals at the melting base of the Laurentide Ice Sheet. The wind has been polishing these rolling, sun-bronzed hills for eons. It rides herd on sagebrush, wild horses, antelope, and men, distributing rain clouds here, blowing them away elsewhere with a careless, unmeasured ease. It was this same wind that shaped the lives of my forefathers who homesteaded here in the arid Paliser Triangle back in the teens of this century.

My first venture inside the base came on a blustery July morning. A flock of lark buntings sprayed up from the dust of the Bingville Road, a track named for a place that no longer exists. A prairie falcon wheeled overhead, and a meadowlark sang defiance. The wind whipped through the open windows of the green Canadian Armed Forces truck and tore at the map I clutched in my hands. Major Brent McDonald, then Base Operations Officer, was at the wheel, and photographer Douglas Leighton of Banff was happily ensconced in the back seat, readying his equipment.

My map contained the legal description of lands once owned by my great-grandfather, Robert Marty, and his son John Claude Marty. I had often heard stories about this place and longed to see it. Last March brought momentous news: Environment Canada and the Department of National Defense had designated a 420-square-kilometre expanse of mixed grasslands, sand hills, and riverbanks at CFB Suffield as a National Wildlife Area (NWA). At the same time, the army, acting on the advice of the Canadian Wildlife Service, announced plans to round up the resident herd of 800 (later revised to 1,500) feral horses to reduce its population here and protect the habitat of the new NWA. The "surplus" horses would be sold at auction, and it seemed likely that those not purchased for rodeo stock, ranch work, or pleasure riding might wind up as meat to feed European and Japanese consumers of horseflesh.

Smelling blood, newspaper reporters rushed into print quoting animal rights activists who fired from the lip, denouncing the proposed cull as a "systematic roundup and slaughter of 500 horses that don't deserve this fate." So the welcome news about the new wildlife reserve was buried in a mudslide of misinformation and emotionalism, and the military, instead of getting kudos for its conservation initiative, got a big black eye.

As a person who is currently owned by two horses, and as one who made a living off the back of a horse during a twelve-year career in wildlife management as a park warden, I knew that the ecological issues surrounding horses grazing at Suffield were complex, too complex to be summed up by headlines in the *Toronto Star* such as, for example, SLAUGHTERING WILD HORSES UNNECESSARY AND INHUMANE. I wanted to see the new reserve and the Suffield herd for myself. Most of all, I wanted to see what had become of this stretch of Alberta since the military took it over in 1941 and homesteaders like my grandfather—those not already broken by drought and depression—had moved out.

"This is the spot," said Major McDonald. A whipcord-tough Calgary native, he is a conservationist and history buff, and on the driving forces behind the formation of the Suffield NWA. He slowed the truck down at a lonely intersection about ten kilometres west of the NWA boundary and turned east. We bounced across the prairie on a cart track at the foot of a range of low hills. Something about this unprepossessing place was oddly familiar to me, though I had never seen it before in my life. It had the flavour of a dreamscape.

The dream shattered when we rounded a corner and saw the stark outlines of entrenched soldiers, their weapons trained on us. The major laughed at my expression. They were only plywood silhouettes, guarding the approach to a mock wooden bridge spanning a river of grass. It had all been part of some old military exercise.

We pulled up on a knoll above the plywood gunners. Below us was a broad coulee that our map said was a lake: it was dry as bone, despite recent rains. We could see that this land had once been broken for farming, that the soil profile was lower in a great rectangle there, though it had not been tilled for fifty years. Crested wheatgrass, a foreigner among the native blue grama and spear grass, formed a yellow rectangle marking the old farm. The wind boomed in my ear, as if boasting of the work it had done decades ago, blowing my grandfather's topsoil east into Saskatchewan. This area has the lowest annual precipitation in Alberta—an average of 272 millimetres—and the wind is capable of evaporating 100 millimetres of moisture per month. I looked at the arid valley and knew the truth: this sod should never have been turned in the first place.

McDonald glanced at his CFB Suffield map. "We're very close," he said confidently. An odd shape stuck up from the grass near a patch of pasture sage, and I pointed it out. We drove over, and I was startled to see the wrought-iron headboard of a rusted double bed sticking up through the prairie sod. Nearby was an old cellar hole, like a sunken grave. It seemed impossibly small to mark what once was a home for my grandparents and their eight children.

"This is it!" said the major jubilantly.

"There are your roots, Sid," said photographer Leighton with a smile.

I stared at the headboard, realizing the import of his words. This was the marriage bed that my father had been conceived upon, sunk now into rust and wheatgrass. I looked down at the map, which showed the two tiny quarters of land worked by John Claude Marty back in 1918, and returned my gaze to the space of cloud and sunburnt grass. I could not relate that draftsman's precise gridwork to this windswept immensity, which showed so little trace of those who had poured so much sweat and tears into its brown dirt. It would take a visit from my father and aunt to this spot, a few days later, to make it real for me.

Stirred to the quick, I stepped down to touch the desert heart of my family's history.

CFB Suffield, one of the largest army training bases in the Western world, contains more than 2,600 square kilometres of rolling prairie lying north of Medicine Hat and west of the South Saskatchewan River. It is used as a live firing range by the Canadian Armed Forces and the British Army. However, the area of the NWA within the base has always been exempt from military training, and been marked and protected by the army as out-of-bounds. At present, a limited amount of cattle grazing is allowed in the southern part of the NWA, and gas wells are scattered through part of the northern portion. Gas wells at CFB Suffield, buried three metres deep to protect them from tank treads and artillery shells, supply 3.5 percent of Canada's natural-gas production.

Though cattle and gas wells are permitted, hunting and farming are not. As Tim Coleman, a habitat specialist with the Canadian Wildlife Service (CWS) has written, the Suffield NWA is "one of the few remaining examples of a native mixed grass prairie ecosystem. It represents habitat for 173 animal species, 29 of which are categorized as being of concern, rare, threatened or endangered." The area includes part of the Middle Sand Hills complex, tracts of wild prairie, and segments of the South Saskatchewan River. The horse herd, we learned, tends to frequent the northeast corner of the Middle Sand Hills: we would visit that part of the reserve last.

The entire base at Suffield has become a haven for wildlife. Base access roads, dirt tracks for the most part, are well named. There are mule deer on the Muledeer Road, and coyotes haunt the Coyote Road. Rounding a curve on the Antelope Road, we spotted the biggest antelope buck I have ever seen. He watched us through his large, wide-set eyes for a few seconds, then broke into a run and raced along beside us for a moment at 50 kilometres an hour before suddenly breaking across in front of the truck and dashing off over the prairie. As a prairie boy raised in Medicine Hat, I am no stranger to this singular beast, which would not look out of place on the plains of Africa. But in one hour on the base I saw more pronghorn antelope than I have seen in the rest of my life. Back in my grandfather's day, part of the Sand Hills formed the core of Canada's forgotten Wawakesey National Antelope Park. Wawakesey was founded in 1922 to protect the endangered pronghorn, whose numbers had shrunk to 1,300 animals by 1910. The pronghorn population made a successful recovery by 1938, and the park was shut down. If it were up to me, this reserve would once again become Wawakesey National Antelope Park, so every citizen could see the splendours of the wild prairie that I was privileged to see there.

I glanced over at McDonald. "They seem used to military vehicles, Major."

McDonald, dressed in green battle dress, grinned from behind his aviator sunglasses. "We were out here on a tank exercise one time," he told me, "smoke and explosions all around. Right in the middle of it was an antelope doe and buck, busy mating. And they weren't about to stop and get out of the way just for a bunch of tanks. Had to split the battalion and drive around 'em—firing all the time. Of course, not one of us had a camera."

The major is dedicated to wildlife preservation, which struck me as an incongruous facet in a military mindset. Last year his troops caught eight poachers trespassing on the base. McDonald is the only game warden I have met whose office displays a collection of defused bombs, rockets, and artillery shells. He definitely has the poachers out-gunned.

Rain splashed across our windshield. I had come to a region famed for its searing drought—in the middle of an unusually wet July. The intoxicating perfume of wet sagebrush blessed the moist air. (The Blackfoot used this plant as a cleanser in their sweat lodges.) Hoping to come across a rattlesnake or a hog-nosed snake, we wandered among beds of flowering prickly pear cactus in the mixed-grass zone above the South Saskatchewan River, observing the burrows of Ord's kangaroo rats among the thorns with their quaint orderly entrances. A soldier had been bitten by a rattler just the day before while fixing a nearby fence, and this news only made us optimistic about spotting the notorious reptile. As a child of four, I once picked up a rattlesnake and whirled it around my head, unaware of any danger until my uncle appeared, killed the snake, and made me weep. Now I yearned for a chance to apologize for my uncle's impetuousness.

But wet weather was forcing the serpents under cover. We were consoled instead to spot a weathered bison horn lying among the bright-yellow cactus blooms. Heat waves shimmered on a nearby alkali flat. Feeling we were being watched, we looked up to see no less than ten sets of massive antlers poking up above the tall sagebrush, as a herd of bachelor mule deer investigated our presence. Closer to the river, white-tailed deer put up their flags and ran toward the cottonwoods with their fawns at heel.

Leighton, an accomplished birder, was thrilled when his keen ears heard the *click click buzz* of a grasshopper sparrow, a species known to be in decline. "And listen," he commanded. "That's a Sprague's pipit." All I could see was another little brown bird. Along with the endangered Baird's sparrow and the burrowing owl, the grasshopper sparrow does not do well in farmed and overgrazed prairies. The presence of these birds is encouraging.

During our stay at Suffield, we spotted marsh hawks, red-tailed hawks, merlins, and, most important, the rare ferruginous hawk. The army has placed nesting boxes throughout the ranges to encourage ferruginous hawks to breed here. At tiny Channel Lake, a river oxbow in the NWA, the army works with Ducks Unlimited and a local rancher to maintain water levels that support a myriad of waterfowl.

A tree on the drylands is a thing to celebrate, and generations of Indians have camped in the shade of the groves of mighty cottonwoods along the riverbank. At a spot dubbed Sherwood Forest, we were saddened to see so many of these giants standing bleached and lifeless. Their saplings are found only close to the water these days. In these years of drought, the floods needed to sustain the trees are too infrequent, now that dams on the St. Mary, Belly, Bow, and Oldman Rivers have tamed the watershed.

As we prowled among the leafy survivors, we saw eastern kingbirds, goldfinches, nighthawks, and mourning doves. The tracks and signs of white-tailed deer were everywhere. Beavers had gnawed down eighteen-inch-thick trees and left them to rot. The broad river chuckled and whispered over its sandy bed. A yellow racer darted across the path, and a great plains toad stirred in the shadows. Somewhere nearby, other reptiles such as the endangered western hog-nosed snake, the short-horned lizard, and the bull snake were having siestas and keeping out of sight. Under a huge slab of dead bark on a cottonwood, bats, possibly the long-eared variety, were squeaking out greetings as they waited for twilight to fall on the river. Sandstone cliffs, gnarled and carved into badland outlines by wind and water, rose 135 metres above us. Golden eagles and peregrine falcons nest there, as well as cliff swallows.

That afternoon we lingered awhile at the nearby Ellis Medicine Wheel site, one of the hundreds of Indian archaeological sites that dot the base. Here ancient stone teepee rings are grouped around a mysterious, ceremonial circle. The site sits on a bluff overlooking the river, where rock wrens call to each other over the mud-brown stream. One can see miles in any direction from this viewpoint. Five white American pelicans lifted from the river far below us and flew directly overhead, like five souls giving us greeting as we stood, meditating, among the white stones and cacti. Towering cumulus clouds to the north threatened a change in the weather.

Bombardier Michael Richards was our driver the next day. We travelled north through a cold rain, past a Canadian Forces Militia camp of soggy tents and rain-streaked tanks. The prairie suddenly looked like Rommel's North Africa—in a monsoon. Travelling east on the Kangaroo Rat Road, it took all of our driver's concentration to keep the four-by-four truck between the ditches of the muddy trail. "Hey, what a day for photo opportunities," grumbled a voice from the back seat.

At last the black clouds parted, and there were the Middle Sand Hills, an endless corrugation of tawny whalebacks. Chokecherry bushes and small, isolated aspen and cottonwood groves growing on their lee slopes offered shelter that the wild horses love. There were freshwater springs nearby to sustain the herds. We topped a rise, and there below us were horses in all directions, of all shapes, sizes, and colours. We saw quarter-horse builds and the heavier workhorse builds and just about all physical types in between. Frisky colts followed their dams in small bands of mares, each band ruled over by a stallion. There was a band of bachelors, too, who nibbled each other's manes for want of mares to horse with. One of these stallions tried to run off a little black filly: she kicked him so hard in the side of the head that he staggered to his knees before running off, tossing his head at the smart.

The whole scene was like a gigantic roundup of modern ranch horses, rather than a herd of "wildies." Major McDonald had objected to my use of that term. "They are not, I say again, not wild horses," he had insisted emphatically. "They are second- and third-generation illegal grazers!" In fact, although some of these horses could be traced back to stock turned loose by my grandfather's generation, most of them descend from trespassing grazers left here by local ranchers between 1941 and 1982. That was the last time the horses were rounded up by ranchers. If they had been rounded up more frequently, they would not have grown from 800 to 1,500 head. According to cws studies, the horses may double their numbers every five years. Unlike the cattle that graze in the south end of the reserve, the horses are year-round users of the range, and that can lead to conflicts with browsing animals like deer and antelope. The Plains Indians often had to winter their horses on poplar bark, and horses compete with deer, browsing on shrubs when grass is in short supply.

The horses milled around our truck, curious about our visit, but moved away quickly when we got out to walk around. They were well muscled; their coats shone with good health though there was no one to feed them oats, trim their hooves, or curb them with a halter rope. Their stable was a chokecherry thicket, their water trough a freshwater spring. But the Sand Hills here in the northeast corner of the wildlife area were churned up by their comings and goings, and the range, spotted with manure, had the look of a stable yard. That churned soil makes life difficult or impossible for some native prairie life-forms.

On Canada's prairies, human incursion has left only 24 percent of the original native grassland in a viable state, most of it fragmented into small areas. This loss of habitat has generated a long list of creatures that are extinct or on the verge of extinction, ranging in size from the plains bison and plains grizzly bear through to the great plains wolf, the swift fox, and the black-footed ferret. Suffield represents a chance to save some of this scarce habitat, especially if many or all of the horses are removed.

The CWS, which has been monitoring this area since the early 1970s, says the horses threaten rare plants such as clammyweed and Carolina whitlowwort, and may threaten the endangered northern leopard frog because of the damage horses do around pond margins. A walk through these hills reveals that only a thin layer of sand grass and other plants hold the sand dunes in place against the ever-present wind. On top of an active dune, where horses had bunched up to fight the flies, I saw how their heavy hooves pushed the sand down, and how a herd could erode a trail, which may in turn be enlarged into a "blowout" by the prevailing wind. As Major McDonald puts it: "The question is—do you let a herd of illegal grazers destroy the land, or do you protect the ecosystem, which we have agreed to do here. A pretty simple choice in my mind. After all, it's not as though there's a shortage of horses in the world!"

I would quickly add that there is even less of a shortage of cattle. But the issue is more complex than that. Scientists don't yet know all the connections between sand movement and plant and animal life. The CWS believes that a small herd of feral horses does have a place on this range. Horses and seasonal cattle herds may help us to understand the role large ungulates, such as bison, played in relation to other wildlife and prairie plants in these hills. That might be especially useful if, someday, it becomes feasible to reintroduce bison to the Sand Hills for limited periods. (Unlike the horses, bison frequented this range only part of the year.) For now, the wildlife service feels a herd of 100 horses should be maintained at Suffield until we learn more about this ecosystem. But political pressure, generated by the public outcry, cancelled last fall's roundup, and the full herd of horses is still roaming freely.

The CWS is eager to learn more about the habitat and the rare and endangered species at Suffield, and it has a qualified staff ready to advise the military on managing the area. Instead, under political pressure, the army hired a consultant: he concluded that some reduction of the herd is necessary. The army had formed a citizens' committee to suggest humane ways of managing the herd and protecting the NWA. For now, at least, the charismatic megafauna has priority over the uncharismatic minifauna like the northern leopard frog and the Ord's kangaroo rat.

No fan of horses and cattle, which destroy bird habitat as well, the bird-loving Leighton suggested puckishly that the nags might make excellent artillery targets. "Just kidding," he added hastily. His mind was in the skies or the chokecherry bushes, and he was not disappointed. In the Sand Hills we saw rufous-sided towhees, brown thrashers, least flycatchers, and a multitude of other feathered delights. A great horned owl flitted through an aspen grove as we approached. The affable shutterbug exclaimed in joy when he finally spotted an upland sandpiper, one of his favourite birds. It alighted on top of a sagebrush with its long, shorebird-like legs, and perched there after elaborate balancing motions with its wings. A rare loggerhead shrike, a threatened species, also put in an appearance. I waited patiently, assured by Leighton that the shrike would catch a grasshopper or a mouse and impale it on a thorn, before dining. But the shrike refused to cooperate, so I accused him of making the story up.

Time passed all too quickly for us in the desert solitudes along the South Saskatchewan. On the last day, we picked up my father, Orland Marty, and my aunt "Dot," Dorothy Kachmar, both retired Medicine Hat residents, and drove them out to the old homestead site, which they had not set eyes on since 1933. My father put on a brave face when he finally saw the old cellar hole, but I could tell that memories were overwhelming him. Aunt Dot stood upon the stone threshold and pointed out landmarks. She recalled how my grandfather, John Claude, plowed one field with a team of horses, and how my grandmother, born Ora Zook, of resolute Pennsylvania-Dutch stock, plowed the other. Glancing down, I saw broken fragments of Delft china glinting in the grass, reminders of my grandmother's vanished kitchen. Father recalled the night the house burned to the ground, when mice, chewing on matches, set the place on fire. It was he who woke first to sound the alarm. How do you get eight kids out of a burning shack? Grandfather picked up my uncle Walter, then a toddler, and simply threw him out through the front window, glass and all. As they recalled that night, I looked down and saw, shining among the sage, pieces of broken, melted glass, coloured with time.

After a few moments, we got back in the truck. Following the long thread of homesteaders' memory, we made our way up the hill until we came to another cellar hole. The building itself had been moved into town decades ago. This was my great-grandfather's place, where John Claude moved his family after the fire. "We called this place the box on the buttes," said my father. "You could see the old shack sitting here from miles away."

I got out to look around. Two Blackhills cottontail rabbits, amazingly tame, had made a home in the thick sagebrush that had overgrown the cellar. My father said, "Just down that slope there, I was roping a calf; I was barefoot, as usual. And I cut my foot wide open, right to the bone, on an old mower blade."

"And I sewed it up," added Aunt Dot.

"Did a damn good job, too," affirmed my father.

I looked around, and the first thing that struck me was that my great-grandfather was a dreamer: our family had been founded by a man with the soul of a poet. This Swiss–Irish American had given up a settled life in North Dakota to strike it rich farming in the desert, lured here, along with thousands of other immigrants, by false promises of ample rainfall and rich land. He was no stranger to wind, yet he had built his home in the most unprotected spot he could find. His brother-in-law, Jesse Smith, had also homesteaded on this hill. But Smith chose to go lower down its slopes. He had dug seven metres straight back into the hill. His home was lined with fieldstone and roofed with sod, and the pillars of his house, as we would discover later, were still standing.

But Great-grandfather had built his home in the sky, and did it have a view! All the way east to the Cypress Hills; all the way south to Montana. It had a view of the Old West that artist Charlie Russell would have painted, had he ever laid eyes on it. And perhaps it was this "Swissman," as Aunt Dot called him, who had left me a gift. For when I looked down I spotted a penny, a little green with age, lying at my feet, not even buried under the grass roots: a 1920 penny with the King's head on it. It seemed to me at that moment as glorious as a diamond. It was a small miracle that I had even noticed such a small treasure in that sea of grass.

On the plain, far below us, we could see a herd of antelope. We also saw deer and the dark apostrophes that marked a small band of wandering horses. I walked down the slope clutching the penny in my hand. I should have been getting used to it, finding the hard evidence of every story my aunt and father told, stories that heretofore I had thought of as mostly myth. Perhaps it was just for doubting them that I nearly cut my own foot, or at least my shoe, on the old mower blade. I picked it up and tested the edge with my thumb. It was still sharp, hardly eaten by rust, though it had lain in wait for me in the desert grass for over sixty years. I decided I would take it home—I don't know why. I also took one stone from the foundation, which the great ice once carried from the Canadian Shield to be a threshold for my great-grandparents' home, as it will be now, for mine.

NOTE: *Although Sid Marty would have liked to see a small herd of feral horses roaming free at Suffield as a tribute to the area's pioneer heritage, the military rounded up the entire herd between 1994 and 1995 and the horses were adopted by people who promised them a safe haven.*

A Woman of Nootka Sound. 1778.
Nootka Sound (King George Sound),
Vancouver Island, S. W. British
Columbia, Canada. Engraving
by William Sharp after drawing
by John Webber.
PL. 39

In the River Currents with My Father

I recently travelled down the Mississippi River from Memphis to New Orleans on a massive 6,200-horsepower, 180-foot towboat pushing 900 feet of barges. On a bend above Baton Rouge, Captain Vollie McCain showed me how to "flank" the big tow. Backing up on his engines, the captain brought the boat and barges to a standstill in the current and then, with perfect timing and considerable patience, allowed the river's currents to turn the front end of the towboat around the bend. The back end, sitting in the slower water by the point of the bend, provided a pivot.

My appreciation of the beauty and harmony expressed in this manoeuvre is rooted in the time that I spent learning about river currents from my father. Especially those times that we cast dry flies onto the surface of the crystal-clear waters of the little Elk River on central Vancouver Island.

Those days that I spent as a young boy on the Elk with Roderick Haig-Brown have shaped my appreciation of that wonderful relation that exists between the earth and the water that moves on its surface, and the consuming human need to return to such places. The Elk was one of those mountain streams that seem to have been made for the dry fly. Shallow enough to wade across in places, it also had pools with deep waters under cutbanks. We walked up the bars on the slow side and cast over the deep: two steps upstream and two casts over the water, gathering the slack in our hands as the fly floated down toward us. As we neared the top of a pool where some faster water would be coming down between the rod tip and the fly, we made little flips of the line to keep the dry fly floating free on the surface: the telltale V lines would expose its artificiality to the fish.

My favourite part of the Elk was the lower part, where the valley widened out above the swamp in which it joined Upper Campbell Lake. The valley had been logged some decades earlier and had grown back to alder and willow, the beginnings of second-growth fir and cedar. In spring, the river flooded and cut new channels through the gravel of the valley floor. I don't remember how many times we fished that river, but I'm sure we never went there without seeing a black bear. Once, one ambled down to the bank just across from where I was fishing. Smelling me she raised up on her hind feet to test the air for confirmation, and getting it she turned and walked back into the alders. Another time we watched a bear swim a particularly fast section of the river and then, swinging one great paw up onto a log at the head of a logjam, pull himself up out of the water. We marvelled at the harmony of animal, water, and land. It was that harmony to which my father aspired when he went on the river.

Another time we were surrounded by a herd of the elk that gave their name to the river. We watched as they walked up and over a logged-off ridge. Lying on the side of the ridge was a deer, enabling us to gauge their size. Along the river we watched the kingfishers and mergansers and talked about what they would be eating. We watched huckleberries and blackberries ripen. We saw the slide where an otter came down to the river. We talked about the feed that the rainbows and cutthroat would be eating. Firm, cold-water cutthroat would come up from the jade-green depths under a cutbank to look at the first cast of a fly before they eased back into security to await the next cast. That indescribable connection with all that the river represents was made when that trout came up to look at the fly on the second cast and then, in a swirl of tail, flashing muscle, and white underbelly, dove with it. To have felt the life-force of the fish and its home river currents through thirty feet of light line and nine feet of split cane is one of the great joys of my life.

When I look back at family pictures of myself as a child, I see that nearly half of them show me with a fishing rod in my hand. As a parent I understand what this means, but as a child I never had any sense that I was being raised to my father's love of fishing. As a parent I have always admired his restraint, and now, as my children grow older, I think I am coming to understand what I am sure he knew. Fishing in our family was not so much an end in itself—or the means to an end. It was the means to a presence. A presence in our environment. A place from which we could take some responsibility for that environment through a connection with it.

I think my father's favourite pool on the Campbell was the Upper Islands, where at least half of the river flowed over a long bar connecting two islands. It was a scary place when you were seven or eight and trying to wade through the current as your six-foot father strode along in felted waders, his pipe smoke trailing aft like a Mississippi steamboat making headway over a shallow. But I followed him there for years because, fishing or not, I knew that this was a special place. It was here that he first showed me the wonder of a gravel-shelled caddis grub living under a rock. So I think I know how he felt the day we went there and found not one but two cars parked at the trail head.

I suppose most fishers resent it when they come to a favourite pool and find others there. For fly-fishers this takes on a particular disappointment when the pool is filled with a bunch of hackers flailing away with spin gear. I don't recall if he swore, but if he did, it would have been a mild "bloody" or "damn." I do remember the disappointment and then that great constant of his life, the optimism: "Well," he said, "that's good that there are people out on the rivers. The only way we will save them is to have people use them."

That idea carries so much of what was important about Canada for the English immigrant who grew up fishing privately owned streams in Dorset. Although one of them was owned by his grandfather, he never thought that chance of birth should be a prerequisite for being able to fish a river. In fact he resented private ownership of resources for our tendency to use that status to confirm our temporal conceits. He preferred an ownership shared with a community of bears, trout, and other humans. He cared not about amassing property to hand down to future generations, but about delivering the land in a condition as good or better than the one in which it was received.

I remember once when I was about ten, driving with him up behind Campbell River to look at the ravages of a particularly big forest fire. His brow was furrowed with concern as he looked at the logged-off hillsides from which the fire had burnt the last of the ground cover. The rains were beginning to wash away the tiny amounts of soil that ten thousand years had nurtured there. In patches the white granite bones of the hill were already showing, and my father was no doubt picturing that soil as silt in the exposed gravel of a spawning bed in the stream at the bottom of the hill. Concerned at his concern, I asked, "Who owns all this land, Daddy?"

We got out of the car and walked over to a ridge where I climbed up on a blackened stump. He assumed the classic pose of the father about to give his someday-all-this-will-be-yours talk.

"You own this land," he said and waited for my predictable exclamation as I imagined the schoolyard boasts that I would make the next day. "You and I and all the people own it," he said, giving me the punch line of life, "and it is our very big responsibility to look after it."

I don't know if I ever heard him talk about rights, but I sure heard a lot about responsibility. Looking back I wonder how he came to such a commitment. What training did he have that enabled him to think differently from those of his countrymen who came here to kill buffalo and dam rivers? Over time I have pieced together a theory. He often spoke of Old Fox, the gamekeeper on the huge Dorset estate of his grandfather, Alfred Pope. My father's father had been killed in World War I when my father was only ten. His mother returned home, moving my father and his two sisters into her father's very patriarchal household. My father's sportsman training had been well started, and now it was left to uncles and the gamekeepers to help him develop a fuller understanding. Spending a lot of time with the gamekeepers, he saw that hunting and fishing were as much about nurturing as they were about catching and killing.

When I visited the estate for the first time some years after my father's death, I got to know a much younger gamekeeper. I think it confirmed my theory. He was proud of the land and the little Wrackle River, which looked just like my father's favourite Canadian creek down to the type of weed growth the two spring-fed streams shared.

I also spent time with my cousin Christopher Pope, who is now steward of the property and who enabled me to see the other part of my father's training. Raised to lead and to make careful decisions for the future, Christopher welcomed me to the estate and showed me the changes that had been made over the years. It was a magical tour, this cousin whom I had never met before acknowledging our shared heritage.

At one point he stopped and showed me a small forest of beech trees that had been planted by World War I German prisoners under our great-grandfather's direction. In the late 1980s, my cousin had thought to take a few trees out of the middle of the forest so that the grouse would go up through the opening and break high when he had his fall shoot. On going with his forester to the spot where he wanted the opening, he found that our great-grandfather had planted no trees there in anticipation of the need for just such an opening.

I was offered and of course happily accepted an opportunity to go with the gamekeeper to fish the Wrackle. I suppose that I thought casting a fly was rather like riding a bicycle—one never lost the knack. I proceeded to embarrass myself by snagging weeds on my cast and then grass on my back cast. The very professional gamekeeper explained that it was a rather difficult spot that we were fishing—it was not—and gently took the rod from me. I vowed to buy a rod and practice when I got home. I came home and bought the rod.

In spite of my lapsed status as a fly-fisher, I very much feel that I am my father's disciple. His teaching was about observing, knowing, caring, and taking responsibility. He taught me to observe in ways that I now make a living with as a writer. Once in the mid-1950s, I went with him on a research trip that took us to the Parsnip River, just into British Columbia's arctic watershed. We fished arctic grayling and marvelled at the phosphorescent blues of their bodies and dorsal fins. But we were, as are most grayling fishers, saddened by how quickly the colour was lost once the fish were taken from the stream. Later I built a stone pond, and we caught several of the fish and put them in there to watch them.

Most of us whose fathers are gone regret things we didn't get to do with them. The same summer that we fished the Parsnip, I bought my first proper mask, snorkel, and flippers and, with my friends, started swimming the rapids and pools of the Campbell River. We swam a lot and made a little money salvaging steelhead gear from the river bottom. In late summer the pink salmon started coming into the river, then into the big springs; a little later the big chinook salmon came up the river. I begged my father to come swim with me, but he didn't. A decade later, when he took up skin-diving, I was working summers on a commercial fishing boat and going to university in the winter. It was the logical continuation of his riverine experiences. I went with him a bit, but my life was busy with other things and I never really shared the underwater with him.

But we talked of it. Not only the fish that we saw, but of the feel of the river's current, how to swim with it while not fighting it. Of the harmony of being weightless and of being connected. I think he fished less after that. I know that when swimming, he did not feel it was right to see a steelhead lying behind a rock and then go home to get his rod. I think it is in this urge to be in and of the water that I feel my father's love and fascination with that wonderful bird the dipper. In his calm way, he never failed to get excited when he saw one of the little birds go from rock to creek bottom to rock. He wanted to go there.

One spring when I had finished university and was teaching in a First Nations community along the Chilcotin River in the British Columbia interior, he came to visit me. He brought along a couple of rods, and after I had obliged him to ride horses with me, which he didn't like, we went down to the river to fish. I had been living there for three years at the time and had camped and ridden my horse along that stretch of river many times. I had watched the people dip net sockeye salmon, and I had seen the steelhead fishermen work their way along the shore ice in early spring. I thought that I knew a bit about the river.

That season of the year is called Green Grass time in the cattle country of the Chilcotin. The snows were melting back around Chilco and Taseko Lakes, and the river was in freshet. Its normally translucent glacial silted waters were roiling muddy brown. We would catch no fish that day, my father announced as he tied a fly to the end of his rod's leader. And we didn't, but we worked our way down those pools, two steps and two casts at a time. I still go back to that stretch of river when I'm up in the Chilcotin because I now know it in a way that only comes from sharing its waters with a master.

In my favourite of his books, *Measure of the Year,* my father writes:

> Because I have learned so much of the river through fishing and watching fish, it is difficult to write of it without thinking of fish. From a fisherman's point of view almost everything about a river is related to fish and fishing. Floods or drought may mean disaster to spawning and hatch, or merely disappointed hopes of good fishing; birds and animals that live along the banks are predators or controls or both; insect life, in the water and out of it, is feed; lime content, temperature, weed growth, logjams, shallows or deeps, all have meaning in terms of fish and fishing. Even trees and brush overhanging the banks, even the work of beavers and muskrats, has bearing. It may seem a narrow view, but the interrelationships are so far-reaching and complicated that it is really comprehensive; if anything is not included, the fisherman is almost certain to include it because observation is one of the keenest pleasures of his sport.

My father saw moving water as the ultimate expression of the earth force, though he wouldn't have used those words. He understood it as a spiritual joining of water and land into which animals be they fish or human could interject themselves in their temporal moment. He spent a good part of his life trying to underpin those ideas with rational scientific explanation and justification. When I go back and read his writing, I know that he succeeded in something much more important: he gave poetic voice to the phenomena of rivers and fish.

For whatever chance of life, my inheritance has not been the fly rod, but the affection for and sense of responsibility to the rivers. As a young man, I went seining with my Kwakiutl father-in-law, Herb Assu. He fished from a sixty-foot boat with a twelve-hundred-foot net. His pride was in understanding that the colour of the maple trees was as important to his work as the turn of the tide. When fishing was slow, he would run the boat back into the inlets and we would explore an abandoned homestead or catch a feed of crabs. When the tide was running at twelve knots in Seymour Narrows, he would push the seine boat up the back eddy and through the riptide. With the back eddy adding to the boat's own nine knots, he would sometimes make it through this dangerous spot. But if he didn't make it and had to fall back to await the slack, that was just as well: he loved the feel of moving water on the boat just as surely as my father loved to feel the river currents in which, I remember, he poled his canoe. It was my father's teachings that allowed me to appreciate my father-in-law's teachings.

I left commercial fishing, just as I left sport fishing. But I live within sight of the Fraser River, and I mourn the little Elk River that was destroyed by the dams that my father fought. As I grow older, I find myself, like the salmon, constantly drawn back to my beginnings with rivers, fish, and people—like Captain Vollie McCain on the Mississippi towboat—who live in harmony with the river currents.

Various Articles at Nootka Sound. 1778.
Nootka Sound (King George Sound),
Vancouver Island, S. W. British Columbia,
Canada. Engraving by John Record after
drawings by John Webber.
The articles:

    1. A bird, made of wood; hollow,
    with stones in the inside, which
    the natives shake when they dance.
    2. A seal's head, made of wood,
    worn upon the head.
    3. A bird's head, made of wood and
    feathers, also worn upon the head.
    4. Another worn upon the head,
    and ornamented with green talc.
    PL. 40

Marine Air: Thinking about Fish, Weather, and Coastal Stories

"The kelp in amorous coils appear to pin down the Pacific"

In early summer, I spent an evening with my friend and my daughter, drifting on Oyster Bay in an old fiberglass canoe. Oyster Bay is a long body of water, part of Pender Harbour on the Sechelt Peninsula, which is dotted with small rocky islands. At low tide, almost the entire bay is a length of mud, the channels of the various creeks that empty into the bay articulating the bottom with rivulets of fresh water. Walking the bay at very low tide, you can see weather-worn stakes of cedar, indicating the location of a weir, driven in the last century or before by a Sechelt man or woman wielding a heavy pile driver, perhaps carved with the head of a dogfish looking away from the striking side.

But we were drifting at high tide, letting the currents take us to the head of the bay, where we planned to ease the canoe through the eelgrass and long strands of kelp, up to the cabin where Elizabeth Smart wrote *By Grand Central Station I Sat Down and Wept.* My friend's family owns much of the property on the northwest side of the bay, and the cabin belongs to them, along with various other outbuildings: another log cabin, an old net-shed, two cabins facing one another over a breezeway where a Japanese family lived until displacement in World War II. Occasionally, the cabin Elizabeth Smart lived in is rented out but not this summer. We headed in that direction to look at it and see if the inscription, THE CUT WORM FORGIVES THE PLOUGH, is still legible above the door. We glided past herons and dunlins on the muddy shore and past a pair of mergansers guarding their nesting site. We kept the canoe on course by pushing the paddles against the sides of the creek, where a Virginia rail *kick-kick-kick-ack*ed in the bullrushes and a blue-eyed snake swam strongly through the eelgrass. The surface of the creek was broken by the flipping of tiny salmon: coming down the creek from the gravel spawning beds further up, they were about to enter the ocean for the next part of their lives.

By Grand Central Station I Sat Down and Wept is not a quintessentially

West Coast book. Intense and passionate, it owes something of its cadences to the Bible and to Shakespeare, and its images of the natural world are subservient to the fierce emotional drama of the narrative. But the passages set in Monterey, where "the Pacific in blue spasms reaches all its superlatives" and "where the sea otters leave their playing under the cliff [and] the kelp in amorous coils appear to pin down the Pacific," are as keenly rendered as much of what we consider to be regional or specific to the Coast. The cabin by Oyster Bay crouches under several enormous broad-leafed maples, cool and green in summer, and Naples yellow, edged in burnt sienna, in fall. I like to think this was what Elizabeth Smart had in mind when she wrote of "the old gold of the October trees, the stunted cedars, the horizons, the chilly gullies with their red willow whips." I've imagined living in this cabin by myself, with the generous life of the estuary at my doorstep. Mornings, I'd drink my coffee and watch the eagles in the stand of firs on the other side of the bay, blackbirds loud in the reeds along the creek. Almost as good, I've begun a novel in which an Irish schoolmaster ends up in a cabin very like this one, on a bay very like Oyster; he scrawls a name for the cabin, "World's End," on a cedar shake with a piece of charcoal from his fire and rows a battered skiff out to the kelp beds to handline for bluebacks (coho salmon in their third year).

At the cabin, we found no sign of the inscription above the door, but my friend thinks that the front area was enlarged in the fifties and the original door used elsewhere. The newer part of the cabin is sheathed in cedar shakes, too, so the proverb might well still be scratched into the logs that are beneath. We looked around and I tried to imagine a writer's life in those years, a woman's life, awaiting the birth of her first child. "On August 26, she felt the first pangs of labour. Mr. Reid, a local fisherman, rowed her by boat to the Mission Hospital," reports Rosemary Sullivan in her biography of Smart. That was 1941. My own daughter, born forty-four years and two weeks later at that hospital's new location in Sechelt, was busy exploring the bluff where you could sit in perfect privacy and watch eagles fishing in the bay.

As far as salmon are concerned, the cedar piles in the bay indicate the very richness of this part of the world. Just up Anderson and Meyer Creeks, which both run into Oyster Bay, are spawning beds for chum and coho salmon. Every fall for the past fifteen years, I've stood by these creeks with my children, watching the mottled fish resting against the sides of the creek, pairing up, using their strong tails to excavate redds in the gravel. We've seen the eagles waiting in the tall cedars for the spent bodies, found ribs and backbones in the woods where bears and raccoons dragged the carcasses. The smell of dead salmon, rotting leaves, and cold water, tea-coloured and fast, is a signature of fall on the Coast.

"You may at once be smelled by Scenting-Woman"

If we'd gone in the other direction that evening, out to Georgia Strait, then north, if we'd had time, and provisions, and inclination, we'd have been heading toward the Kwakiutl fishing grounds. Not that we would make such a journey of an evening, but in the days I'm thinking about, people thought nothing of going great distances in their magnificent cedar canoes: families heading for fishing camps in sun and rain. The villages of Nawitti, Fort Rupert, Alert Bay, with their poles and planked housefronts, fish traps and racks for drying salmon, branches of kelp hung with herring roe, the smell of oolichans and wet cedar—these places had their own poetry, were purposeful and mindful of the importance of ceremony. In his books, ethnologist Franz Boas preserved some of the fishing chants. One ritual had the fisherman stringing nine river-caught sockeye salmon on a ring of cedar branch or withe while chanting:

> O, Swimmers, this is the dream given by you, to be the way of my late grand-fathers when they first caught you at your play. I do not club you twice, for I do not wish to club to death your souls so that you may go home to the place where you come from, Supernatural-Ones, you, givers of heavy weight. I mean this, Swimmers, why should I not go to the end of the dream given by you? Now I shall wear you as a neckring going to my house, Supernatural-Ones, you, Swimmers.

Then, placing the salmon on a mat in his house, the fisherman would continue:

> O Swimmers, now I come and take you into my house. Now I will go and lay you down on this mat which is spread on the floor for you, Swimmers. This is your own saying when you came and gave a dream to my late grandfathers. Now you will go.

I think of this prayer when I'm choosing my sockeye on Ron Malcolm's boat, the *Sapphire Sky,* each body a kind of frozen perfection lying in the hold. I like to think that the souls have left the fish and continued up the river, in this case the Skeena, perhaps as far as Babine Lake. We make a ceremony of the season's first salmon, cooking it outside and inviting friends to share the meal. I use a variation of Susan Musgrave's recipe: instead of marinating fillets in a dish, I brush the marinade over a whole five- to seven-pound sockeye laid out on heavy foil, putting lots of marinade in the body cavity. I then let it sit for an afternoon in the fridge. It takes about forty minutes to cook on a fairly low barbeque and tastes like the northern rivers: wild and sweet on the tongue. There's seldom any left: every morsel is plucked from the skeleton until the backbone lies on the platter like a delicate comb.

GRILLED PACIFIC NORTHWEST SALMON

1/2 c unsalted butter
1/3 c honey
1/3 c brown sugar
2 T freshly squeezed lemon juice
1 t natural liquid-smoke flavouring
3/4 t crushed red-pepper flakes
pinch of allspice (optional)
2 LB salmon fillets, skin on, in two pieces

Combine all ingredients but salmon in saucepan. Cook over medium heat, stirring, for about 5 minutes or until smooth. Cool to room temperature. Arrange the salmon in a dish just large enough to hold it. Pour the cooled marinade over it and let stand for 15 minutes. Turn, baste with marinade, and let stand for another 15 minutes. Prepare hot coals for grilling (or gas barbeque). Oil the grill well and cook the salmon, skin side up, over medium heat, for 5–7 minutes. Turn and cook until fish flakes easily, about another 5–7 minutes. Transfer fish to a platter and serve immediately.

The Kwakiutl halibut songs are also intriguing. The fishhooks, called Younger Brothers, were beaten with burning spruce branches as the fisherman sang:

Now, good Younger Brothers, I am putting on you this sweet smell, good Younger Brothers, that you may at once be smelled by Scenting-Woman, Old-Woman, Flabby-Skin-in-Mouth, Born-to-be-Giver-in-House, when you first fall on the roof of their house, and then take hold of Scenting-Woman, Old-Woman, Flabby-Skin-in-Mouth, Born-to-be-Giver-in-House when they come near you, good Younger Brothers, and do not let go of your hold when you take hold of them.

The hooks must have been tremendously strong, steam-bent wood— yew was used by the Makah, and other peoples used fir, balsam, spruce, hemlock—barbed with bone and later with iron. As the fisherman paid out a line made with spruce root, he exhorted the halibut to be quick about taking her meal, which consisted of octopus or small fish threaded onto the barb. When the fisherman made his catch, he hauled in the line until the head came out of the water. Striking the head with his club, he said,

Indeed, this does not sound bad on your head, Old-Woman, you Flabby-Skin-in-Mouth, you Born-to-be-Giver-in-House, for indeed, I came to do so to you with my club.

and then sent the soul of the halibut away to tell members of its family that it had the good luck of coming to the fisherman's canoe. The hooks were washed, and prayers said to them.

Our halibut comes from Ron Malcolm in autumn, one of a number of fish that he brings back on the *Sapphire Sky* intact but for the viscera. The call goes out from person to person—"Halibut's in!"—and we make our way to Ron's dock to pick up our fish, usually a sixty- or seventy-pounder. Halibut can be *really* huge, the females reaching four hundred pounds or more, and are odd to look at. More symmetrical at birth, they swim like salmon: dorsal fin upright. When they've achieved adulthood, they have adapted to lying on their left side, and their left eye has moved over the top of their head to a new position just above and slightly behind the right eye. Because they are bottom fish, living in very deep water, there is something of the ghost about them, their colouring, and their eerie gaze, even in death. I cut ours outside, on a piece of clean plywood, using a very sharp knife that will cut through the hard bones, portioning it into tough plastic bags. It freezes beautifully, keeping its good texture. The bones are simmered with shallots or an onion, some white wine or dry French vermouth, a bay leaf, and some black peppercorns for stock. Any scraps left after I've made steaks and thick slabs for barbequeing go into chowder. My friend Mary White uses clams and scallops in her recipe, which I've adapted for halibut:

GOOD FISH CHOWDER

about 1 LB of halibut, cut into bite-sized pieces
1 tin of clams or the equivalent fresh
1-1/2 C fish stock or water
1/2 C white wine
2 T butter
2 T olive oil
1/4 C flour
2 diced red or yellow onions or equivalent amount of scallions
4 large red potatoes (use other boiling potatoes if red ones are not available), unpeeled, scrubbed, and diced
2 C milk
2 C light cream
ground pepper to taste
lots of fresh minced parsley

In a large soup pot, cook onions in butter and oil until soft but not brown. Add potatoes and flour, and cook, stirring, for 5 minutes. Add stock and wine and simmer for about 10 minutes or until potatoes are tender. Add halibut and clams and simmer gently for about 10 minutes. (If you're using fresh clams, scrub them and steam them open in a heavy pan, shaking the pan, while the potatoes are cooking. Remove the meat from the shells, strain the juice, and add both meat and juice to the chowder.) Add milk, cream, and pepper. Heat through until steaming. Garnish with parsley.

NOTE: This is terrific with the addition of a little smoked salmon. Not mild cure or lox but the barbequed tips you can often get quite cheaply. A little—quarter-pound?—will add great flavour.

In his comprehensive *Ethnology of the Kwakiutl,* Boas included many fish recipes collected and recorded by George Hunt, of Fort Rupert: roasted salmon, blistered salmon, dried salmon, old salmon, green salmon, and boiled salmon, among others. What is most impressive is the variety of methods for using every part of the fish in ways best suited for that part. There are recipes for salmon spawn with salmonberry sprouts (I've eaten these sprouts, and they taste a little like celery, a welcome early green on the Coast); boiled salmon guts, cheeks, tails, and fins; seal and porpoise; herring spawn, chitons, and sea slugs; and dried halibut head, the recipe for which calls for soaking the head in the bilge water of a fishing canoe. There are also recipes for lily bulbs, lupine roots, clover, crabapples, viburnum, elderberry, and huckleberry, among other succulent plant foods. Reading this lengthy section of Boas's book, one cannot help being impressed by the resourceful spirit of these cooks, preparing meals that were true reflections of the world around them. No wonder the feast dishes were so beautiful: they were created both to acknowledge the origin myths of the family and to provide suitable receptacles for honouring the food and family. One chant, recorded by Boas, exhorts the fish:

> Go now and tell your father, your mother, your uncle, your aunt, your elder brothers, and your younger brothers, that you had good luck, because you came into this, my fishing canoe.

"The sky is turning over"

In the Provincial Archives there is an 1868 photograph of salmon drying on racks by Hell's Gate: strung on poles, the fish catch the warm wind and sun funnelling through the canyon. There is evidence that people have lived for at least nine thousand years in this area, relying on rich runs of fish for sustenance. Cultures that depend upon something as intimately as the coastal and river First Nations peoples depended upon salmon generally express the dynamism of the relationship in every aspect of their lives, from practical fishing gear to songs and prayers to vessels that hold and cook the fish to ingenious methods of preserving fish for the winter months. One has only to look at the pile drivers, halibut hooks, tobacco bowls, clothing, baskets, and hilts of daggers, or to read some of the transcriptions of prayers to see how interwoven those cultures were with the means of their subsistence. Some modern writers have written out of a similar relationship. In those cases where a people's nourishment is not so dependent upon fish, it might be argued that fish and fishing, the life of the ocean, speak to a spiritual hunger for connection.

In my own community, Pender Harbour, Native fishermen have been netting salmon and digging clams for hundreds of years. My friend on Oyster Bay lives in a house constructed over and among shell middens, and when the tide is low, she can see the piles from the ancient salmon weirs sticking out of the mud like signposts. Digging in the garden, her family has found pieces of slate blades from fish knives. Once my friend's husband thought, as he sat on some rocks, that generations of people had likely been cutting up fish on the same rocks. Turning, he found a complete slate blade on a little shelf of rock where it had been placed and forgotten a century or more ago by someone sitting where he was sitting, perhaps pausing in his work to watch eagles pick off merganser chicks from the water near the small rocky islands. White fishermen have been leaving the harbour in boats for a hundred years, heading to various fishing grounds for herring, halibut, salmon, black cod, and prawns. Each fall, when all the boats are back from the north or from the west coast of Vancouver Island or from the mouth of the Fraser River, there is a homecoming dance in the community hall. All the old fishing families are represented (the white ones, that is, because the Native boats sail out of Sechelt now): the MacKays, the Malcolms, the Reids ("Mr. Reid, a local fisherman, rowed her by boat to the Mission Hospital . . ."), the Camerons, the Warnocks. And some years the boats are represented, too, by a photograph or a flotilla hung on the walls among the balloons and streamers: the *Sapphire Sky,* the *Gallivanter,* the *Scotia,* the *Belle Isle,* the *Ocean Viking,* all of them home safe and their skippers dancing on dry land for a change and not untangling gear in a storm or sitting in Prince Rupert in the rain, waiting for an opening.

Several years ago, my son Forrest conducted a census of the cutthroat population of the lake near our home. They are a rare population, spawning in the fall, while most freshwater cutthroat—as opposed to coastal cutthroat, which have a residency period in salt water—spawn in the spring. Forrest began his project as a result of spending a day with a Ministry of Environment technician who was clearing debris from the spawning area. The technician said no one had a clear idea of the number of fish in the lake and suggested that Forrest undertake a census, providing the forms and listing some steps to follow. Mostly the project involved regular visits to the creek that the fish spawned in to determine when they first migrated from the creek to the lake. After school each day, Forrest went to the creek at a set time and counted fish for half an hour. There was a way of extrapolating real numbers from this brief but regular count. The census was completed when there were no more fish to be seen in the creek. Most days I went there with Forrest and walked the shore, alert to the movement of trout in the clear water. Some idled under the low limbs of cedars and alders; some shot up the quick rapids and darted among the big rocks. We saw lots of cutthroat and were lucky enough to observe all sorts of birds, too: ouzels and dippers running along the creek bottom, a heron waiting on the bridge rails, a kingfisher squawking from a high tree. A neighbour, out with his dog, told us he'd been walking the creek all fall and one day had seen seven otters feeding off the carcasses of trout. We kept our eyes open for otters but didn't see one. When the census was complete, Forrest turned his findings into a project for his school's science fair. What I remember most about those days we walked the creek and counted cutthroat, often in rain, was the fresh smell and the damp air, our hair and skin jeweled with mist.

When we go to look at the salmon spawning, it's always the smell of fish, the living and the dead, that I notice the most. The living fish, on the final stretch of the long swim home, have shredded tails and patches of deteriorating tissue all over their bodies, and the dead fish have been pulled from the creek to be eaten by birds and mammals. But the cutthroat spawn a number of times and return to the lake after depositing eggs in the gravel. We found on the bank of the creek, perhaps carefully removed by an otter, one perfect specimen, dead but with no sign on its body of a struggle, no eye nipped out, its belly intact. Leaning over to rearrange it slightly for a photograph, I could smell only the earth it reposed on, mossy and rich, and the wet stones of the creek bank.

Last fall we took to walking the creek again, watching for cutthroat. For some days, nothing. Then one Sunday we pushed through salmonberry and thimbleberry bushes to an area just up the creek from the lake. A deep pool, formed by a natural dam of fallen trees that painted turtles reclined upon in summer, was hung over by a few huge cedars. Looking closely we could see at least a dozen big trout idling in the shadows cast by the limbs of cedar. Shafts of sunlight poured through the higher branches, the light refracting as it hit the surface of the creek. I thought I'd never seen anything so lovely. Occasionally another trout would swim up to join the others in the deep pool, and sometimes one would suddenly dart away to the faster water racing under the bridge. We watched for some time and then walked to the trail that leads along the creek to where the water races and tumbles on its urgent way to another lake a mile or two away. We could smell, just faintly, the heavy sea air coming in from Agamemnon Channel on the wind. I knew in the deepest possible way why there are poems for fish. Hilary Stewart, in her book *Indian Fishing: Early Methods on the Northwest Coast*, gives us one such poem:

> I will sing the song of the sky.
> This is the song of the tired—
> the salmon panting as they swim up the swift current.
> I walk around where the water runs into whirlpools.
> They talk quickly, as if they are in a hurry.
> The sky is turning over. They call me.

Migration of the Zucchini

I

In August when the orange petals
have fallen off in disrepute

and the garden has become crowded
and dry, the zucchini begin their migration.

No one knows where they are going.
And at first the zucchini themselves

aren't certain. At night, the stems
of their old selves reach out and drag

them unceremoniously over the dirt
and it hurts, the way it always hurts

to get started. But by then
they're underway, their pale bellies

shifting so slightly upon the crushed
petals that line the predetermined routes.

Above them, switch after switch of starlight
blinks on, as if it would light the way

for these bruised souls, who have imagined
themselves as great nomads

and therefore will be surprised
no matter where they are tomorrow.

I I

For zucchini, hell may be nothing more
than a matter of being
left behind

and to compensate
they have learned how to
imagine themselves as something else.

They have been canoes
overturned by heavy weather.
They have been primitive snakes.

They still have the shape, they say,
of small pills and all their promises.
Some are pontoons.

Some are ancestral watermelon.
They lie upon the ground
like old socks dreaming of feet.

There was an old worm
in the sediments of the Burgess Shale
that looked just like a zucchini.

Before it popped, the child
had a red balloon twisted into
the shape of a dog with four legs.

And yes, then it popped.

They are moored to the ground
like a fleet of zeppelins
with their dreams of hydrogen.

And yes, look how it burns.

I I I

If you enter the garden
after midnight

you must be
merciless.

You must find the
largest zucchini.

If it is pointed
towards the North Star

you will know
that departure

is imminent.
If you remove

the largest zucchini
from the garden

you will create such
unthinkable chaos

that those remaining
become immobile.

You will create plenty.

IV

What is the front
of a zucchini?

With lettuce
there's a head.

With pumpkins it's easy—
they get a face, although
this is admittedly
a social construction.

But with zucchini
the questions
are more difficult.

We know
they are blind from birth

that they are guided
by a low-frequency sound

played deep
within the course of events

that they lie
on the September garden
like the carcasses of tongues

that for every dead zucchini
a small constellation
is added to the sky.

And still, we don't know
their orientation.

Unless, of course, they
are moving. Then we think
they must be facing the future

and all we ever see
is the backside of the zucchini.

v

The passage
of the zucchini

wears ruts in the earth
so shallow

that you could not see them
except that

after the zucchini are gone
nothing else can grow there.

They are different in scale but
similar in look to the

slight depressions worn
under swings in the playground

brushed bare by so many feet
wanting to fly.

V I

One Halloween
after a particularly generous garden
we gave zucchini to kids
trick-or-treating at our door.

Ghosts and witches and
angels, they all dragged
pillowcases weighted
with apples and kisses
and one 4-lb. zucchini
down the cold October
sidewalk

back towards paradise.

Our Small Republic

On Saturday afternoons a wind blows from the west, off the water. An old man shivers inside his coat and sucks at his cigarette as he waits to buy his ticket for the matinee. Because we still allow smoking in our theater, the tips of cigarettes glow in the darkness, ephemeral as fireflies. From our balcony we watch as the old man buys his ticket, then shuffles into the theater. *Le Notti di Cabiria* plays today, as it does every Saturday. Because he sees the film every week, the old man knows the screenplay by heart. He repeats whole scenes, at the café, when he's drunk enough, in Italian, though he doesn't understand that language. Maybe after we make love we'll get up and watch a few minutes of the film. We might catch the scene with the fortune-teller, or the scene in which the young man steals Cabiria's money but can't bring himself to throw her over the cliff. She walks down the road, in despair, crying, and the carnival music starts and the bicycles pass and she smiles. Maybe we won't get up for the movie at all. We might just lie in bed, as we so often do on Saturday afternoons, dozing and making love again, waking entirely only when the kids march down the street on the way back from the park. Maybe then we'll stroll to the beach. We walk for a while, wading out as the tide recedes. You name the soft creatures in those pools for me, and I forget the names as fast as you utter them. We step inside one of those concrete bunkers left over from the last war, the one nobody remembers anymore. The bunker smells of seawater, and of the lovers who huddle there, shuddering together. Back in town, we stop at the café. We pause outside, studying our local vulture as he wheels over us. The old man is inside, working on his first *vin rouge* and describing the film. He's delighted, surprised, as though he's just seen it for the first time. We settle at a table with our coffees, listening as the old man plays each scene word for word, gesture for gesture—Cabiria in despair, Cabiria in love, Cabiria laughing. As we listen we wait for the kids to return. Tonight they're a little late, those kids with the rope they tie around the doorknob of the café. Then they pull, slowly, with patience, with the strength and persistence of children, pulling until the town comes loose from its moorings, and the café and the movie theater and our balcony slide downhill toward the sea, across the sand and into the water. They drag us under the waves, burying our republic in the depths of the sea, as they do every Saturday.

Ginny

My mother didn't like it when I arrived at my grandma's birthday party with my short boyish haircut and long skirt, which looked like old-fashioned underwear to her. You know how mothers look when they disapprove of something. They are worse than fathers. My grandma didn't care. By the time you're eighty-six you have a right not to care about certain things. That's what I'm talking about. My grandma is like me: she doesn't wear makeup and she says what she thinks. When I came in through the door and she saw me, she called immediately, "There is Ginny! Come, sit on my lap, my little beauty!" She pulled me close to her while all our relatives and friends stared at us. I had to sit on her lap at the table where everybody else was busy emptying cups of coffee and plates of cherry strudel. I didn't mind. My grandma still smells good, fragrant like old wood—the wood of an old, solid piece of furniture that has absorbed some of the life lived around it. The smell reminds me of ancient fairy tales about deep and strange forests.

I don't like to be touched by my mother. The other day she tried to touch my head and I screamed. She got scared and backed off like a little schoolgirl. All she said was "Ginny" in a thin, hurt voice. I felt bad for her, but I can't help it. I hate when she comes close because I never know what she's up to. When she is in her teary mood, she is around me like a dry sponge. It's not that I hate her; I just don't like to be near her. She is too much of a pleaser for me. I remember when I was ten and we were at Lake Pontaqua swimming. It was a very hot day, so hot that we couldn't walk on the concrete without burning our small feet. I was feeling sick from all the swimming I had done, being in the water most of the day, when she got on my nerves with her sweetness. "You make me barf, Mom! Stop it!" She hit me hard on the mouth and sent me back to the small cabin we had rented. "You're like your goddamned dad!" she screamed. Then she didn't talk to me for two days. Most of that time I had to stay inside the cabin. I still remember the monotonous sound of the ceiling vent and the swirling mixture of shadows and light reflecting from the polished dining table. She was brooding outside in the humid August heat. When we returned to Millborough, she had long phone conversations with friends, and the dark bluish rings underneath her eyes grew larger and larger. I think she was reliving something with my dad, some old stuff she had never talked to me about. One morning before school she told me that I had to see a psychologist that evening. I didn't know what seeing a psychologist meant, but I just said, "Fine, Mom," because I wanted to be in good with her again.

After she had talked first with my mom, the psychologist tried to make me do all the talking, but I was quiet. So she brought out a bunch of toys and puppets. The one I really liked was a crocodile that smiled. I'd never seen a smiling crocodile before, and I was so taken by it that I started talking to it. When I noticed that the psychologist made some notes on a pad, I stopped. My mother seemed to be wrapped up in her own thoughts and didn't say much. When I refused to play with the toys anymore, my mother canceled the next session. She thought it was a waste of money—me sitting there saying nothing or playing with a crocodile for fifty-five dollars an hour.

Grandma laughed when I told her about it. With Grandma I laugh a lot and talk a lot. She couldn't believe that I was silent for one whole hour. The two of us never were. There was always something interesting going on. "I would be rich," my grandma said, "fifty-five dollars an hour." Then she took me into the kitchen and made me a giant sandwich with strawberry jam, the kind I could make my friends envious with. It was loaded with butter and homemade jam, and I had to hold it with both hands so it wouldn't collapse. While I was walking carefully out into the yard, she gave me a kiss and said with a smile, "That'll be fifty-five dollars for the sandwich." With Grandma it hasn't changed in all those years. She can touch me. Now she likes to touch my face. My friend Carol likes it too. She says it's good to feel the pure skin, no makeup, something clear and open.

I was thinking about shaving the hair under my arms and around my crotch, but I know it will itch and I hate that. I remember when I was sixteen and had lice: the doctor told me to shave it all off in order to get rid of them. He said that to punish me because I had told him that I had slept with a boy and had gotten it from him. I didn't know then but heard it later from friends that this doctor always asked girls about their sex lives and prescribed medicine or treatments that were uncomfortable in order to punish them. Since then, I don't really trust doctors. Carol's gynecologist fondled her during an exam.

I didn't think about gynecologists or shaving my pubic hair when I was at Grandma's party, but it was kind of boring. For a moment I wished Jim, my boyfriend then, had come with me. But he doesn't like parties or family gatherings. He would rather spend an afternoon roaming with a pack of wolves across a plain in Alaska or observing the intricate life of an anthill than be inside a room with people who talk and talk. The party got more interesting after I asked a guy I didn't know a few questions. He was a representative from City Hall, some kind of an administrator, who was there to "honor one of the elders in the community," as he said in his toast. I asked him later if he had seen my grandma's social-security check for two hundred and sixty-seven dollars and if he thought that was part of honoring the elders. He coughed politely and smiled. After that, Aunt Birgit started complaining about the treatment she had received in the hospital for her paralyzed arm. She is my mom's half-sister and was one of the first female commercial pilots in the country. She wears her red, curly hair long, and it looks untamed, especially after three or four cognacs. The City Hall guy left shortly after that, without fanfare.

Mom had made her excellent carrot cake. The way I like it, with a lot of lemon peel, ground hazelnuts, and a few apples. I have to admit—she is a very good cook. She is happy working in the kitchen. She usually turns on the radio or listens to a tape of oldies. She smiles standing at the sink and looking out the window. Her eyes are far away while she is cracking an egg or cutting bell pepper. If she really feels good, she starts to sing. She has such a beautiful voice that even after a nasty fight with her, I think I would forgive her anything if she would ask me in her singing voice. She could do it like one of those opera singers who sing about love or their upsets over a miserly or jealous husband. When she was nineteen, Mom sang in a band. The band even did some recordings in a studio, but the producer took off with the tapes and the advance money and they never found him. Her voice reaches very high without being shrill or loud, and it gives me goose bumps every time I hear it. It is hard for me to understand how such a beautiful voice can be within an ordinary person like my mother. In a moment of good feeling for her, I make a promise to the unknown music god that if I ever have some money, I will pay for her to have her music recorded in a fancy studio equipped with the best microphones, amplifiers, and mixers. I imagine her hearing her own voice over huge loudspeakers, filling the studio or an auditorium, and leaning back against the podium with a happy face—listening with that same face she had when she was nineteen. Maybe after the recording it would be OK for her to come up to me and hug and kiss me.

Kinko can touch me anytime. It's so much easier with children. There is nothing corny to it. He is my favorite nephew. He is three years old, and he is as wide as he is tall. His head is as big as a basketball, and he loves to talk. Whenever he sits in my lap, I get into a good mood. He cuddles up and tells me about his world, about small light points drifting through the air, or about a grandpa grasshopper he met that afternoon in the backyard or about his plans to marry Great-grandma when he is a grown-up. Kinko was sitting in my lap when Grandma got up to give her birthday speech. Her veined, old hands pushed back the coffee plate. "I like to talk, as you all know, but I hate speeches. Because I am a bit older than you are, you expect me to have something wise to say." With her lower lip pulled in, she paused and looked around the room. I knew that meant that she was giggling inside. "There is nothing great or mysterious about getting old—it is just one body part after another giving up until the vital ones go. But I want to tell you one thing that might be true: one doesn't wither from the blows one receives but from the ones one didn't give; I mean the justified ones kept inside." She paused again, looking around the room. "Enough! Sally, hand me that bottle of rum." After my mom handed her the bottle, she poured a bit in her coffee and then raised her cup. "This is to all of you, who I have given a blow one time or another, which is nearly everybody here! I hope you forgive me or are even thankful for it! Thanks for not giving up on me!" She emptied her cup while everybody got up and cheered her. My mom wiped some tears from her eyes. I'm not sure, but I think she felt all the love Grandma had for her family, even if it often seemed she was rough. Later that night I went over to Grandma and put my head on her chest. She kissed me on top of my head. It was a strange sensation to have those old lips touch my bones. Someone touching me like no one else can.

I changed into jeans and a dark-green sports jacket, which I had in the trunk of my car, and drove away from her house feeling free to live and free to die. It was weird: there was nothing holding me back. None of my self-doubts or guilt—just a sense of largesse in my body, an inner space that had grown between my organs. I turned on an old Eric Burdon tape and listened to "Ring of Fire" and drove the shortcut around the park on 37th Street. Suddenly I had this urge to stop and walk on the grass. The grass looked so green and sharp. I don't know why I stopped. I have asked myself that question countless times since that day. Was I too full of certainty that there was love inside me, that my life had a destiny?

They were down the small slope behind the maple-tree line, doing drugs. They probably hadn't much to lose, or to win for that matter. No jobs, but lots of anger. Strong and invincible. Great guys. Cool. Looking at the sky and into nowhere, I saw them too late. When I sensed the danger and tried to get back to my car, it was too late. I am a fast runner, so fast that I outran my older brother all through high school. But two of them were already cutting off the path, lit by some old-fashioned wrought-iron lanterns. I could hear the traffic behind me along Lincoln Boulevard. But here—nothing! Not a single car, no citizen walking his dog. Just grass, trees, and those guys.

In war movies they sometimes have scenes where soldiers wear night-vision glasses. That's how it was for me: I could see everything very clearly and in great detail. No colors at all; just pure black and white. Three of them were coming directly towards me. The one in the middle was wearing a wide leather belt with a big silver buckle. I think a bird was embossed on it, a flying eagle. I was wearing jeans and a jacket, so they thought I was a guy they could rough up and have fun with. They laughed when they realized I was a woman, "a bitch," as they shouted. I was still as a rock and didn't say a thing. When they started pushing me around, I saw nothing but their hands. Suddenly the rock in me broke, and I furiously kicked and bit. I had my teeth in the arm of one of the guys, just above the elbow, when an explosion happened in my head, starting from the left ear. I slid to the ground when other explosions hit my forehead and my stomach. I am not a church person, but I thought of Jesus and felt like a slaughtered animal, blood dripping from my mouth and forehead. Then my vision became grainy, and all the signals coming from the outside seemed to take long detours inside my body till they finally arrived in my brain. I smelled the alcohol, then felt them pulling on my clothes and legs. I tried to push all those fingers and bodies away, but my muscles didn't function. It seemed that every muscle, every nerve and joint, was disconnected. Their bodies were on top of mine, opening it up, and my brain told me, "Ginny, they are inside you," but there was no connection to my genitals. My body was hanging down from my head like a big broken limb. The last thing I remember was that strange sound of a bone in my face breaking. It was a dry sound, like when a branch snaps under the weight of snow, and there was only a dense, pulsating silence in which I floated on top of bloody cotton.

Jim was the first thing I saw in the hospital. His face came slowly into focus and then went out again. I wanted to leave my head, which felt like a huge turbine transforming thoughts into unbearable pressure and every small eye movement into a torrent of pain. "Stay still, Ginny," he said. His voice was very thin and distant, but it was him, and I could sink again into the sea of cotton. As the time in the hospital went by, it was easy for me just to lie on the bed and let my mind hang somewhere in midair, or let it travel outside the large window and look back at this person others called Ginny. When my friends or relatives came for a visit, my mind would come back and join me again, and I guess I looked quite normal under the circumstances. Grandma came often, and those visits were the only times I can remember that we were silent together. She was there to make sure my mind didn't fall and crash. Being quiet together in that hospital room, I felt we were the same age, she and I. I didn't know if I had aged or she had become younger—we were of one generation of women who had lived for a long time.

A nurse had shaved my head for surgery. That's when I thought about leaving it shaved. It was even cleaner and more straightforward than my short hair. Everything superficial seemed to be stripped away. There was no pretense. Just like death. Real. No imitation. Like a naked body. The way some wild people in the Amazon carry birth, death, truth in their naked bodies. Some keep the skulls of their ancestors in their huts and look at them every day, even sleep on top of them. Even elephants, I heard, visit the skeletons of relatives and touch them with their trunks. I think that's what Grandma and I were doing.

After several weeks of lying down, it felt awkward to be in an upright position again and to walk. When I laid back down, I remembered how I went down with the first hit. The scars on my head started hurting. Now they function as new senses: they detect the most subtle things. Sometimes it is too intense, and I think about growing my hair again, to cover them up so I'll be less sensitive. But then I think it is only right that people see my scars. We all have some.

A few weeks later I was on my way home from the hospital. Jim, my mother, and Carol picked me up in Carol's new convertible. She drove slowly, and Jim and my mother were sitting with me in the back seat, holding my hands. I wanted to have the top down and feel the air, but my mother wouldn't let me. I wasn't in the mood for fighting and I knew she felt protective of me. Lucy, Fernando, and my brother John were at my apartment. Everything was clean and there were lots of flowers. They had twenty candles burning. "For the birthday you missed," Lucy said. "You overslept in the hospital."

"You never liked to be celebrated," John added. We all laughed.

Later I told Jim that I wanted to be alone in my bed and he could sleep on the couch. Even after weeks, when I felt a bit turned on, I didn't want anybody close to me. I just wanted to feel the sheet on my skin and nothing else. I just wanted the ceiling and the walls around me. I don't know where all this will lead. I wish I could leave my body sitting here for a few weeks and then come back and feel the difference, feel what time is doing to me. Then I could enlarge those subtle, minute changes and see the direction my life is taking. Often my feelings seem to be together inside me, in a blender going at low speed. I look at myself in the mirror and see my eyes flashing out underneath long, dark eyebrows. The face doesn't stop at the hairline but goes all the way into the skull. The scars are dark and look like they are hot. I have less patience for stupid games and the bullshit people do to each other. Some say that I'm rude. People who don't know me think it is because of the assault, but that's not true. I was like this before. It is just clearer now. The truth is that I don't have enough time left to get all the blows out of my body. I don't want them in me for the rest of my life. I want to make room for something else. I told my mother that I wanted her to write a song for my next birthday.

Jim is still a good friend of mine, but we're not lovers anymore. I need a bigger guy, someone with more weight and muscles. Although my body has healed and I'm strong again, I need a bigger body. Jim feels too much like a child who was never hurt. I know that he cannot understand the loss that I feel and also the weird joy of survival. Those guys tried to make me sterile for love. But they didn't succeed. I have this longing for a child. It comes out of nowhere. I'd like for Grandma to have her first great-granddaughter through me. I will let her choose a name.

Whoopers

I avoided Mr. VanderWaal as much as I could that fall. It wasn't easy, since he helped at our place a lot after Dad caught pneumonia. But if facing Dad was hard for me, talking to Mr. VanderWaal was almost impossible.

When I shot Mr. VanderWaal's cow, he didn't act all that upset. It was Dad who wouldn't let go of it. He took away my gun. "You get it back when you can convince me you deserve it," he said. "A gun is not a toy. You don't make mistakes with a gun."

I still don't know how I hit that stupid cow. I was shooting gophers along the edge of the coulee, down past the correction line. They would stand up at the edges of their burrows squeaking at me. At the shot they would collapse, kicking in the dust, or drop down the hole.

I had twelve gopher tails and was just heading back for the road when I spotted two gophers. They were chasing each other about at the edge of the big field Dad had just finished seeding to winter wheat. Both ducked into a pile of rocks. One came out and stood up.

I sat, settled the sight on the base of his little rodent head, and squeezed. He dropped, twitching, and at the same moment there came a horrible bawling from the coulee. I stood up. Sweet Jesus, one of Mr. VanderWaal's cows was thrashing about in the buckbrush a quarter-mile down the coulee!

Her calf ran to her and nudged her side. She tried to stand and collapsed again. I felt sick to my stomach. My bullet had put her down; I hadn't checked behind my target. I also knew that nobody shoots a cow by mistake.

I thought of running away from home, pretending to be sick so nobody would find out who shot her, even—for a moment—of shooting myself. In the end, though, I could find no way out of facing Dad. I jogged for home along the fence line.

We drove over and picked up Mr. VanderWaal. Dad was too mad to even talk to me. Mr. VanderWaal gave me one long look and then ignored me. I sat between them and felt like a piece of crud.

The cow had stopped struggling when we got to her. Her belly was wet with dark blood and covered with flies. I hung back as the men leaned over her.

"She's a goner," Mr. VanderWaal said.

"Shit." Dad flashed a look at me.

Mr. VanderWaal took his rifle from the truck. He fed one brass shell into the chamber, and closed it. He held the end of the barrel a couple inches from the back of her head. The cow's eyes rolled, bulging with mindless cow-fear as she tried to watch all of us at once. The calf pleaded hungrily from the coulee bottom. The rest of the herd watched solemnly.

At the blast, the cow went rigid. One eye bulged half out of her skull and stayed there, horror fading to blankness. Her whole body stretched. One hind leg flexed, kicking. The leg reached and stretched, tense, as if it were trying to resist what had already happened, then dropped limply. Blood dripped from her shattered mouth.

I threw up. Neither of them even looked at me. I had never seen something die like that before; not the dozens of gophers I had murdered for a dime a tail, nor the chickens whose heads Mom so matter-of-factly hacked off, nor the partridges and prairie chickens Dad and Mr. VanderWaal shot each fall along the coulee.

Later, after we had hauled the quartered carcass back to Mr. Vander-Waal's place, Dad gave me his lecture about guns.

By then I had begun to feel persecuted. I had only made a mistake, after all. It hadn't been like the guys from town. They came out every now and then and shot up signs and mailboxes and things deliberately. It wasn't as if Dad had never made mistakes.

Like the time he and Mr. VanderWaal shot the whooping cranes. He had been a lot older than I when they did it. He had known it was against the law, too.

We had a picture of the dead cranes in one of the family albums. Dad was holding one at arm's length by the neck. Its feet scraped the ground. Mr. VanderWaal was grinning. Dad had a mustache, and his face was rounder and smoother than now. I could not help thinking he looked like somebody I wouldn't like if I met him today.

I studied that picture a lot after they told me about shooting the cranes. It was like a cipher. If I examined it long enough maybe, I would find some clues about what Dad had been like when he was younger—who he had been.

We had been hunting prairie chickens the day they told me about the whooping cranes. It was an Indian-summer day, the coulee slopes red and gold with the fall colours of saskatoon, chokecherry, and buckbrush. We already had seven or eight chickens when we stopped for lunch.

They were talking about how they used to hunt ducks in the stooks, before the days of the big combines. "They used to just pile in," Mr. Vander-Waal said. "All you had to do was throw out a couple dozen tar-paper decoys, burrow down in the stooks, and wait."

"Remember the whoopers we shot that one time?"

They had been sitting huddled into a stook in light drizzle. It was after sunset, and the light was nearly gone. The only way to see the ducks was to look for dark shapes moving fast against the clouds as they arrived, wings whistling in the wet, gabbling quietly to one another as they set their wings and dropped toward the tar-paper outlines below.

Dad shot and saw a duck fold. It fell with a thud among the stooks a dozen yards away. He was standing to retrieve it when Mr. VanderWaal grabbed his arm and pulled him back.

"What?"

"Look."

Ponderous and heavy, wings lifting and falling in great slow-motion beats, seven huge birds materialized from the rain mist. They were flying so low that they had to lift, one by one, to cross the fence line.

One croaked, and then the others began to call, a resonant, two-noted trumpeting.

They flew in staggered single-file, each riding the turbulent wash of another's wing tips. They were so white they could have been mirages, ghosts out of the Pleistocene past. Their wings hissed and creaked, up, down, up, down, as they passed within a dozen yards of the watching hunters.

At the last, without a word being spoken—probably without a thought being thought—Dad and Mr. VanderWaal stood up. The cranes were so close, Dad said, that even in the poor light he could see their heads turn, the primitive little eyes suddenly aware of the men.

Both men shot. Three birds fell. Two were dead when they hit the ground but one jumped to its feet and ran with long, awkward steps into the dusk, dragging one huge, snowy wing.

There were only two cranes in the photo. "You never found it?"

Mr. VanderWaal shook his head. "Coyotes must of got it or something. I never even saw a feather when I went back the next day."

"Never seen a whooper crane since then, either," said Dad. "They were even pretty rare then. Most of them were further east."

"Geez they were pretty things," said Mr. VanderWaal.

It was something about the prehistoric look of those two huge birds, something in the way they seemed to represent a time already past when grain was stooked rather than swathed, when ducks darkened the fall skies, when Dad had a mustache and went hunting on horseback with his school buddies. I kept going back to study that picture. Dad had an old leather wallet full of brightly coloured wet flies his own dad had left him; they gave me the same feeling. There was something important back there that I had missed.

I don't know what I wanted. Lots of those little sandhill cranes were still around. Sometimes I would stop and watch them, turning them into whooping cranes, putting unbroken prairie and undrained sloughs into the big grain fields. But they were not much bigger than geese and I usually saw them on the winter wheat the same as the big honkers that came up off the river each fall. It just didn't work.

I would look at Dad, his lined face, whiskers like steel filings on his cheeks, the bald spot on his head, and try to picture him young and unmarried. It was impossible. He was my dad; he had always been. I don't even know why it mattered. For some reason I just really wanted to know how it had felt to be young at a time when there were whooping cranes to shoot.

We had no shortage of sandhill cranes the fall he caught pneumonia. It was a wet one. The grain was sprouting in the swaths, and it was mid-September before a chinook blew the fields dry enough to combine. Meanwhile, the ducks, geese, and cranes got fat and happy on the swathed grain and the sprouting winter wheat.

Mr. VanderWaal lost time on his own land because of the time he spent on ours. Dad lay in the hospital in town and watched the sky outside the window, or paced the halls coughing. He was not used to being sick. The germs seemed to take advantage of his inexperience. After the first week and a half, he rarely got out of bed at all—just lay there and tried to sleep.

I didn't like visiting him at the hospital, although Mom insisted. I still felt rotten about the cow. So did he, especially since he had to sit there feeling useless while the man whose cow I had shot did his work for him. That's how I figured he felt, anyway. He hardly ever mentioned the work he couldn't do. Mostly he either slept, coughed, or talked about the early days when he had been starting the farm.

I wish I hadn't shot that goddamn cow. I would have spent more time with him.

The rain had ended. The skies were clear, everything fresh-washed and golden in the late-afternoon sun when I looked out the school-bus window and saw the big white birds way out in the winter wheat. I could see three, and one smaller, reddish one. Sweet Jesus: whooping cranes!

The bus turned the corner at the correction line. The birds were gone from sight. "Damn!" I said.

Mom was on the phone when I busted into the house. She didn't look up, just motioned for me to be quiet. I found Dad's binoculars, dumped my books on the couch, and headed back out. Mom put her pale hand over the phone receiver.

"Don't go taking off," she said. "I need you here."

"I'm just going up the coulee a little way." The door slammed before I finished the sentence.

Thinking about it now, I'm almost embarrassed with how worked up I got. It was like I was so charged with adrenaline or whatever it was that swelled my face and sent my feet flying effortlessly across the ground that I was not even myself. The excitement was almost sexual. For four birds. I can't remember having ever felt like that before, or since.

A big pasture of unbroken prairie stretched down from the bluff behind our house to the coulee. It was easier running there than on the field that stretched from the house to the big field, and shorter than going around by road. I flew across the close-cropped prairie grasses, dropping to roll under fences and skipping over badger and gopher holes. Rose prickles and thistle leaves filled my socks. I barely noticed them.

A quarter-mile down the coulee, I figured I must be just about even with the birds. I slowed to a walk and began to climb the slope, heart pounding in my head. I could barely breathe, more from suspense than exertion.

Over the rim. Nothing there. The field was empty.

Sweet Jesus: too late.

I felt sick with the letdown. I did not even know for sure that they had been whooping cranes. Maybe they had just been swans or waveys.

Then I heard a resonant trumpeting unlike anything I had ever heard before. It was like someone blowing across a bottle lip, but higher, louder, and more rolling, a sound that made the sky vast and the distance empty. I shaded my eyes with my hand, staring desperately . . . and there they were.

They were in flight, already half a mile off, flying straight away. All I could see was the white flash of wings as they caught the sunlight on each upstroke. With each downstroke, they disappeared into sky glare.

I watched them going, sick with regret. I willed them to come back, and I knew that they wouldn't. It was out of my hands. They were gone. White over gold, flicker, vanish, flicker, vanish until, at the last moment, they veered to bypass our house and disappear for good behind the poplar windbreak. Even then, their great rolling cries drifted back to me out of the empty sky.

If I had stayed at home, they would have gone right over me.

I stood still. Nothing stirred. The whole prairie was gold and black, utterly still. The sky was barren. The whoopers no longer called.

It was like when Mr. VanderWaal had finished off the cow and I had watched it try not to die when it was already too late and nobody could change what had happened.

How could I have so narrowly missed something I wanted so badly? How could they have gone just then, when I was so near—when it was that important to me?

You can't call things back. You can't turn time back. You can't ever have the things you missed. And when I saw our pickup pull out into the road and accelerate down to the correction line, then turn and disappear behind the swell of land that hid town from view, I ran again, back down the coulee side and through the wet grass toward the house. Only now my feet no longer flew. What I ran toward was gone.

Of Swallows and Doing Time

The wind always blows here. It gathers itself into a steady pulse from the south and breaks across the prison yard with its load of blond talcum. I'd forgotten about the wind. I've been back only a day and already it greets me with its forlorn touch. The feeling wants to overwhelm me. The barn swallows welcome me too, the graceful birds darting here and there in the wind like dark hands throwing gang signs. They know how to take advantage of the wind. But do they know how to deal with the loneliness, the melancholy, the time?

Had anyone said I'd see this place again after gaining my freedom in December 1994, I wouldn't have believed it. My release was a miracle, and now, it seems a miracle I'm back. Eighteen months after a superior-court judge ordered me home to my wife and three daughters, the appellate court overturned his decision and returned me to prison to finish the outstanding four years of my twelve-year sentence. Not that I can complain; I am guilty.

In 1986, I was voted teacher of the year by the Mesa public-school system. I had been teaching only five years and had already found success. I believed I was invulnerable. Then, at the end of that school year, I became infatuated with one of my students. Infatuation led to romance and then obsession. That summer, while I was working at the same youth camp where I had met my wife, the student and I decided to run away together to start a new life in Colorado. I left my wife five months pregnant with our third child. After two weeks in Aspen, we were seen in a bookstore by another teacher from Mesa. The police arrested me while we walked hand-in-hand along the plaza. The girl went back to school, and I went to prison. I was twenty-seven years old; she was fourteen.

The miracle was not so much that my wife, Karen, could get me out of prison in the first place . . . but that she would want to. I had deserted her, degraded her—the stigma of being a convict's wife on welfare relatively minor in comparison to being the wife of a nationally recognized sex offender—and yet she set aside her humiliation and shifted from housewife to law student. While raising three girls on her own, she earned paralegal and political-science degrees. Six years after my arrest, she began working for a criminal-law firm in Tucson. It was her work on my case that got her hired and, with the assistance of two sympathetic (unpaid) lawyers, won my release.

Now I'm back, and it feels as if I've been arrested and convicted all over again. Unlike the swallows, which migrate in and out of this place, I have been left defenseless, insecure, disoriented. Four more years. The time weighs heavily on me.

I find Brad in an empty classroom where he is waiting for his next student. He teaches the men, mostly Mexican nationals, how to read and write: regardless of where you're from, English literacy is a requirement in the Arizona correctional system. I haven't seen Brad for two summers, and he's pleased to tell me about his barn-swallow observations during my absence. Brad is dying. Has been dying for twenty years, but he's getting closer now. He's in his seventies and can't squeeze much more time out of this place, already outlasting cancer in his bowels, a colostomy, and the necessary bag his blue T-shirt could never hide.

Brad's moleskin face splits open and his eyes unglaze when he talks about the birds. He's been watching a nest on the run near his cell since the swallows daubed the mud-pellet cup to the block wall four summers ago. "Three successful nests this time!" he says, exposing several gray and black-rooted teeth. The dentist will pull those soon, I think. "First time ever they've raised three broods in one summer," he continues, then laughs. There's swallow-pleasure in his eyes, and I believe for a moment that the birds allow him to forget about this place, his dying. Like the man in my creative-writing workshop who also watches the swallows and who writes about them in haiku. If the guards even suspected that there are men here who escape on those dark, narrow wings, if only in their minds, they'd shoot the birds.

"There are those birds you gauge your life by," says Terry Tempest Williams. "Each year, they alert me to the regularities of the land." For her, the birds are burrowing owls. For me, they are the barn swallows. I was here, in the Santa Rita prison unit, when the swallows arrived for the first time, in the spring of 1990. Theirs was a tentative advent. Only three pairs came to breed under the visitation ramada, hauling thousands of beak-sized adobe bricks one at a time to construct their pueblo nests. I watched with my visiting wife and daughters as the dark crescents rolled from the sky to streak through the vaulted structure, each one spinning and weaving in an aerial dance as precise as if it had been choreographed and practiced a thousand times. We were familiar with the common birds in the yard: the greasy-black grackles and cowbirds, the beggar house sparrows. Even my three-year-old, Melissa, could name them. But the swallows were different, Stealth Fighters by comparison. Our eyes were drawn to the sleek bodies with their metallic, blue-black sheen and pumpkin breasts, long tapering wings and deeply forked tails. Such poetry from a pointed, seven-inch frame. And voices to match: a cheerful, liquid twittering of notes on descending and ascending scales. That summer, the transients raised twelve offspring, and by the end of September they were gone, migrating south as the first Pacific cold fronts prodded the Southwest. I remember hoping that they would return, wondering if their experiment in nesting here at Santa Rita had been successful enough to make them come back.

Meanwhile, I began to gather stuff on barn swallows. The prison library offered some information, but it was general, encyclopedic. I wrote the Tucson Audubon Library and connected with a kind and helpful woman named Joan Tweit, who sent me more material and never concerned herself about corresponding with a criminal. (Joan proved an invaluable source for me over the years. I finally met her after my temporary release from prison, at a book signing for her daughter, Susan, a natural-history writer.) My wife also helped tremendously by perusing the periodical stacks at the University of Arizona Science Library and photocopying articles from professional journals like *The Auk* and *Condor*.

Soon I was learning things about swallows. And, because of this knowledge, I started wondering why they had come to Santa Rita.

By the end of March the following year, as the mesquite and desert willow finally shrugged winter from their dark branches, I was watching for them every day. I worked as a teacher's aide in a classroom next to the visitation ramada, and every birdlike movement outside the picture windows attracted my attention. During evening church services, held in the same classroom, I waited for that quick flash of wings and sicklelike projectile, that phantom silhouette that could only mean *swallow*. Then one Friday in mid-April, as the sun flattened on the western horizon and the sky turned cayenne, something dipped under the ramada. I stared, and a few seconds later I saw it again. I was sure. They were back.

Over the next month the birds reclaimed two nests from the previous year and refurbished them, packing fresh muddy pellets onto the lip of the old nest cup and reinforcing the work with bits of dried grass. A third nest, also left over from last season, was in dispute. My family and I amused ourselves with the drama of two flustered swallows attempting to drive out some obstinate squatters. A pair of house sparrows had built a grassy nest on the top of the swallows' nest and wouldn't budge. I became convinced that bird vocabulary includes swear words; the arguments lasted two weeks before the swallows finally resigned themselves to sticking a new nest on some other joist. A month or so after their arrival, three pairs of barn swallows were brooding clutches of four or five speckled white eggs. By the end of June two more pairs had joined them. It was small, but it was a colony.

I had read that barn swallows often nest in large groups: as many as fifty-five nests have been found in a single barn. They also seem to prefer human-made structures—barns, bridges, boat docks—especially if they're near open fields, meadows, marshes, or ponds where insects are abundant. The birds are voracious bug-netters, one swallow scooping up hundreds of insects in a day. At the prison, swallows will work a large field in the morning and evening, sailing low to the ground and weaving a block pattern, dipping to intercept their prey, which usually consists of lacewings, flies, and moths. It's these fields, I believe, that originally attracted barn swallows to Santa Rita. The fields and their insect complement.

In 1989, before swallows first nested at Santa Rita, the Arizona Department of Corrections changed the way the Tucson complex dealt with its wastewater. The prison was overcrowded, tents had gone up, cells were being double-bunked. We were taxing the sewage-treatment plant, and its settling ponds had begun to flow. The reclaimed water needed somewhere to go, and we didn't have a golf course. So what was once dust and creosote between the complex's main units (there were three of them at the time: Cimarron, Rincon, and Santa Rita) suddenly became an artificial wetland of weeds and grasses, kept verdant and flooded by a new irrigation system using sewage effluent. Twenty-one hundred men flushing their toilets had turned the desert green.

I noticed the difference in bird life almost immediately. As usual, ravens probed the trash dumpsters; sparrows, starlings, and Brewer's blackbirds winnowed the dirt behind the dining areas for crumbs; and cowbirds roved the soccer and softball fields en masse. But as the evening floodings fertilized the air and the new wetlands, I started counting mallards, gadwalls, killdeer, and great blue herons. When a flock of whimbrels flew over, I was certain the birds were lost. Mourning doves by the hundreds, all coming from separate directions by twos and threes late in the afternoon, would congregate in the grass before flying off together to their roosts. My life list for birds seen in prison doubled, then tripled as I added western meadowlark, lark bunting, Say's phoebe, olivaceous and ash-throated flycatchers, western kingbird, yellow-headed blackbird, Cooper's hawk, and burrowing owl. And once, for most of the morning, a great egret, all legs and beak, stationed itself in the center of the field. I'd never seen feathers so white; it was a blank cutout from a green page. When it wandered into an area of standing water, I half-expected it to spear a fish. As I write this now, I find I'm not surprised that the insect forage of the wetland created by the prison's water-reclamation project drew the barn swallows. Certainly they're more common in the desert than whimbrels and egrets.

For the ramada colony, 1991 was not a good year at Santa Rita. Another breeding pair had constructed a fifth nest in August, but not a single chick had fledged in the entire colony. It was getting late; something was wrong. The only chicks I had seen were scrawny and featherless. On one visit, my daughters had found two under a nest. Both were dead. What confused me was the apparent contradiction I had discovered about half a mile away at the Cimarron unit, where I traveled every Sunday for a creative-writing workshop. By that same August, two swallows at Cimarron had already raised six offspring and had started a second brood. Why was this solitary pair of swallows producing healthy birds while the ramada colony was not? I believed there were two keys that unlocked this riddle: the nature of bird colonies in general, and the nature of the weather at Santa Rita in particular.

I didn't jump to this conclusion in a moment of inspiration; the idea came slowly. As I read the work of scientists who had studied barn swallows, one question kept arising: why colonies? The best argument I found *for* barn-swallow colonies involved the bird's preference for nesting places that were already established in ideal habitats with a history of reproductive success. (Talk about your chicken-or-the-egg story!) However, field observations seemed to support the idea that the cost of nesting together was too great: more competition for nesting areas, food, and mates and a greater likelihood that predators such as raccoons might discover and destroy a whole colony would conspire against colonial nesting. Solitary nesters had none of these problems: no competition for resources; less chance of predation.

I knew this, but it was the second key—the weather—that really helped me solve the riddle. In southern Arizona, the summer of 1991 turned out to be one of the driest in recent years. High temperatures averaged 105 degrees. The monsoon storms were late, shrinking the normal amount of rainfall for that year by inches. One result of this unusual weather, and a serious problem for the brooding ramada colony, was a drought of flying insects. I had an idea that limited food resources, due to the failed monsoons, were working against the Santa Rita colony because there were too many birds in the area. In contrast, the solitary barn swallows at Cimarron were doing fine.

I sent a letter to Mary Bowers, then editor of *Bird Watcher's Digest*, telling her about my conclusions and suggesting that I write a feature about the barn swallows at Santa Rita. She had already published my article about Harris' hawks, saying in her acceptance letter, "I get a lot of articles from prisoners, most of them invariably bad. Yours is different, however . . ." We were developing a good relationship, and she asked to see my barn-swallow piece. She published it in the March/April 1993 issue with a photograph of a single swallow gripping a strand of barbed wire. Quite appropriate, I thought, for an article from a writer "based" in Arizona.

When I wrote about the barn swallows for *Bird Watcher's Digest*, I didn't know where the ramada colony was headed. I continued making notes of its progress—counting the number of nests and chicks—for the next four seasons, until my release in 1994. The colony seemed to be just holding on.

Now that I'm back I notice it's gone. Perhaps I had been right: the prison yard and its flux of insects couldn't support it. I could blame the weather. I could also blame the visitation guards who knocked down the nests to keep the ramada free of the "mess" the birds made and who thereby destroyed the attractiveness of the site to the birds. Once, I tried to explain to an officer the necessity of leaving the nests alone even after the birds were gone. He looked at me as if I were crazy and said nothing. I felt like a fool.

But even though the colony has dissolved, the birds still hang on. Solitary pairs have begun building nests under the eaves of the runs at some of the cellblocks, spreading them out so that there is only one or, at most, two nests on each of the four yards. Like the swallows at Cimarron, the birds have found an alternative to colony life. And now, out among the inmates, they're better off for it.

Today, Steve brings me a swallow he's found injured and wants to know what he can do. I see one wing has a red bruise underneath it and tell him the bird may survive if he can get it to eat. Risking disciplinary action for keeping an unlawful pet, he carries the tiny bird to his cell and makes a simple perch for it under his television. While the swallow sits quietly, Steve stalks the run for flies, swatter in hand. He offers the freshest morsels to his charge, but the bird ignores them. It refuses his nudges and proddings, but he won't force it. Tonight, the swallow will slip from its perch and flutter mothlike on Steve's bunk. He won't know what to do except hold it until the spasms stop, watching as one foot extends to grasp at nothing.

The men whose cells are near a swallow nest continue to impress me with their sensitivity to the birds. Men like Steve. Or Brad, who is fiercely protective of his swallow family, monitoring its growth year after year, counting eggs and chicks, marking off the days to hatching and fledgling, watching for additional broods. "I counted thirty this morning," he told me yesterday. "All of them singin' and carryin' on. I'm gonna miss 'em when they're gone." It's September, and I've noticed too: the swallows are gathering in preparation for the migration south. I wonder how I will have changed by the time they return . . . and if time will still have weight.

Years ago, the swallows had allowed me to feel the weight of time and, in doing so, to feel the pain of remorse for what I had done. I had accepted this: the first steps toward change, toward health. Now, as I see them in this place again, a measure of hope returns. There's more than the heaviness of time.

Thinking about it, it seems ironic how overcrowding in this prison and the solution to the consequent wastewater problem have affected the inmates, have affected me. Twenty-one hundred men flushing their toilets has done more than settle the dust under a mat of vegetation. It's turned this bleak place into a wildlife island, a rest stop and refuge for wings and beaks and talons. And every spring, and for five or six months following, it's given us the swallows, gifts of grace on narrow wings.

I gauge my life by the swallows. Their nature, like many things in the world, is cyclic; they live inside the regular heartbeat of the land. Ebb and flow, rise and fall. It's a pattern I can live with, one that gives me hope. As long as the swallows come in the spring and go in the fall, come and go and come, I'll feel their rhythm, measuring it out as a change of seasons. This is the source of my hope: the swallows not only make me feel the weight of time; they also cue me to the passage of time. Where ancient peoples raised stones to track equinoxes and solstices, the swallows are my Stonehenge. In a place where clocks and calendars are meaningless, where hours and days and months percolate into one homogenous, stagnant pond, I mark the swallows.

Lionbird

I

North-central Nicaragua, Holy Week, late in the dry season. I caught three rides quickly, but then my luck broke down sixty kilometers past Matagalpa and fifty short of Waslala. A store owner and his family had given me my last ride, to their own doorstep, and predicted that I would get no further.

I parked my backpack in the shade of a tree. There was no public bus that day, and we'd seen no commercial traffic either, but I was sure someone else was fool enough to be on the road. I sat on a wooden gate and chatted with Luis, the store owner, and with his daughters. When they went indoors for lunch, I stayed by the road with one last companion, a short-haired dog asleep at my feet. His coat would have been black if you'd clapped the dust from it. Intelligent dog, that one, taking his siesta in the heat of the day. I was getting sleepy myself. I stood and stretched and rolled my neck back. I was under an evergreen tree whose needles broke into rigid, laminar patterns.

I suddenly saw a huge bird among the needles. It was stone still, perched on a branch about twice my height above me. When Luis and his daughters returned, I pointed to the animal.

Luis nodded. "He's been there for three days. He's dying. One of my men hit him by accident, and then put him in that tree. He's been there ever since."

"Are you sure?" I didn't like this news. "Owls are stupid in the daytime. Maybe he hunts at night and comes back here to sleep during the day."

"To the same position?" Luis asked dryly.

I began searching the ground for owl pellets. There were none. Luis took a long stick and prodded at the animal until I told him to quit. "I only wanted to show you his beak," Luis said. "He has a huge beak."

The girls were urging me to join them at the river, but I had to say no. I couldn't afford time away from the road. Luis collected the family in their yellow pickup and they left; I waved good-bye and settled in the shade to wait. It was after 2 P.M. The dog barely moved, the bird not at all. Not a single vehicle passed in over an hour. Occasionally a man rode by on horseback; once a few women and children walked down the dusty road in bright churchgoing clothes. But generally there were no sounds and no traffic; the air was so still that I began having auditory hallucinations of approaching vehicles.

I kicked in the dirt and uncovered an AK shell, green-rimmed. Three years after the cease-fire we were still picking up bodies. One of my earlier rides had cautioned me as he dropped me off: "Be careful. There was combat recently near Waslala. There was one dead."

Waslala had always been a tough area, and I was neither surprised nor particularly scared. "Where?" I'd asked. "This side of Waslala or the other?"

"The other."

"When?"

He had ruminated. "The eighth."

My mind had been on the traffic and not on the conversation, so I'd thanked him and then stood by the roadside to catch another ride. Now I was stalled and had time to think: Oh yes, the eighth. Near Waslala. What day is it today? Today is the—uh—ninth.

And then—was it?—a real noise; a blue pickup with yellow license plates. I put out my thumb and the pickup drove past without pausing. An international-mission vehicle and it hadn't picked me up even to ride in the back! I was astounded. The engine faded and left me with my hallucinations.

Another dusty dog had come to join the first, and both were asleep at my feet. I sipped lukewarm water. Across the road a few men began to collect, waiting for Luis's family to come back and open their store. Another group of men was passing on the road when the bird suddenly came down from the tree like a stone with feathers. Wings outstretched, it fell forward on the ground. Then it pushed itself upright, curling its wings inward for balance. It stood sixteen inches high at least. The head was twisted to one side and back. One eye was completely out of its socket.

I stood and stared, trying to separate what was only the bird's daylight clumsiness from what might be actual injury. Meanwhile the men gathered around. The bird staggered and rested half-upright. The wing feathers were white and gray and black; the chest was mottled brown. I used the only word I knew for owl in Spanish—*buho*—but the men corrected me: it was a *pájaro león,* they said, a lionbird. One of the men waved a branch near the animal's beak. The jaws snapped open and they were huge; I could have put my fist down the bird's throat. The men cheered. *Muerde duro,* they cried. He bites hard.

Rural Nicaraguans aren't offered much formal education. Their biology lessons are impromptu, and so they often experiment in order to learn.

The men prodded the bird, but not cruelly, so I held my tongue. I was thinking: Three days. Now it's Good Friday and time to die. Have I wine or vinegar? No, but I have boiled water. I uncorked the bottle and poured water carefully around the lionbird's beak. Its jaws smacked open and shut a few times, and then shut absolutely. I laid a piece of cassava at its feet. The head rolled slowly forward and then back again until the beak was pointing at the sky. I totaled the damages: spinal injury, one eye out of socket, barely able to stand. Whatever the men were about—study or entertainment—this bird was not a good subject. I started blocking their sticks. Finally we all agreed to put the lionbird back in the tree.

The men poked at its feet with a stick for it to grab on to. The animal opened its beak and a noise erupted—a ratcheting, almost mechanical growl, as though a massive door were grating on stiff hinges. It took me a while to gather in all the noise and assign it to the bird. The men cheered again. "You should hear him at night, when you're alone!" they said.

At last the bird took the stick in its claws, but when it was lifted it could not grab onto the tree branch and fell to the ground again, near the sleeping dogs. The dogs did not stir; they were oddly uninterested in the lionbird. Finally a kid grasped the tip of one wing, climbed onto the fence, and slung the bird into a thick web of needles near the top of the tree. It wedged there awkwardly. For ten minutes the men and I chatted about nothing, and then down came our lionbird, cradle and all.

Now the men were all business. "Kill it. So it doesn't suffer." I agreed. Four or five began selecting stones. The kid again picked up the bird by one wing—the span of that wing alone was about three feet—and braced the body on the slanting face of a boulder. The men fanned out at a distance. Rocks whistled; a few struck. The lionbird growled. The men moved in with larger stones and now the animal was shrieking. This was a huge and horrible noise, and I bent and tried to loosen a rock from the ground so I could crush the bird myself. But I couldn't get the rock free, and anyway the men knew their business. By the time I straightened up, the bird lay quiet. Someone was being congratulated and clapped on the shoulders—"Those seven years are yours," the men told him.

I went closer. There wasn't much to see; the feathers hid the damage. Blood oozed from the beak and from around the injured eye. The animal lay chest up, and I put a hand on it. No breath, no heartbeat. My fingers easily covered the top of the rib cage, and I thought: My God, it's a bird, just a little bird with a lot of feathers. It was all head and feathers: the body was nothing. I took the dead lionbird back to the tree and propped it on a branch. On the ground I found a chest feather that had come off in the melee.

A half-hour later a truck picked me up, and I rode to Waslala among sacks of rice and sugar in the open bed. The driver had rescued another stranded traveler as well, a man from a village near Waslala. I told the man the story and showed him the feather. With long, gentle fingers, he inspected it. "Anyone who kills a lionbird gets seven years bad luck," he said. "They're not pests. They're actually helpful." He seemed reluctant to return the feather.

II

About Caprimulgiformes, the scientific name for this order of birds, the 1979 *Encyclopaedia Britannica* states: "There is now a tendency to replace the name goatsucker with the more appropriate term nightjar." I hope the *E.B.* is right. The word "goatsucker" has been hijacked recently by an entirely different and extremely improbable creature—a pointy-mouthed, goblin-like being, possibly of alien origin, that sucks the blood of small mammals. Rumors place it in Mexico, Central America, and southern Florida.

The original goatsuckers are not mythical creatures accused of real deaths—rather, they are real animals accused of mythical crimes. Centuries ago, people saw birds flitting around their goats or other livestock at night, and they suspected that these birds were stealing milk from the goats' udders. Hence the birds' eventual scientific name: Caprimulgiformes, from the Latin *caprimulgus,* milker of goats. But the birds were after insects, not milk; they were eating the insects that were feeding on the livestock.

Whippoorwills are goatsuckers. You may have seen them—the orange-eyed birds that frequent country roads at dusk and rise up and criss-cross in front of your car. Or you've heard the three-note call for which they're named: whippoor*will,* whippoor*will.* I hear them even late at night, which is unusual, since I sleep deeply. Frogs, wind, rain, owls—even when I notice their night sounds, the noises weave back into the darkness and I sleep on. Start up a *whippoorwill,* though, and suddenly I am wide awake. The bird's voice is crisp and musical, like a perfectly played woodwind. It's also *loud.* Hence *nightjar.* Along with being insectivorous and nocturnal, most Caprimulgiformes have in common their loud and rather unearthly cries.

Now take this bird south. The season for feeding on insects lengthens. The size of some insects also increases; the cockroaches, for example, are beyond appalling. Sooner or later the predator of such prey will also grow. The largest goatsuckers—the potoos—are so outsized that some tropical-bird books place their pictures on the owl page. That is where, finally, this confused nonspecialist located her lionbird. Owls were presented facing frontally; the potoos were shown in profile. I recognized my bird for certain when I read the vocal credits: "deep, gutteral, strangled cries." Everyone put in their two cents on the vocals. I agree with "explosive, bawling *bwarrr,*" but even more with "loud, far-carrying . . . *GWOK!*" and "guttural, snoring *GWAWWWRRRR.*"

Take a second characteristic. "Bills relatively small . . . but gapes enormous." The mouth "is large enough to close over a tennis ball." And here I'd been accusing my memory of telling me fish stories; no bird mouth could be as wide as all that.

A third characteristic. "The potoos are noted for a peculiar stance. . . . When alarmed in daylight they slowly flatten their plumage and stretch their bills upward in a stiff posture." This is camouflage: a potoo's protection is its treelike coloring. It perches on upright branches and snapped-off limbs; it looks like an extension of the tree. When frightened, it assumes what texts call the "cryptic" pose—beak in the air, head feathers flattened, becoming less birdlike, even more like a tree.

My list of the lionbird's injuries was falling apart. The lionbird had trouble standing? Because it is a tree-percher, not a ground bird, its tail gets in the way. The lionbird's head rolled back on its spine? Well, so does mine—that's how I caught sight of the bird in the first place. The lionbird was found in the same perch day after day? Documented behavior: healthy potoos have favorite perches. The lionbird's eye was out of its socket? Perhaps—or had I mistaken the huge-eyed glance of a night-hunting bird?

I had not. That, at least, was real. Based on the pictures, I think potoos may have a propensity for dislocated eyeballs, rather like Pekinese dogs. But perhaps, as with some dogs, one can reposition the eye without permanent damage. The bird's head was twisted to one side, but I can't *assume* that meant a spinal injury, not when my other assumptions had been so poor. The bird was weak and couldn't fly to feed itself, but that needn't have been fatal. Had I known its diet, I could have fed it, starting with those appalling cockroaches. A little patience, a little expert knowledge, and killing may become unnecessary.

Which is not to say that potoos—even healthy potoos—would be easy pets. You wouldn't be able to let them hunt without losing them, so you'd be obliged to collect their insect and rodent dinners yourself. And they definitely wouldn't endear you to the neighbors, croaking as they do like the fatal entrance of Duncan under your battlements.

There are half a dozen identified species of potoo, but only two presumed resident in Nicaragua: *Nyctibius grandis,* the great potoo, and *Nyctibius griseus,* the common potoo. To confuse matters, however, there is *Nyctibius jamaicensis,* the northern potoo, which resembles the *griseus* in all but voice, and which some experts speculate is either concurrent with or else replaces the *griseus* in certain areas.

I suspect our lionbird had been the largest potoo, the *grandis,* which can reach twenty-one inches in length. Although our bird had seemed shorter, I hadn't calculated the tail, which had been bent along the ground, making the animal stagger. It isn't that I want to claim a rare sighting. I might have preferred to meet the common potoo, the *griseus:* it has a famously beautiful voice. On the other hand, I'd just as soon *not* meet the *griseus*—or any other animal—under the circumstances in which I met the *grandis.*

Still, I would like to have heard one. Apparently, the common potoo's song is enough to make a grown man want to leave home. In 1930, in Argentina, Robert Lehmann-Nitsche published a collection of indigenous South American legends about goatsuckers. Most interesting to me was a purportedly true story involving *N. griseus* in 1860. An absentee landowner received a note from his overseer: the overseer could not continue in his position; his family was frightened; to whom should he hand over care of the property? The landowner, greatly surprised, traveled to the country to investigate. The people in the area were terrified: every night, strange wails came from a particular tree, yet the dogs did not bark or growl when they approached, so the people believed something otherworldly—perhaps agonized souls—was in the branches. The people left paper, pen, and ink in the tree's fork so that the souls might communicate the cause of their misery, but they received no reply, and the wailing continued. The overseer's wife recounted the prayers and rosaries she had said for the souls, to no avail.

The story concluded, as you might expect, with the landowner shooting one of the birds in the tree and frightening off the others, thus ending both the mystery and the wailing.

As you can see from both this story and mine, there is something curious about the dogs' behavior. My two dusty twentieth-century Nicaraguan dogs and Lehmann-Nitsche's nineteenth-century Argentinean dogs refused to bark at potoos. They acted as if asked to bark at the tree itself.

III

I could not find a good photograph of a potoo, but I discovered that there are three tawny frogmouths at the National Zoo in Washington. Frogmouths are also goatsuckers, Australian cousins to potoos; they are almost as large as the potoo and perhaps a bit scruffier. The coloring is similar—a forest camouflage of mottled gray, brown, white, and black. When I went to see them, the frogmouths made no exotic neck movements, nor did they scream, but I still recognized them, even after four years. It was like seeing ghosts. Or agonized souls.

In the same birdhouse live two mottled owls. When you have the animals in front of you and you can walk back and forth between the owls and the frogmouths, they are easy to distinguish from each other. The owls are smaller, neater, with short, blunt tails and a determined slumber. The frogmouths waver between sleep and wide-eyed staring. They have an emphatic, V-shaped tuft above their eyes, which gives them a fierce expression. Bristly muzzles surround deceptively small beaks. Only the two long lines dropping from the beaks indicate how wide the mouth can open.

An outdoor cage at the National Zoo houses the granddaddy of owls, an Asian brown fish owl. He's two feet tall and catlike, with ear tufts and claws and a noble, upright stance. His head rotates, but the movement is deliberate, not sinuous. He and the mottled owls keep every feather and every motion under tight control. The frogmouths look unkempt, and maybe this is more than just camouflage. Maybe the irregular feathers trap insects, so that when a frogmouth is done with its evening flying, it can snack between its feather-shafts. But I'm presuming now, as dangerously as ever. There was no one around at the zoo to ask, and two weeks later the birds were gone.

IV

In the morning, in the tree's fork, I find a note. It reads: "You see a potoo and picture an owl. The feathers are rough, so you slick them down. The tail is awkward, so you cut it off. The neck rolls about, so you clamp it in a brace, if you're so inclined, or you just shoot it, if you aren't. Because it looks malformed to you, ugly. Or because you want to put it out of its supposed misery. But years later you will still be picking up the bodies, because potoos will persist in being potoos."

V

The frogmouths had gone underground. Their permanent exhibit was being renovated, and they were in a temporary cage. There, the male flew to the open cage door and puffed himself up to twice his normal size, glaring at me. Round, severe, huge, unblinking eyes. The bird was all face; his face was all eyes. It was like confronting a baleful, feathered Halloween pumpkin. "He bites," said the caretaker, "if you let him."

The two females remained on a high back perch, but they were wide awake and their feathers lay sleek against their bodies, as sleek as owls' feathers. Apparently they can, like actresses, control their unkempt look, but may puff themselves up during sleep or under threat. Only when they're *really* frightened do they "disappear": nose in the air, invisible, an inverted ostrich. The caretaker said she'd witnessed this only under certain conditions—being zoo animals, they were used to lots of activity. "Construction sets them off," she said, "or else seeing-eye dogs."

On later visits I came to recognize the birds not just as a species but as individuals. The posturing male who swaggered if you looked at him and fell asleep if you didn't. The smallest female, an exquisite bird, was nicknamed Ghost because she often tried to disappear. Her plumage was tipped in white and sparkling. And the larger female, who one day stared at me, unblinking, unthreatening, for at least twenty minutes, until my knees got tired. I stood up, but when I looked back she was still staring, her head tilted up to meet my eyes. She was still watching when I left.

A Man of Prince William Sound.
1778. *Prince William Sound, South
Alaska. Engraving by James Basire
after drawing by John Webber.*
PL. 46

Slow World

*

Two weeks of thirty-five below and the fat sway of the river
                              is jammed four feet down,
but on the creek between hills, behind
                    beaver dams, ice slumps under snowshoes and
there are no deer tracks.
Fire thrums and lounges godly in the stove.
Big lynx prints behind the hut; heavy
thatch of the Milky Way;
coyotes; the red of the willows
is poor.
Deer coats are poplar ash.

Green ice of the river where a
          hoof has scratched snow crust.

*

Under the wedge of light,
you know nothing.
You'll sing the inside of the snowberry.
A cold with scales heaves up the valley;
          the dark flower of the cold ignites the dark
               flower in the hump of fat things carry.
There is waiting.
You will lay your cheek against the float of the grass.
There is winter in her body;
          there are grains of winter in her body and a low sun.
There is the colour of horror over the snow.

*

I went under the
        earth and the river
gave me a rag, a leg bone to hold.
We looked into one another's
face. Don't say I'm here.
I am feverish with grass.
A dark in things, in wild rose,
            a stalk, a line coming out of the mouth and
curving, is weight, privacy, sleep,
            a cache of fat
the seeable thing sucks on, turns to and
        lives with.
The bull of the weather moves from here to there,
the purple and the bulge
in the heft of moving, unfallen snow.
The complete moon is still there
when I carry a poplar trunk out of the bush
to cut it by the road.
An inhaled wind moves in things; quiet
        flickers there, receiving a spread of weight.
The dark tower and at its top
        an almost buried light in cold trees.

*

The river is a man who's just ducked into a doorway,
            who's changed his name and lives in the crawl space.
The river has worn through itself and is turning up its hands.
A man and a dog come across it late in the afternoon
        to a stump-bank near Bohemian waxwings in a cottonwood in
            crouched sun.
Ice plinks and wangs, some thinking
    going on in a room in the castle of the river-ice's private ear,
whale-moan, other-side moan of the ice.
Under the ice, the long hair of what is not there.
Low in the dogwood's throat,
        under dead leaves, the river has its name tied up in some cloth.
The river is widowed.
The rabbit island willows and *Periphyseon*
            and *The Divine Names* are the same thing.

Seeing the willows, their forehead light, you walk into the thicket
                    of the book and are poor.
Willow showing red, mild week in January,
                    a red that drops its eyes
              when you look at it.

*

Late light, grass-thin and a bone star,
              shimmy of fox tracks beside the black stumble
                    of water, along the river's snow-ice ledge.
The willow has gone into the small room of its redness
where there is no book; the new cold
              lowers a perfect rope to climb into ash.
Way into the burley water, you could hear something.
The woman has looked a pelican descent into me,
                    her weight and her slope,
her weight and her slope into me.
You go into the bush and the bush shrugs.
The woman has tipped into me the far corner
              of her eye; I'll build a fire where I am and wait.

A Sea Otter. 1778. *Nootka Sound
(King George Sound), Vancouver
Island, S. W. British Columbia,
Canada. Engraving by Peter Mazell
after drawing by John Webber.*
PL. 43

Two Poems

WILD BLUEBERRIES

After hours on the shallow northern lake, green
then silver, then green, we drift into the far shore, a brief
crescent of beach behind reed. The hiss of sand
as the prow runs aground. We lift the boat out of the water, hand
over hand. At the edge of the beach, fringed
gentians. Their blue
not sapphire, not Prussian, not sky. A blue
with blood in it.

We walk up through juniper
into a meadow flocked with low-growing berries.
Blueberries ring our ankles like amulets on sprung stems.
We glance at each other, think
bear. She must be there, farther back, watching.
Sun wedges through spruce, hot, monolithic.
We feed each other handfuls of berries, they spray
our teeth blue, taste of light tempered
by conifer. In the background, indigo
shadows, and live, wind-shipped darkness, stippled
like fur. We kiss, slow but wary, eyes open.

Time to go. We want more
blueberries, but we feel her, the she-bear, the breath of her
waiting. We walk back down through juniper to gentian,
launch the boat, our smudged mouths knowing, for the moment,
what the bear knows. Blue of late summer, blue of northern duff,
a meadow of peeled light, and beyond, the entrance to caves
of spruce, birch, aspen, the bent trunks of wind.

GARDENER OF SNOW

Winter's first daylong fall, a
squall out of nowhere, finds her
snow blind but still gardening.
She struggles to recall last
plantings, where she buried
new tulips, those small papery
apples, delicious fruit of next
year's bearing. She worked bulbs
in wherever she found room,
and later, when the ground froze
spread a mulch of dry leaves,
their smell like tobacco, perfume
of the late garden, ritual
cosseting. And now she covers
the same vulnerable sleepers
with snow. Godsend
snow, fallen starfield of seeds
cast by cloud, profligate
grains that grow nothing but more
cold, more petrified
water. November in Saskatchewan
means she must shift bushels of snow
onto all the fertile beds,
onto the green and red and yellow
and magenta of aster, lilium,
sedum, delphinium, hemero-
callis, aconitum.
After this she's free to go inside
and forget the many names the world
has given chlorophyll, until the days of
unimaginable April, that
moment when sun calls out heat
and the helpless earth answers
with spring, when the slowly warming
syllables of humus grow
wonderfully articulate and speak
in green tongues of original
resurrection.

Winged Victory

The motel, with its "pay per view,"
is more scenic than the scenic drive
and more exotic, with you
putting your forehead to mine
to check for fever, prescribing cola,
and charting our road, first with one finger,
then your whole hand . . .

The next day it's tempting to touch
the cavern walls, but we don't,
knowing the oils we secrete
indelibly mar and stain.
Those draperies and columns, thrones
and soda straws—I'd like to see
the Winged Victory among *them,*

not to compare and choose,
but to be doubly bowled over.
The Winged Victory, and what's left
of the Parthenon! But then,
when they turned out the lights
down there, seven hundred feet down,
and it was absolutely unlit,

pitch black, and for a moment
they had us hushed (until someone,
a crying child, broke the silence
and everyone began making noise),
wasn't that hair of a second in total
quiet and darkness, though fleeting,
one of the best moments yet?

That, and the amphitheater at dusk,
watching the cave's long exhalation
of bats, and then the first stars.
The world has so many ways to woo us,
so many unexpected vistas,
and miraculously so much of it (your face
at rest, eyeglasses off) near at hand.

The Invitation

Marina and Oleg fell silent in front of their unfinished plates of kasha. The orange AM radio on top of the refrigerator announced the beginning of the Goodwill Games. The windows were sealed shut, and it was hot in the high-ceilinged apartment. Outside, on Nevsky Prospect, small uncatalyzed cars shot through the wavering heat. Sometimes a passing truck or a tram made the windows rattle. The radio droned, low.

Marina stared at the plastic tablecloth. "It's the best way to get her to America," she said. "I've been planning this for days."

"We don't even know him," Oleg said.

"I told you—he's the brother of Masha's husband," she said. Her hands were clasped under the table.

He looked blankly at her.

"Masha—my cousin."

Oleg rubbed his nose. "Your third cousin."

"Anyway, it's too late. He's coming tonight."

"Fine," Oleg said, shaking his head. "But you can't say I haven't warned you." They finished eating in silence.

Oleg read the newspaper *Izvestiya*. With a pencil Marina crossed out Rossiysky cheese, pickles, and beef tongue from her grocery list. She was adding mushrooms, duck, and *studen* when the radiator clanked. Oleg raised his eyes from the paper. Marina stopped writing. The radiator clanked again in staccato, quicker and quicker, then went silent. Oleg got up and touched it.

"It's warming up," he said.

Marina frowned. "They're finally fixing it—in July." Last winter, though mild, had been difficult. For one long month the central heating of the building had been down. Marina and Oleg had moved about the apartment with coats and gloves on, their mouths steaming. They had washed once a week, a small electric radiator set up next to the bathtub. The constant cold forced them into bed early, with their clothes on, and they never slept as much as they did that winter. In the mornings, the quilt on their bed glimmered with ice crystals.

Marina began to wash the dishes. Oleg finished reading his newspaper while drinking black Cuban coffee from a small cup.

"Can you buy vodka and cognac on your way home?" she asked. Oleg glanced at the plastic kitchen clock. He folded the paper and stood up.

"I'm running a little late." He moved close to her. "I'll take care of the drinks," he said. "This one time."

Marina did not look up from the sink. She heard the front door close behind him and the lock snap. She washed his cup, then dried her hands with a towel. Sitting at the table, she placed the phone before her, picked up the receiver, and dialed.

"Olya," she said. "It's Marina. I need to borrow 50,000 rubles for tonight's meal." Listening, she nodded and tangled her finger in the phone cord. "OK . . . I'll be there in half an hour." She hung up and went into the living room, where she pulled a box of chocolates from an oak cabinet.

Carrying the box against her chest like a book, Marina walked down Nevsky Prospect toward the metro station. The sidewalk was crowded with tourists and merchants selling tepid sodas, cigarettes, Russian dolls, and watches. Rusty trolley buses screeched past, and among the small Soviet and Czech cars, powerful Mercedes and BMW sedans zoomed by. At the entrance of the Gostini Dvor station, Marina stopped at a florist and bought an arrangement of crimson carnations for 2,000 rubles. A bony man played violin by the door. At his feet lay a hat with a few coins in it. Marina funneled with the crowd through the photo-sensor gates of the station, careful to wait for the light to turn green after she dropped her token into the slot. She stepped onto the long escalator going down to the platforms and watched a young couple kissing as they passed her on their way up. She remembered that Oleg did not kiss her that morning. Waiting for the train, she stared at a billboard advertising a colorful pair of Nike sneakers and wondered why there were ads for things that couldn't be found in Saint Petersburg.

Marina got out at Vladimirskaya and rushed down the street clutching her flowers and the box of chocolates. In the distance, the golden dome of Saint Isaac shone. Three young boys sat on a stoop smoking cigarettes. They wore T-shirts that were too small, and their faces were smeared with soot. There was no one else in the decrepit neighborhood, away from the Neva River. Marina went up the dark stairwell of a yellow building and rang the bell of Apartment 6. Olya, skinny and middle-aged, let her in. They pressed their cheeks in greeting, and Marina gave her the carnations. They went to sit in the kitchen, which was cooled by a small, humming air conditioner. Iron pots and pans cluttered the greasy counters. "It's tonight?" Olya asked.

"Yes," Marina said.

"I hope he agrees, for your daughter's sake."

A pot of boiling water began to hiss. Olya got up and made two cups of tea.

"What a dream," Marina said, "air conditioning."

Olya smiled, tensing her lips. "It was very expensive and difficult to get. But it's well worth it."

Marina nodded and finished her tea, enjoying the cool air drying her skin. "I have so much to do," she said. "It's not easy with all the tourists making the prices rise."

"Here," Olya said, taking a roll of bills from her pocket and setting it on the table.

Marina placed the money in her purse. "Thank you very much," she said, wondering what she would be asked to do in return. After a pause, she added, "I can't find duck. I looked everywhere." Olya said nothing, then took a deep breath. Marina waited, staring at her with slightly raised eyebrows. The kitchen clock was ticking through the silence.

"You want me to call that butcher by Avtovo?" Olya said at last, leaning back in her chair.

"I would be very grateful."

"I don't think it will help. I'm not even sure he has duck."

"With your influence," Marina said, "maybe there's a chance. You're very respected."

"My influence can't perform miracles. If there's no duck, nothing can be done." Marina looked at a crack in the mottled kitchen linoleum, thinking about this life, her life, of always waiting and trying and getting nothing. She hoped it would be different for her daughter.

"Of course," Olya said, "you come to me at the last minute and you expect miracles." She sighed. "Olya, 'the miracle woman.'"

"I'm sorry," Marina said, getting up. "I shouldn't have asked. It was silly. I was desperate."

Shaking her head slowly, Olya remained in her chair, her hands flat on the table. "I'll make a call," she finally said. "When you get there, ask for Boris. He may help. He owes me a lot."

"Thank you so much." Marina grabbed Olya's hand and pressed it.

Marina went back to the Vladimirskaya station. In the subway car, she stood, squeezed by the sticky crowd and holding on to a ceiling handle. When she was two stops away from Avtovo, the last station before the suburbs of Saint Petersburg, she got a seat. Smelling of sweat and vomit, a drunken man was snoring next to her. Two street boys got close to him and stared at his watch. When Marina got off, one of the boys took her seat and the other one stood before the drunken man.

The prefabricated buildings all looked the same, like shoeboxes. Marina walked up a side street and stopped in front of a small shop that was on the ground floor of a brown building. A long line of women, all stooping and dressed in gray, coursed in slowly, like a tired snake. She tried to make her way inside to see what was still available, but the women stood close together and would not let her pass.

"Wait like everyone else," an old, balding woman said.

"Do you know if there's duck?" Marina asked her.

"Why not venison while you're at it," the old woman replied.

"Only scraps and fat," another woman said. "As usual."

Marina waited in line. Her forehead shone, and her bra moistened below her breasts. The old woman ahead of her was carrying a plastic bag of frozen whitefish dripping onto the pavement.

"Get rid of that stinky fish!" a woman with a black eye shouted.

"It's for my cat," the old woman said. "The bastard only eats fish." The women laughed. The line slowly moved into the shop, where blackened strips of flypaper dangled from the low ceiling. A fat woman was shouting and shaking her fist at a man behind the counter. The air was stale and pungent, and the line seemed to stop.

When Marina got to the glass counter, she saw nothing but fatty ground meat in steel buckets. Black flies hovered about. The butcher wore a gray apron stained brown and red.

"Is Boris here?" Marina said.

The butcher eyed her. "No."

"When is he coming back?" she asked, her voice getting higher.

"Not today."

"I need duck."

The butcher laughed. "There's no duck." She looked around furtively, then she pushed the box of chocolates onto the counter. "Boris isn't here," he said.

"Can *you* help me?" she said, staring at him.

The butcher turned away. "Next!"

"I'm willing to pay the price," she said, leaning over the counter. "Twenty."

"Go out back," he said under his breath, not looking at her. The next customer was already placing her order. Marina left the box on the counter and went out.

She waited behind the building in a little yard. A black cat, its tail flaring, fumbled in a garbage bin reeking of rotten meat. She stood there, in the sun, a long time. Down the street a dog barked. She checked her watch: it was already noon. With the tip of her shoe she flipped over a paperback that lay on the ground. The back door opened and the butcher stepped out. On a sheet of newspaper he held a skinny, soggy duck, its head dangling to one side. The skin was yellow and gelatinous. Marina's lips tightened.

"That's all I've got left," he said. "You're lucky. Boris doesn't have anything." She took 20,000 rubles out of her purse and handed it to him. He took the money and shook his head. "I thought you were willing to pay," he said, leaning closer. He had a broad, red face, and his eyes were small and bloodshot. He smiled, revealing widely spaced teeth. As she stepped back, he grabbed her wrist. She stiffened. "What about a little extra?"

"I paid." He shook his head and dropped the duck on the ground. "Let go of me," Marina said, trying to yank her wrist loose.

The butcher pulled her to him. "C'mon, now," he said in a low voice. "If you want, I've got better meats . . ." The rear door opened. The butcher let go of her wrist and turned around. A man with greasy hair said, "We need you up front!" Marina picked up the duck and rushed off, not looking back. Two streets down, she stopped and leaned against a wall, trembling, her knees weak. She breathed deeply and set forth to get the caviar.

With her hair sticking to her temples, Marina stepped out of the third store. Still no caviar. The duck was warm and soggy in her hand. Her mouth was dry as she walked along the Fontanka River towards Inna's apartment. On blue taxi boats, brightly dressed tourists were taking pictures of the embankment.

In the shade of a maple tree, she sat on a bench facing the river and rested her feet for a moment. A few children were swimming near a small oil spill and a floating Coke can. She took her shoes off and wiggled her toes. Her toes and heels were dark and gritty where the shoes had not covered them. She gazed at the statues of the Anichkov bridge: four strong men trying to hold down rearing wild horses. She thought about Oleg shaking his head for the past week, showing no faith in her plan, in her power to make something happen: she would prove him wrong. She slid her shoes back on and got up.

Marina sat in Inna's tiny kitchen with a glass of cool tea before her. A squeaky fan plowed through the hot air. Her friend was rolling meatballs on the vinyl tablecloth with the palm of her hand. A small black-and-white TV showed athletes running a two-hundred-meter race for the Goodwill Games.

"Here's the *studen* for your meal," Inna said, pointing to a foil-wrapped plate on the stove.

"Thanks," Marina said. "I'd never have had the time."

"This foreigner will know what good Russian cooking is."

"If he doesn't like it, I don't know what I'll do. I've been through trouble for this." Marina took a sip of her tea, thinking that she only had one evening to convince the foreigner. "I thought I'd never get the duck."

"How's Natasha doing?"

"She says she's OK, but I don't know. I'm afraid she'll do something stupid so she can move out of the filthy dormitories."

"Like you did when you were at the university?"

Marina nodded slowly. "I didn't get a degree. But I got Natasha. And

Oleg." They were both quiet for a while. Inna rolled three more meatballs, and Marina stirred the tea in her glass, then swilled it as if it were vodka.

"You could've done worse," Inna said.

Marina said nothing, then, "I can't bear this heat. We're not meant for such heat."

Her friend nodded. "In other countries, at least they have deodorant."

Marina remained silent, her eyes unfocused.

"It will be ок," Inna said. "After your apple-baked duck and my *studen,* he won't be able to say no. Just ask him at the very end, when he's got a good glass of Cognac Napoléon in hand."

Marina smiled briefly, her eyes weary. "I've got to go. I couldn't find caviar. I'll have to buy it at Elyseevsky."

Inna whistled. "That's a place for foreigners and racketeers. It's expensive."

"I know," Marina said, waving her hand briskly, "but I have no choice."

Inside Elyseevsky, the windows, the counters, and the tiled floor shone. A few tourists dressed in casual yet expensive clothes browsed, buying nothing. Ahead of Marina in line, a New Russian's wife in a sophisticated French toilette pointed at a plate of truffles behind the glass counter. Her hands were manicured, and her nails long and glossy. The saleswoman smiled at her and scooped a few spoonfuls of truffles into a plastic container and weighed it on an electronic scale. The wife nodded, and the saleswoman glued a computer-printed label on the container and handed it over the counter. The wife took the truffles and walked over to the cashier, who stood by the entrance. The saleswoman turned to Marina and stopped smiling.

"What do you want?" she asked.

"A jar of black caviar," Marina said.

"What kind?" she said, her head slightly cocked.

"The cheapest."

The saleswoman scowled, bent behind the counter, and took out a small jar of caviar. She placed it on the counter but kept her hand clasped around it. "Ten dollars," she said, looking Marina in the eyes.

"I've only got rubles."

The saleswoman wrinkled her nose. "Then it will be 30,000 rubles."

"The rate is 2,100 rubles to the dollar," Marina said. "That's 21,000 rubles."

The saleswoman glared at her. "What do I care? If you don't like it, go somewhere else."

Marina counted 30,000 rubles out of her purse. She knew that people were staring. Her fingers trembled a little when she handed the money to the saleswoman.

"I'm not the cashier," the woman said. "Go pay at the cashier and come back with the receipt."

Marina pulled her hand back and turned towards the cashier. Two young women in elegant clothes looked at her, smiling softly. She averted her eyes, and as she walked over to the cashier, her legs felt heavy. Never, she thought, never this for my daughter.

Marina climbed to the fifth floor of her apartment building, carrying the duck, the caviar, a basket of mushrooms, and the *studen*. Her wavy hair was damp, limp on her head. The dark hallway smelled like cat urine. She leaned on the wall and fumbled for her keys, careful not to drop anything. Unlocking the door, she pushed it open. A whiff of dry, burning air startled her. Fire, she thought. She rushed into the apartment and dropped her groceries onto the living-room table. She glanced around, and her eyes stopped on the big accordion radiator under the window. The air in front of the window was undulating. She didn't move for a moment, staring. She approached the radiator slowly. It was too hot to touch. Perspiration slid down her scalp, and her dress stuck to her skin. She hastily rinsed the duck in the sink and put the groceries into the refrigerator. Then she ran across the hall and knocked on her neighbor's door. When it opened, the same burst of hot air startled her. Her neighbor's shirt was drenched with sweat. Marina could hear the heavy traffic outside—the windows had been opened.

"What's going on?" she asked.

The young woman shook her head. "Someone fixed the heat and left it on. Nobody knows how to shut it off. Nobody even knows which committee to contact." A little girl in yellow underpants came and stood close to the woman.

"This can't be," Marina said. "This just can't be."

"I know," the young woman said. "We all know."

Marina returned to her apartment and called Oleg at work. "What's going on?" her husband asked in a low voice.

"The radiators—the heat is on," she said quickly. "The apartment is an oven."

He was silent. She could picture him closing his eyes and rubbing his wide forehead. "I'll see what I can do. I'll try to get off early."

She said nothing.

"Are you OK?" he asked.

"I think so."

"Did you find duck?"

"Yes." She paused. "I have to open the windows."

She hung up the telephone and went into the living room. Burgundy velvet curtains hung along the tall, wide windows. She pulled the window lever down and tried to push the window open, but it was stuck. She pummeled it until her fist was red and she was sopping with sweat. Stepping back, she kicked her shoes off and slipped out of her dress, hanging it on a chair. She stood with only her underpants and bra on, her pallid body webbed with little blue veins. She got a hammer from the toolbox in the broom closet and began hitting the central frame of the window. As she pounded, slowly at first, then faster, dust and chips of paint fell from the frame. The window moaned and finally opened. The roar of the outside traffic filled the apartment. Marina wiped her face with her dress. She opened two other windows the same way. Then she was in the bedroom, working fast on the last one. It wouldn't budge. Her bra cut into her flesh, so she snapped it off and continued working. Red marks glowed on her white skin where the straps had been. The living-room clock chimed—it was four o'clock already. She bit her lower lip and began to hammer the window frantically, her sweat blinding her, until the glass shattered. Shards fell into the street, and she heard screams from below. She dropped the hammer on the floor and leaned through the large star-shaped hole. Small white faces stared up at her as a piece of glass pierced her right breast and then plummeted, exploding on the pavement. She moaned and jerked back. Blood dribbled from the cut under her nipple and mixed with her sweat. Dizzy, she sat, then lay on her bed, closing her eyes. Her rib cage heaved fast, then slowed. After a few minutes, the blood began to coagulate. On her gleaming body the dried blood looked like the mouth of the Nile on a map. She got up, leaving the wet print of her body on the sheets, and went into the bathroom.

Marina checked her wound in the mirror: it was small but deep. She rinsed her face and washed the blood from her torso and breasts. She tried to put a clean bra on, but it hurt too much. She went into the kitchen and began to cook, cleaning and seasoning the duck and then placing it with the apples into the oven. Perspiration blurred her vision, so she tied a scarf around her head. She put the beef tongue to boil, then sliced the mushrooms and soaked them in oil and pepper. The heat in the kitchen was dizzying. The walls suddenly turned red, and Marina almost fainted. She held on to the counter for a few seconds, then, feeling better, went into the living room and set the table with her pre-Revolution blue-and-white china. She returned to the steaming kitchen and pulled the beef tongue out of the boiling water, splashing her belly. When she turned, cursing, to place it on the counter, Oleg was standing in the doorway holding a grocery bag. She was startled, and blushed. His mouth was slightly open, his eyes wide.

"What's going on?" he said. She stood in her wet underwear and a head scarf, her breasts exposed, her body lustrous with sweat. "Are you crazy? Have you gone mad?" She pushed past him into the bedroom and put on a T-shirt. He followed her, still holding the grocery bag. "What on earth are you doing?" He noticed the broken window and the hammer on the floor. "What happened?"

"What do you think? I'm getting this meal ready." She glared at him. "Stop looking at me like that," she said, walking past him back to the kitchen.

"Marina, there will be no meal," he said behind her. Using a dishtowel she took the duck out of the oven. "Marina, have you gone completely mad!" he shouted.

She looked at him but didn't seem to see him. "There *will* be a meal," she said, placing the duck on a silver plate. "We need this invitation."

"Marina, don't you see it's a sauna in here?"

"Didn't you find a way to get the heat turned off?" she asked, her dark eyes glowing. He did not answer. "It will get cooler soon," she said.

"Look around you," Oleg said. "Look at the living-room walls." Marina's head turned and her lips parted. Two strips of wallpaper had detached and crumpled onto the floor. The plant next to the couch had wilted. She saw flashes and red spots before her eyes, and then she stumbled to the bedroom and fell on the bed, crying and punching the pillows. Oleg came and sat next to her. He lay his hand on her back and looked out the broken window, silent. Marina buried her face in a pillow, sobbing, feeling her husband's warm hand on her back.

Early the next morning Marina woke up, naked and drenched. Next to her, Oleg snored softly, his naked body shining. She watched the sun through the window. Outside, the first trolley buses were rattling. The air above the radiator was still undulating. Everything in the room was covered by a thin film of black dust from the car fumes.

Marina wanted to get up, but it was too hot. She wanted to reach for Oleg, but she remembered his voice on the telephone the night before, trying to reschedule the meal in vain, and her daughter in Moscow needing an invitation to leave for America. Then she began to cry. The clock-radio went off: . . . *forecast record heat today of thirty-seven degrees by noon. Malfunctioning of the ice generator has caused cancellation of the figure-skating competition . . .* Oleg opened his eyes and took Marina in his heavy arms. "Don't," she said between sobs. But she didn't move; she lay there until her skin no longer burned against Oleg's and she could no longer feel herself touching him.

from *Lo, This Dreamer Cometh* _____

Although it was now late February and the days were getting longer, it was still the deepest part of the winter. The tiny cabin was wrapped in frost; even inside, the ceiling was coated with rime, and icicles hung like stalactites from the beams. Robert and Elvis were asleep.

It was a very small place: a cabin for one or two people. With their heavy down and blanket-cloth arctic sleeping bags, Robert and Elvis almost filled the place up, Elvis sleeping on a makeshift bunk that also functioned as a table, and Robert on the bare, packed earth of the floor.

When Robert had last been here at this time of year, he was twelve years old and had his whole family with him: his father, his mother, and the two sisters who came after him, as well as Danny, then a toddler, and Michael, an infant.

That winter they had not seen the track of a single large animal. Robert's mother and sisters had fed the family with rabbits from a snare line; some nights all seven people sat around a stew made out of a single rabbit. They had had fish too—fish in profusion when the spring finally broke the ice in the river. The fur price had been low—the way it was this winter.

Now all was silent, broken only by the deep breathing of the two men.

Robert was dreaming. He dreamed of Rebecca standing in the shack in the morning light, the way she was the last time he saw her: her hands clasped and a look of sparkling amusement on her face.

"Do you want me to stay here, Robert?—then I'll stay."

Suddenly the scene changed, and he didn't know where she was; he couldn't see her, but she was calling to him. "Oh, Robert, why did you have to go trapping?"

"I just didn't see what else I could do," he spoke aloud.

"You ran away, didn't you?"

Robert sat up suddenly, opening his eyes.

"Dreaming again, eh?" said Elvis, now also awake.

"I guess so." He opened his sleeping bag and got up on his knees to replenish the stove, which was almost out. He put in a few big chunks of wood, then opened the draft. The place was so small that the ancient, half-broken oil-drum stove could heat it up in no time.

The fire flickered through the draft hole of the stove and cast a little light in the room. It was enough light for Robert and Elvis to see by, for their eyes were attuned to starshine and moonlight; at this time of year, there were only a few hours of full daylight to work by.

Elvis yawned and opened up his sleeping bag to stretch. *"Brrr,"* he said.

"Don't get up, Elvis. Everything's frozen yet," said Robert. He got back into his bedroll and lay down with a groan of discomfort. Then he began to think about the dream.

Robert had been dreaming about Rebecca every night for a month. And he spent most of his waking time thinking about the dreams: on the long trail while they were laying the traps or back at the cabin, thawing and skinning the bodies of the animals—marten and fox and wolverine—and setting them on the stretchers.

He had put together every scrap of knowledge he had about her and her family, including things he heard when he was a child, and only half-understood, about her father's wild history of drinking and womanizing before he became a Protestant evangelist. Robert divined many things about Rebecca in this: she was the oldest in the family and therefore, like himself, the rebellious one, the one who had been through everything with parents. He also remembered what she had implied about the breakdown of her marriage, and in dreams he saw her in scenes of degradation: passed out from too much drink, befouled with her vomit, giving herself to men she was too drunk to remember later.

He now understood that the idealism in her character came from her crazy, religious nut of a father. Somehow, slowly, she had pulled herself out of the slough she was in and, with her quick intelligence, her spirit, her sense of humour, had created another Rebecca: the beautiful, sparkling creature he had been dreaming of. Robert had been in a fever of desire and indecision when he left Prohibition Creek; now he was sick with love.

He felt Elvis's eyes upon him. "Cold weather for trapping, isn't it?" he said. Elvis laughed. Robert rose on one elbow, and they were almost face-to-face. Elvis was grinning down at him from the edge of the table. Robert was not really aware of what poor company he was: he talked to Elvis about once a day, or if he noticed Elvis wanted him to, and then usually about the weather. "What is it?" asked Robert.

Elvis's small, wrinkled face lit up with amusement as he laughed again. "Well, we've all got our own problems."

"What do you mean by that?" Robert straightened up, prepared to deny whatever Elvis had heard him say in his sleep.

"It's still too cold to get up," said Elvis. "Tell me a story, Robert."

Robert stared at him, surprised. Like all the other old people, Elvis did everything by taboo. When they found a rabbit in the snare, they reached up under the rib cage with their fingers to dislodge the heart. The spirits were satisfied only if they killed the rabbit this way. Other animals, like moose and caribou, could not be clubbed or beaten with sticks. And there were ways of setting traps, particularly for the larger, more intelligent animals like wolf and wolverine, that reflected an ancient understanding of animal personality. Even on this trip, Robert had learned a lot from Elvis about the old ways of doing things.

If there was an old-time story to be told, Elvis should tell it.

"There were two brothers," said Robert. So many stories began that way.

"But the older one's mother died of TB when he was only a little one," said Elvis, startling Robert by taking over the story. "His dad married again. The younger brother was born when the older one was five." He had Robert's full attention. "Then the younger one's mother died of TB too," said Elvis.

Robert remembered that there had been some girls. But they had come along later in his grandfather's third family. The old man had been a patriarch with thirteen children from three wives. But only one child had survived in each of the first two families, in each case a boy: his father, the eldest, and his uncle Elvis.

"The younger brother never had any mother except the older brother," said Elvis. "The older brother started taking care of him when he was a baby."

"He must have looked after him when they went to that school too," said Robert, his memories of school coming back to him in a rush of bitterness. He had been separated from his sisters when they were put in the girls' residence; he hadn't even been allowed to see them.

"Yes, he did. But the older brother was a crazy guy," Elvis reminisced, smiling. "He liked stick gambling and poker more than just about anything else—except chasing girls."

Robert grinned. "I guess he was a good-looking guy, that older brother."

"Yeah," Elvis agreed. "The younger brother was skinny and kind of ugly."

"Come on!" said Robert. His uncle laughed.

"The older brother got married," said Robert. He knew that Elvis was leading up to this, and it was the part of the story he wanted to get to as well.

"The girl was an orphan," said Elvis. "Both her parents had died of TB."

Those had been bad times, Robert knew.

"The younger brother got married after a while too. But his wife and kids died of TB."

The record of how bad those times had been was locked in the memory of the old people like Elvis: the waves of disease that had decimated the Athapaskan bands and created a legacy of grief. No family had been left intact. First came flu and measles, which could strike and kill half the people in a settlement in a few hours. Then came TB—an epidemic that rended the families, taking the sick away to sanatariums in the south and leaving parents, husbands, and wives not knowing, sometimes for years, who had lived and who had died.

It had been a holocaust: a whole society almost destroyed. To the Dene, society was first and foremost the family.

"So," Elvis continued, "the younger brother went to stay with the older brother and his wife. She was a real good one, smart—and good-looking too."

Robert could not remember that. He could only remember his mother crying day after day when she and her children were deserted and then her working like a man and wearing the clothing of a man.

"So maybe I know what happened to the older brother and his wife," said Robert, impatient to move on. But he realized that he didn't know. He had just been in a hurry to put his father's cruelty behind them: it was a known fact, something that didn't need to be discussed. But the story was still in Elvis's hands.

Elvis had lain down on the bunk above, and Robert couldn't see his face anymore.

"After that pretty girl had a couple of kids, the older brother didn't pay attention to her anymore. She was unhappy, and the younger brother couldn't stand to see what was happening to her."

Robert hesitated to ask, but he wanted to know. "So did she fall for him? Even before the older one took off?"

"Fall for him? That skinny little guy?" Elvis peered over the edge of the table mischievously, and they both laughed.

"She didn't want to," Elvis said a moment later. "God wouldn't let her."

Robert had been expecting that all along: for his mother, the main consideration was what God would let her do.

"She made him stay away from her. They wasted a lot of time."

Robert thought of all the years that Elvis worked away from home, on the DEW line, on the oil rigs, way up north on the coast.

"Finally, a long time later—a long time—she let him move in." Elvis paused. "But then she made him go trapping."

"She did?" Robert was surprised. "I thought that was your idea."

"One of her sons didn't like it—the way that old man moved in with his mother."

It was my brother Danny, Robert thought. The hypocrite.

From the edge of the table, Elvis was now giving Robert a penetrating look. "Do you think they should have wasted any more time, Robert?" he asked.

"No," answered Robert. "No, I don't."

At once Elvis sighed and lay back down, crossing his arms under his head.

A thin daylight was now creeping through the chinks around the door of the little cabin. Robert got out of his sleeping bag and began rustling around to start the day. He pulled on his pants and vest. Then he fixed the fire again and put the billy for tea on the stove. He rummaged through the bag of food and found a piece of dry meat and a bannock for both of them. They sat opposite one another on their bedrolls, munching thoughtfully. The billy boiled, and Robert poured the tea.

"*Masi.*" Elvis reached for the sugar bag, put a spoonful of sugar in his cup, and stirred with deliberation.

"Now tell me your story, Robert," he said.

"My story?" Robert had forgotten that he was supposed to be telling his story. He was still thinking about what Elvis had told him, digesting it slowly.

"There were two brothers," repeated Elvis, starting him off. There seemed to be a good reason why so many of the stories in the Book of Dene began this way.

"Well—"

Elvis nodded imperiously for him to go on.

"They were in love with the same woman," said Robert, surprising himself with his words.

"Oh, they were, were they?" said Elvis.

"The younger one was married. But he slept with her anyway," said Robert.

Because he had lived so much of his life away from home, Elvis didn't know any gossip. He could identify Robert and Danny as the two brothers, but Robert thought he wouldn't know much else.

"The older brother found out the woman didn't care about the younger one," Robert went on. "And he— Boy!" He broke off. "Do you really want to hear all this?"

Elvis folded his arms. "Yeah," he said.

"He wanted her himself." Robert hadn't said any of this out loud before, except when he was talking in his sleep. Saying it was like coming to terms with his dreams.

"So what did he do about that?" Elvis asked.

"Nothing," said Robert. Big fat nothing, he thought.

"Is that the end of the story?" Elvis looked disappointed.

"Look," said Robert desperately, "I helped you tell that story we just had. Maybe you could give me a hand with this one."

"Let's see," said Elvis. "The younger guy was still married, right? So maybe he cared what everybody would think—if he took up with that other woman."

"He didn't care what they'd think," said Robert.

"You said she was his brother's woman."

"She wasn't really his woman. She just made a mistake—that was all. She'd had kind of a crazy life."

"Well, maybe the girl didn't like the older guy enough," Elvis suggested. "Maybe he couldn't get her anyway."

"Maybe not," replied Robert. "But I think he could. The way he dreamed about her all the time."

"This story is getting better," Elvis murmured. The elders attributed a great deal of significance to dreaming. And he had been witness to the amount of dreaming Robert was doing lately.

"Once she even appeared to him as a caribou doe when he was awake. You were there when that happened." Elvis was listening with his mouth open.

He could tell this part as a real story. The clear, cold mountain air on the ridge. They had been climbing all morning, and the caribou were a long way down on the other side. They were having a tea break, trying to decide what to do, when Haga spotted the doe, standing quietly almost right behind Robert. Her two little ones were in front of her, and they started to walk towards the men. While Haga fumbled with Elvis's .30-30 the doe began to flee down the stony hillside, looking over her shoulder, then slowing down for her two young ones as, panicking now, they followed. Luckily, Haga was bowled over by the kickback of the gun and lay howling on the ground.

"But how did you know that was her?" asked Elvis. He only meant by what supernatural sign or means, for he was not at all sceptical.

"She told me about it afterwards. How she saw us and everything. The two little ones were her two kids."

"This is a really good story, Robert," said Elvis.

"Yeah. Except that nothing happens at the end."

They had finished eating and drinking by this time, and the daylight was much stronger. The cabin had no window, but the light found its way in anyhow, around the door and through the broken chinking of the logs. A broad beam of bright spring sunlight fell between them, and tiny particles of ice sifted down from the ceiling with the iridescence of a thousand prisms.

Robert began to pack up the food bag. They were late getting out on the trail this morning and had to visit forty miles of traps in one direction, fifty in the other.

Almost thirty years ago, as a child of twelve, Robert had gone these rounds with his father. They had used dogs. It was one of the last winters his family had kept dogs and one of the last good times between his mother and father. In the bush his parents had worked together cheerfully, and there had been an equality between them: the work the man did on the trapline depended on the sewing, the fishing, and the snare line of the woman.

A whole way of life had come and gone, and although Robert remembered what it had been like—cold, hard work and being cramped at night in the tiny cabin while the baby cried—he thought that the life then had been better than the one he had now.

He and Elvis were two lone men, perhaps both destined to be lonely old men, driven out here together almost as if they had been ostracized by their own people. It felt as if they were the last human beings on earth; they were among the last who would be willing to make their living this way.

"You know, we've been out here a month," said Elvis, watching Robert put the lard can, the sugar bag, and the billy in his pack. "I want to go home."

Robert laughed. "You don't want to waste any more time—is that it?" he said.

Elvis laughed too. "Well, I think you're right about that."

With Elvis's skidoo, they could go around and get the traps in a day, he figured. Then, if they travelled all night, they could be in the Forks by the next day, sell their fur and . . . They began to roll up their sleeping bags.

Elvis said, "You'll tell me the end of that story sometime?"

"Well—if it gets one."

"What do you mean? A story like that, with dreams and people turning into caribou—it's bound to have a pretty good ending," said Elvis.

Revenge of the Pebble Town People:
A Raid on the Tlingit

"Revenge of the Pebble Town People" is an attempt to reconstruct a moment of Northwest Coast history: a nineteenth-century Haida raid on the Tlingit. The tale on which it is based was told around the turn of the century to American ethnologist John R. Swanton by Richard of the Middle-gîtî'ns. Swanton's version appeared in his book Haida Texts and Myths[1] *under the title "A Raid on the Tlingit." The poem is followed by Charles Lillard's commentary on the process of reconstruction.*

Qandawas was going to make a potlatch in Masset. She owned ten slaves, and she had eight storehouses in the Kaigani country, and she owned a copper worth ten young slaves. She intended to sell it for that price in the Tsimshian country. They offered her nine slaves and an eight-fathom canoe. She said she would not part with her copper because there were not ten slaves. So Qandawas returned to Raven Creek. Later, as she was sailing north to House Point with a south wind, a squall drove the canoe into the Kaigani country. There some Tlingit, who were gathering seaweed, invited Qandawas and her crew ashore. After these Tlingit had fed everyone, they killed them all.

Thinking of this while we were growing up,
we grew up only to war with the Tlingit.
In the very middle of winter we began to drink medicine;
and from Kitgoro,
the black-cod fishery, we went to war in two canoes.

That night we camped at Tlell, the next at Nai-kun,
in the morning we crossed over to the Straits Country.

And while it was yet daylight we saw rocks along the shore.
We waited for night. And when it came, we landed inside the kelp.
In the early light we hid our canoes.
Then we drank four buckets of saltwater.

We were thirsty and ran to freshwater,
we drank it from spruce-bark pails.
And then we ran to the sea, our bowels steaming.[2]
That was when our lookout saw four Tlingit going by in a canoe.
When evening arrived,
we went looking for the people we knew lived in the inlet.
We found their smoke,
and before daybreak we found their camp,
four houses above a long stretch of steep shore.

Nearby we beached our canoes,
then Ankusta whipped our souls as a shaman must,
then two men sought a closer look at the houses
but a big dog barking scared them away,
so Ankusta performed again:
he pretended to tie the dog's mouth shut,
and he told us,

"Now, friends, go look at the houses again.
     Now, that dog will see you but he'll not bark."

Three of us went this time.
Only a mat hung over the doorway,
so I lay there listening to the snoring,
then I tied my knife to my hand and entered,
and I found by feeling
that there were only women asleep there.

We returned to our waiting clansmen and I said,

"Chiefs that I have for elder brothers
     strengthen yourselves!"

Then we formed groups to enter the houses.

   Huk

we called to ourselves.

   Huk.

Abalone went ahead
and his younger brother followed me,
but when it came time to run in I looked back.
Instead of following, my crew were waiting,

A Woman of Prince William Sound.
1778. *Prince William Sound, South
Alaska. Engraving by James Basire
after drawing by John Webber.*
PL. 47

preparing to shoot—
so I returned to the canoe in disgust,
and when they asked why, we almost quarreled.

We started off
and when we found a place to land among the driftwood
Ganai's canoe followed us in.
He called out,

"Come, friends, light a fire,
I've got sockeye, they'll be good."

But I scolded Ganai for wanting to break our fast,[3]
so they left us as my crew argued whether to stay or follow.
And I said,

"My father-in-law is a chief.
If those who've been in our company kill some of the Tlingit,
and he receives nothing, we will feel sorry—
let's go down the inlet after them."

    Paddle after.

    Paddle after.

        My brother may find people to kill.

And there they were around the point—
Tlingit in a big canoe,
men standing in lines down the middle,
holding their rifles high.
There were a great number of guns in that canoe.

    Huk

    HUK,

I called out to my men.

    Let's kill people.

Seeing they were outnumbered
the Tlingit began fleeing, still they shot at us twice.
Then something struck me on the head,
and I fell. When I came to myself,

I was in the bilge, and I stayed there
in the bloody water until I grew stronger.

Then I tied my knife to my hand,
the men told me my younger brother was dead,
Beloved was hanging over the water,
then I told my men not to let him slip overboard.

Now we were closing in on the Tlingit,
they beat their paddles against their canoe,
shouting,

  A'lala a'lala

until one of my men stood up and shot their steersman.
As he fell away into the water
we, too, started shouting,

  A'lala a'lala.

They shot at us, and two of their bullets
went through the skin of my head.
Ankusta shot the one who was trying to steer, and that man
fell into the bailing place face first.

  A'lala a'lala

we sang, rapping the edges of our canoe,

  A'lala a'lala

we mocked them, and when Ankusta shot again
another Tlingit cried out.
And though the riflemen stood there in lines
between the paddlers,
and though it was a large canoe
and the number in it beyond counting,
they waved us away and called for a truce.

The Tlingit sat down,
their rifle barrels pointed skyward,
then Ganai moved his canoe in close
and a man stood up and pointed his rifle.
One of my brother's crewmen speared the man
with a bone spear with a short handle,
and that man sat down quickly enough,

trying to pull out the spear,
but it was entangled with his guts, and when the spear
came free, his guts spilled out on his knees.
When he tried to push the spear back in,
one of our spearmen jumped in the canoe and cut his throat.

Now it was our turn.
I jumped into their stern,
everyone had long knives. I fell into the stern.
And someone stabbed at me. He hit me on the shoulder
and my insides seized up,
but I stabbed him in the side
and I felt his insides splash on my legs.
Another came at me and I struck him in his guts.
When I struck him again, he died.

Another man came at me.
I dodged and struck and he went pale.
I told the man behind me to kill him.
An unarmed youth in the bow held up his arms.
I picked him up and threw him into the canoe.

Next the famous Yan came at me,
I had heard of his powers—
people were afraid to pass before his town,
he was too strong,
but when I knifed him, I left a slash down his back,
then he went into my canoe willingly.
No one believed it.
The famous Yan became a slave.

Then the Tlingit saw their leader gone and heaved a sigh,
but they were strong and proud Wolves,
so they fought on.
    Too bad their luck had fled.

In the stern our men were pulling in the slaves.
There was one woman we did not take,
she'd been shot in the leg, and there was one man
who acted crazy, but when I was about to stab him,
the man held his hands out, so I tied them
behind his back, then I tied his legs together.

The property was captured at once.
Ganai's canoe had taken ten heads,
we had five; there were only nine slaves.

Then we began paddling,
and the warriors sang their songs, but mine were sad;
two of my younger brothers were dead
and I sang for them,

> *There is no place where people do not die.*
> *I do not know where my brother is.*
> *If only I knew where to find the trail of the dead.*

When we were almost out of the inlet
someone shouted,

> **Look, there—**
> **the Tlingit are pursuing us.**

Full canoes were behind us.
The canoes were close together.

We were brave in our canoe,
but the people in Ganai's canoe
started to paddle away from us. I stood up
and said,

Do not let anyone tell a bad story about us.
We have avenged the murder of Qandawas
and our friends. That is why they will kill us.
Before they destroy us,
we will destroy a whole canoe-load of them.

No one listened.
Ganai was fleeing.
My crew paddled away in fright,
singing a fleeing song,

> **Waho-o-o he-ooo waho-o-o he-o-o-o.**

After we had paddled away for a while in fright,

I looked back.
Instead of my seeing Tlingit I saw nothing
but seagulls sitting on top of driftwood.

Soon Ganai found a creek
where there were many humpbacks.
There they roasted humpbacks for us. We drank some whisky

and after we sent food through the fire
to those who had been unable to escape,
we ate and fed our slaves.
I tied cedar bark round the arm of the man that they shot.
And the one shot in the head also returned to life.
He told us he would not die for some time yet.

Then we went away to Cape Chacon
and by evening we could see
North Island and then Red Bushes Point.
While we were coasting along together
someone ahead of us shouted:

What warriors are those?

Then Ankusta shouted:

Those are warriors from Masset,
    low-class Eagles of no account.

And they came out from their concealment.
They had new guns and two cartridge boxes apiece.
And when we came round the point,
the Masset people came down in a crowd.
They had a Kaisun man living at Masset
question us.
They gave him the following directions.
    If you recognize them, ask them,
      "Is it you?"
and if you do not know them, ask,
          "What warriors are you?"
That was the way in which he questioned us.

One of the Eagles held a gun.
Two cartridge boxes hung from his side.
They said he was a brave man.
He said,

Tell me, Pebble Town People, what did the
Tlingit do to the people of your family in former times?
When the Tlingit formerly beat them every time, why do you
    do this?
I could do something to you for your foolishness.
You might be shot to pieces.

And, when he aimed his gun, he pointed it at us.
His name was Stawat.

I felt as though I had been struck in the face.
He had pointed a short gun at me.
I seized my long one, and I jumped ashore.
I ran to him.
I struck him at once with the gun.
I struck him in the neck.
And when he was about to strike me
I got my gun ready for him,

Strike me and I will shoot you.

Two of my friends came ashore behind me
and they struck him with their rifle barrels.
Ankusta said to him,

This is not the first time men of your clan
have acted so brave and made trouble.
Why don't you strike back?

Then someone said,

Stop it. You have struck him more than enough for his talk.

It was late and we were tired.
So the people took us over to the camping place.

Ganai did not trust these low-class Eagles,
so he went around Entry Point.
The Masset people went down to the canoes in a crowd.
And, when they had nearly reached our slaves,
I handed my gun to Ankusta's father.
I then ran down to our canoes.
I made fast my knife in my hand.
I then pushed them away and anchored the canoes outside.

They then began to offer us food.
And we had on our cartridge boxes.
We also kept our guns at our right sides,
and we had our knives hanging down in front.
At the same time we ate.
Then we finished, and they gave us tobacco.

In the evening my Masset clansmen
made me an offer for Yan.
They offered sixty blankets for him,
an unused musket,
a whole suit of clothes,
two bags of shot,
a big canoe,
and many things of all kinds.
I refused everything.
   Yan was mine.

We remained awake that night.
Some of the crew slept ashore.
Very early on the next day
we started for the west coast.
And, when we were ready to go,
Ankusta's father went after some water.
He was gone for a long time.
While he was still away, Ganai's canoe set off.
The wind was in the north.
I then left directions for Ankusta's father.
And we left him.
The Masset people afterward took him in.

And that day, when it was almost evening,
we sailed by the long town of Skidegate.
The Skidegate people came out in a crowd to watch us.[4]
We did not stop.
They stood behind us watching.
We spent that night at Water Hole on Maude Island.
The wounded one in our canoe was still alive.

And we started from there at night.
Then we made a campfire on the inlet above Chaatl.
From there we started very early to Kitgoro.
At that time we sang a war song.

We went into Kitgoro, singing songs of victory,

   Hu hu hu hu.

We sang songs of victory for many nights.

   Hu hu hu hu.

NOTES

1 John R. Swanton, *Haida Texts and Myths,* Bureau of American Ethnology, Bulletin 29 (Washington: Government Printing Office, 1905; reprinted Brighton, MI: Native American Book Publishers, 1991).

2 "One of the purificatory war regulations was to drink a great deal of salt water and then take fresh water after it, when the whole would be ejected." Swanton, 370, note 8 [99, note 6].

3 "Because they had not yet met an enemy or taken a slave, and therefore had no right to break the fast regulations." Swanton, 370, note 12 [100, note 10].

4 "The people of Skidegate, when they had an opportunity, were wont to intercept West Coast war parties on their return through the channel and take their slaves away from them." Swanton, 370, note 16 [103–04, note 14].

COMMENTARY

The original account of this raiding party's foray into Alaska was told to the American ethnologist John R. Swanton by Richard of the Middle-gîtî'ns. It was the winter of 1900 to 1901, and both men were living at Skidegate, Queen Charlotte Islands, British Columbia. Swanton later published the story as "A Raid on the Tlingit" in *Haida Texts and Myths.*

I have heard it said of this story, and many similar ones, that it makes perfectly good sense as it stands. Perhaps. More likely, the effort to wade through the unexplained allusions, cross-references, repetitions, unusual names, geographical confusion, and (for us) arbitrary use of pronouns has deterred everyone. Only this explains why this story, despite its sagalike qualities, has been ignored for ninety years.

Having grown up near Tongas and Gash, both places that I explored as a boy, I have been intrigued by this story ever since I discovered it in Margaret Bell's library at Naha Bay, the site of another Tlingit village (but one too far north to be considered the camp Richard and his companions discovered). In the late 1950s Margaret—whose juvenile novels (particularly *The Totem Casts a Shadow* and *Daughter of Wolf House*) are set near the Haida villages on Prince of Wales Island in Alaska—and I talked about methods of exploring early Coastal history. I experimented with various ways of retelling the myths and stories collected by Swanton and others, but none satisfied me. They didn't sound like much of anything, and their appearance was not quite right.

That was in the 1970s. Recently I began thinking about reconstructing history; that is, taking a fairly complete story and, using details from similar stories, building a more complete structure. It is hardly a new concept. Reconstructions have been a common practice since Homer's time.

"Revenge of the Pebble Town People" is an attempt to reconstruct a few moments of Northwest Coast history. It is now literature, not a story lost in a book that has been out of print for almost a century and that cannot be found in most public libraries. But those who compare my version to Swanton's will find that little has been changed, though a deal has been left out and, if anything, it is now more Richard's story than it was in Swanton's account. This may be to our benefit, for in his *New Science* Giambattista Vico tells us that "History cannot be more certain than when he who creates the things also narrates them."

There is another consideration. As the author of *Just East of Sundown,* a history of the Queen Charlotte Islands, and as editor of *In the Wake of the War Canoe, Warriors of the North Pacific,* and *The Ghostland People,* all of which contain nineteenth-century accounts of life among the Haida, I know how rare it is to find firsthand nineteenth-century Haida accounts. Mostly we find Haida words that have been paraphrased by explorers or churchmen, or stories caught in a limbo beyond our reach. Straight autobiography is rare to nonexistent, and, as we will soon see, Richard's story may have important autobiographical qualities.

Of Richard of the Middle-gîtỉ'ns, Swanton had this to say: "The storyteller was an interesting old man who . . . had lived a life full of adventure. He belonged to the Middle-gîtỉ'ns . . . a branch of the Pebble-Town Gîtỉ'ns of the west coast, but, while still a young man, had gone to live with members of his family in Alaska. After that he and his uncle were in the employ of the Hudson Bay Company for a long time, until he finally came back to Skidegate to live." In other words, Richard was probably born and raised in the town of Chaatl, on Chaatl Island at the western entrance to Skidegate Channel, and thus only a few miles from Skidegate. Chaatl was not the original Pebble Town, but the people from that town moved to Chaatl some time in the mid-1850s. This date is firm.

Another date is only slightly less firm. In another story, Richard told Swanton that "[w]hile they were still trying to kill one another, when I was yet a boy, there came a great pestilence, and, when the people on the Haida islands were being destroyed, they stopped fighting." The "great pestilence" obviously refers to the smallpox epidemic that swept the Queen Charlotte Islands in 1862 and 1863. If we think of a boy as someone just short of puberty—say, eleven or twelve years old—then Richard was probably born about 1850.

If 1850 is the pivotal year, then it is possible that his war stories date to the late 1860s and early 1870s, when Richard was a teenager and a young man. This makes a certain amount of sense, as he does not mention Whites in his story, and we know there were no White settlers on the Queen Charlotte Islands, or in the area around Cape Chacon and Tongas, until the late 1870s. However, by 1880 the Church of England at Masset had become an established fact of life and there were Methodists at Skidegate. About this same time in southeastern Alaska, American and British entrepreneurs began developing salteries, which were usually located near Haida or Tlingit villages.

Beyond these assumptions, there is no way to date Richard's story. Although Port Simpson—which was established near the mouth of the Nass River as Fort Nass in 1831 and moved to the vicinity of present-day Prince Rupert in 1834—is mentioned in the original story, that inclusion is clearly part of an interpolation. Skidegate and Masset were busy towns throughout most of the nineteenth century. At some point there was a village in Kitgoro Inlet, but when Dr. C. F. Newcombe visited the place in 1901, its name was not remembered and he was told that "long ago" the village had been raided. All the men were killed and the women and children enslaved.

So far as internal evidence is concerned, cartridge boxes, muskets, and spears were contemporaneous on the islands, and the Haida were wearing European clothes by the 1790s. Canoes were in use throughout the nineteenth century and were so popular that by the 1870s they were being sold to tourists at Fort Simpson.

Slavery among the Coastal peoples was not made illegal in Alaska until 1880; while slavery had been abolished in the British dominions in 1834, the law was rarely enforced on the coast. As late as the 1870s, able-bodied slaves were selling for 200 to 300 blankets each.

Chronology is an important feature of any reconstruction, for it is one of the yardsticks with which we can measure the historicity of a text. In this case the pieces form a reliable picture, and there is more than a touch of poignancy to this story. Richard was one of the last Haida warriors, perhaps *the* last. There could not have been many men on the Queen Charlotte Islands, where the Haida lost most of their population during the epidemic of 1862 and 1863, who retained the strength and willpower to continue a way of life that was as serious and honourable to them as was the code of chivalry to Sir Galahad.

Once the text's historicity has been established, we can turn to geography. Where was Qandawas murdered? Richard names all of his Queen Charlotte Islands campsites, but his voyage into Alaska is a voyage into the rainshadows, where there are neither echoes nor headlands. It is at this point that I took a limited number of liberties with the text.

With some assurance—where else would they have gone?—it can be said that the original raiders, knowing how slight the chance of finding a small and undefended Tlingit camp near any of the Haida villages along the shores of Cordova Bay (which separates Dall Island and the west coast of Prince of Wales Island), had no choice but to seek out camps on the east, and predominantly Tlingit, coast of Prince of Wales Island. Farther east at Gash, near Cape Fox, and Tongas, near the mouth of Portland Canal, were prominent Tlingit villages. This assumption is supported by the mention of Cape Chacon.

This cape reaches so far south as to almost touch the British Columbia–Alaska boundary. Haida on their way to visit their kin in Alaska knew it as a landmark, as did Haida traders bound to or from Fort Simpson and the Nass River. Prevailing winds or inclement weather often forced the Haida to use Cape Chacon as a halfway point on their trading voyages. A westerly such as the one Qandawas encountered would not necessarily have driven her canoe into Tlingit territory, but her attempt to get to Cape Chacon might well have taken her to the east coast of Prince of Wales Island. There, I believe, she and her men were slaughtered. As the Tlingit and Haida were busy traders at Sitka, Fort Simpson, and Fort Victoria, it was not long before her family learned of her fate.

Another geographical point mentioned in the original was Fort Simpson, but for reasons already mentioned I deleted that portion of Swanton's text. It is worth noting that the Haida had been visiting the post since the 1830s and that this was their window to the Tlingit world. Tongas and Gash were only some twenty-five kilometres north of Fort Simpson.

I have not given the linguistic evidence much consideration. Some will think my handling of names, for instance, has been unnecessary. I do not agree. Richard's story is a chronicle: there is no characterization in the story; point of view is never developed; and there is no plot. Perhaps, if we had Swanton's Queen Charlotte Islands papers at hand—as well as someone who could read them—our situation would be different. As this is an initial reconstruction, and one that attempts to add a few more minutes to what we know of the history of the Islands in the 1870s, names are unimportant so long as they are authentic. These are.

Still, linguistic problems worry me, or rather their shadows do. How good was Swanton's Haida, Richard's English? How much rewriting did they do? Whose fault was it that the warriors started out in two canoes in "the very middle of winter"? This is hardly the time to be crossing Dixon Entrance. Besides, the people would be in their strongly fortified and well-guarded winter villages. But the warriors go, they find a small camp, they find other travellers, and they find salmon spawning. Somebody is at fault here, and it would be satisfying to know who.

The appearance of the text on the page is not as novel as it may seem. Certain influences are obvious: David Jones's *The Anathemata,* Christopher Logue's not-always-happy adaptations from the *Iliad,* Peter Matthiessen's *Far Tortuga.* But, to give credit where credit is due, I owe an equal debt to Wendy Wickwire, who, in her *Write It on Your Heart: The Epic World of an Okanagan Storyteller,* observed: "I searched for a presentational style to capture the nuance of the oral tradition—the emphasis on certain phrases, intentional repetition, and dramatic rhythms and pauses. I have, therefore, set the stories in lines which mirror as closely as possible Harry's rhythms of speech." And, as I am still learning, Dell Hymes has a good deal to say about oral presentation in his *"In Vain I Tried to Tell You": Essays in Native American Ethnopoetics.*

KIMIKO HAHN

Reflections Off White

for M

The werewolf is on. During her sister's wedding reception, May and I curl up in the minister's cottage on a bed larger than my parents'. A sunny room with strict shadows. White chenille spread. The bumpy texture presses designs on our legs. We are seeing a horror movie for the first time. Is it 1962? Is it before color?

May's first wedding is in Colorado. I am in a purple dress. She wears a creamy lace dress. On the plane home a rock star tries to pick me up, but I don't recognize him and I squint at his lines.

I am a bridesmaid. I have watched all of Pia's preparations from registering at Bloomingdale's to studying meals apropos for early evening. An Italian American, she marries in the original Saint Patrick's on Mulberry. Strawberry-gold bands. Before the year is out, they will shatter all their dishes against the wall.

My first wedding: a white moiré taffeta strapless gown with short jacket. Even his great-grandmother attends. I don't remember the cake—white with yellow roses? I decide not to keep the album after we split up. Only five photos—none with the cake. In one his mother smiles at him.

My second wedding I am three months pregnant and drink only one glass of champagne, which I throw up.

My sister marries a musician. My eighteen-month-old daughter wears a pink sailor dress and cheap red "patent leather" slippers. There are several bowls with ice and the shrimp our parents shelled all night. Even their hands look pink. I don't recall the music.

At my first husband's second marriage, I wear a small black dress and red fishnets. He wins a bet with an officemate who figured I wouldn't show up.

My husband's co-worker's niece's wedding is at the Sacred Blood Church in El Barrio. We don't know her. I weep when we all throw rice on the front steps. Her bridesmaids are in peach.

At our close friend's wedding before he came out, the music is mostly R & B. Several of the gay men comment on the pity of it. One wears an immaculate sharkskin suit and shades.

A friend calls to say she's eloped with her sweetheart so as not to have to deal with family. They go to City Hall, then rent a car and drive to a bed-and-breakfast. The room smells of cedar. In the morning in the empty parlor, there appear cranberry juice, cranberry muffins, and coffee, all in glassware. The juice looks like blood. They never see—only hear—other guests.

My haircutter's mother designs the gown and has her grandmother's tailor in Red Hook sew it. He has cataracts but produces a terrifyingly delicate dress. She knows she will save it like a flower pressed in a Bible. She wears white roses in her hair.

A friend's teenage daughter studies bride magazines: from the veils to the satin pumps. She wants to fall in love to marry. She wants everyone to turn as she enters the church with her father. She wants everyone to cry, especially her mother. She wants the groom to sweep the veil back and kiss her so hard her back bends.

A colleague marries in her fiancé's—in *their*—apartment. They look like an immigrant couple, he in pinstripes and she in antique lace. Standing beside two poets, I weep during the whole ceremony. The couple stands by the window, and backlit by the midafternoon light, the groom doesn't have a face.

Prayer for My Father

At the Blue Jay Motel the four of us brothers dress in our funereal suits and white shirts and drab ties with sensible black shoes and dark socks, showered and hair combed, shaved and ready to rumble off into the void of the Druid chapel, the Catholic Mass at Saint Cecilia's that would be held, and then the cortege of rented limos and vans that would wend its way from Clearwater to Saint Petersburg, on to the grounds of the soldiers' cemetery, my father's final resting place. There was no time to eat out, so Brendan and I drive to a McDonald's nearby and come back with breakfast specials, orange juice, and big containers of coffee. We eat by the pool, watching the herons and gulls poking through the clear, still water for fish. All of us eat the food but Tommy, who has decided that it is beneath him.

"He's the uppitiest homeless person I ever met," I say, half jesting and half serious.

"He's worse than that," Brendan says. "He's a fucking pain in the ass."

Oh, to hear how my brother Brendan says that word *fuck,* full of New York's working-class toughness, resentful and poetic. On Brendan's tongue, it is a word full of animistic fury and unbelievable magic, each consonant and vowel delivered with a lyrical violence. My oldest brother, Jimmy, always said that people from Long Island—and Brendan was totally Nassau County, as opposed to his older brothers, who were part Nassau, and part Brooklyn—had a thicker New York accent than those from the boroughs. He was probably correct about that. Listening to my brother Brendan, I could see—I mean hear—his point. Fucking Tommy, he'd mumble. Fucking son of a bitch. Who the fuck do they think they are? I'll fuck them up good. Fucking bastards. The fucking guys at the airport. The fucking guineas (echoing his father). The fucking Arab and Indian taxi drivers. The fucking cops and airport security. The fucking family. Yeah. The fucking family. Because that's what it comes down to, the fucking family, all assembled here, though one of them, Tommy, pisses off his younger brother Brendan once again, and I have to be aware, though I am nearly a stranger in their midst, rarely seeing or socializing with them, that they see each other regularly and that Brendan has become, over the past decade or longer, Tommy's caretaker, his meal ticket and his crib, his brother confessor and soulmate. Poor Brendan. So fucking Tommy is at it again, getting under Brendan's skin. This time he is playing the pampered role. Who knows what it might be next? Probably one of his outbreaks of religious indignation, Bible-thumping and all, about how we are all damned, no matter that we didn't drink, all of us cursed too much, took the name of the Lord in vain, were disrespectful to our parents, did not go to church on Sundays, etc., etc.

"Fucking Tommy," Brendan says again as he watches him disappear upstairs, not even close to being ready to go to the funeral.

"He's going to be late for his father's funeral," I say.

"Christ," responds Joe, "Tommy's going to be late for his *own* fucking funeral."

"Not if I can help it," Brendan says. Then he shouts up to his beleaguered older brother, "If you ain't ready in fifteen minutes, we're leaving you here, Tommy."

"That's right," I say, piping in, getting on the bandwagon, because I am determined to get to the chapel early, to be there and be ready to serve and assist, lend a hand and be generally useful to my mother and the rest of the family.

"Even *you?*" Tom asks me.

Et tu, Mickey?

"I thought you didn't get involved in this kind of fighting," he says.

But now I am as annoyed as any of them, all dressed and ready to go, the funeral Mass not that far off; we are ready to leave, but Tom is not ready. He still needs to smoke a few more cigarettes, get his bearings, chitchat about this and that and nothing at all, then leisurely, no matter the hour or the conditions, get ready. He comes down the stairs and begins a conversation with the Polish proprietor about the curios and knickknacks scattered around the grounds: tiny plastic gnomes, a donkey pulling a cart, plaster flamingos (nearly as flawless as the real ones in the water).

"Get ready!" Brendan shouts.

"I think your brothers want you to leave for the funeral," the proprietor says.

Tom ambles up the stairs and into his room while Brendan fumes under his breath and Joe talks about antique furniture and the cost of heating a house in upstate New York during the winter.

The brothers get into the white van, and we drive off. Joe drives; it would seem he has become the designated driver during our stay. As he drives, he sings "Something" along with Joe Cocker on the radio. I can't help but think that he once looked a little like the British singer. Brendan sits in the killer seat, smoking cigarettes and looking tense in his neck and shoulders.

Tom, following his own script, speaks with himself in the rear seat. I look out the window blankly. Each day that I spend in Clearwater the sadness not so much washes over me as soaks into my marrow. But it is not just sadness. I begin to see how tragic all our lives are, and just before we expire, the end usually is not graceful, painless, or artful. Perhaps I don't mean that our lives are tragic but that they are pointless. Death is artless and dumb, but totally democratic in that it gets everyone. There! It comes. It is here. It is among us. Smell it. Taste it. Don't even try to fathom it because it cannot be comprehended. What an insignificant little man my father had been, and, in turn, so am I, and so is everyone else, Napoleon, Dante, James Joyce, Caesar, Michelangelo, ashes to ashes, everyone all falls down, reduced to anonymous dust no matter who they had been. Death is the only equal-opportunity experience I would share with the rest of humanity. So it is not just sadness, but despair, and how, as I did in the past, I mask these sensations by feeling rage and anger, though this morning I am not able to set off the hair-trigger explosion. I'm bloated by these feelings.

I also feel a specific grief: that my father and I never came to any closure, much less a discovery, about our relationship. It is as if he disappeared before I could find out what was what, shout and scream, before we could have come to some kind of terminal resolution, expressing our heartfelt feelings for each other while still acknowledging our differences. This was not to be, not for me, nor for any of my brothers and sisters, because after four days in Florida, I see in ways I never saw before that I am not unique among my siblings in my feelings toward my father. Each one of us carries around this same baggage, and each one of us brought it to Clearwater, maybe expecting to air our dirty linen, though no true opportunity presents itself, no dramatic moment comes. Instead of revelations, we have our dull little aches, physical and psychic, plaguing us like an inherited arthritic condition, a pain in the little bones of the feet, an ague in the cheeks of the ass and up the lower back and down the top of the legs, a headache on one side of the head, a stiff neck, upset stomach, hemorrhoids, in-grown toenails—all the maladies that we inherited from that devilish man, the little civil servant in the pinstriped suit, laid out to be mourned, waked, vilified, and eulogized this day from which he is to be expelled from our consciousness into the eternal vastness of the universe.

Joe sings "You Can't Always Get What You Want" along with the radio, which blasts from the speakers as we speed, windows up and air conditioner on, over the causeway and back into Clearwater and on to the chapel. As soon as we pull into the Rhodes Funeral Parlor parking lot, the fun ends. We get serious.

"Wipe that grin off your face," I say to Joe, trying to make myself sound like our father. "Or I'll wipe it off for you."

"OK, Chief," Joe says, sounding just like the old man.

"Hey, this is serious," Tom warns us.

"Screw you," Brendan tells him.

Then, straightening our ties, buttoning our jackets, polishing our shoes on the bottoms of our pants, we enter the funeral parlor.

I had thought that the Chief would be put away already, that I wouldn't have to see him ever again, but there he is, front and center, surrounded by the horseshoe rings of flowers and well-wishings—a note on one of the floral wreaths says, TO JIMMY, FROM YOUR GODFATHER—still vigilant and scrutinizing his sons and daughters. I get hot and clammy; I don't like this Florida weather at all. Heat always brings out my dengue fever, causing me to get headaches and feel vaguely hallucinatory, like some second-rate Joseph Conrad character. Clearly I haven't traveled through the five stages of grief I learned about when I had to mourn the loss of my alcohol at Smithers Alcohol Treatment Center on East 93rd Street, off Madison Avenue in Manhattan; I need to go through these stages in order to be well, though for the life of me, I can't remember what the five stages are other than denial and anger, oh yes, I think, acceptance too, so I have three stages of grief at hand, fumbling to remember the others, as though that act of remembering will be a substitute for actually feeling them.

I cannot kneel in front of the coffin, but maybe, I think, I will be able to say a prayer from this perch in the back of the room. It would be my own kind of prayer, not denominational, not religious, but a practical utterance to God concerning my father. Yet I have no words, only a vague feeling, and I ask myself, If there are no words, can it be a prayer? I think not. Maybe a meditation, but not a prayer; prayers need words, and not only words, you need to believe what you are saying. I don't believe yet a thing I am saying. Besides, I'm not saying anything at all.

After the aborted prayer, I saunter to the back of the room as relatives enter, sobbing and veiled, no longer talking away; now they whisper. Even amid sheer chaos, a kind of order obtains. There are rules. If I don't know the rules or seem to understand them, these mourners do. I sit on the sofa in the back of the chapel, the young children playing around me. I try to put together a thumbnail portrait of my father: he became an orphan when his own father became incapable of raising him, forever drunk and in trouble, so that my father lived for a time with his late-mother's relatives from New Jersey. Eventually, he left New York for Washington, where he briefly attended Georgetown University, hoping it would be his entry into the foreign service.

During his Washington years, he lived in a boarding house. The happiest stories I ever heard him tell were about those days, and when he said those words *boarding house,* they rolled off his tongue like poetry, part James Joyce short story, part Sean O'Casey play. When he talked about his boarding-house days, I pictured a house with wooden stairs outside, as if it were in New Orleans, not Washington. But his boarding-house days came to a close when his father became ill; he had to leave college and his job in Washington and come back to the city to watch after his sickly old man.

It was after he returned to Brooklyn that he met my mother, introduced to him by his best friend, the man who married my mother's sister Harriet. After my father married my mother, he went off to war and she raised their children in Greenbelt, Maryland. He got stationed in his beloved Washington, no longer a single, boarding-house dweller but a married sailor in naval intelligence, assigned to processing West Coast Japanese into the internment camps in America during World War II. By war's end, he had three sons, and soon after that a daughter on the way, and by the time they moved to Long Island, getting out of Brooklyn, there were five children. They had double-digit children by the end of the fifties, though nine would remain the magic number, the number of children that was most often used when people asked him how many children he had.

"Nine," he said, using all the fingers on his two hands but the left thumb.

Like Charlie Chan, who referred to his sons as "number one" or "number two," my father called me the third son. When he wanted to put a Brooklyn spin on it, he said, "He's tray," using the Italian word for three, or "He's t'ree," in the more vernacular speech of East New York.

My father might not have liked the Italians on the docks, but he spoke fluent Italian, often dazzling stewards and other crew members on the *Michelangelo* or *Leonardo* or *Raffaella,* Italian ocean liners that used the Hell's Kitchen piers when they docked in New York Harbor.

Seeing my father again is almost like seeing him yesterday. I get nervous and afraid, tight in the throat, worried, and unsure. And looking at his placid face now, I remember how animated and antagonistic it used to be. When I was a teenager—the last time I was in his thrall—I used to hate him; gradually I mended this emotion to angry spite. Finally, I realized that I was angry at him because he awarded me the booby prize in the Catholic sweepstakes: being born. Everything else was gravy. His rotten personality. His evil disposition. His murderous tempers. I can forgive him all that, but I still have this grudge against him for causing me to be born not into infinite grace, what I yearned for, but into the misery of this Catholic childhood, its guilts and shames, its sins, both venal and mortal, and its everlasting punishments for the damned, and how I also used to think that if God were this mean, He probably would change the rules anytime He liked, so that instead of the good being saved and the bad condemned forever to Hell, maybe God might condemn the good to eternal torment and admit the bad boys and girls into the pleasures of eternal life in Heaven.

That is what I experience standing in the back of the chapel, hanging back, actually, as I look at my shriveled father in his coffin. Maybe all their Catholic rules would not work, I think. Still, I go forward, kneel at the casket, and finally say a prayer for him, not some *Our Father/Hail Mary/Act of Contrition* kind of prayer, but one of my own intensity.

"I forgive you, Dad," I say, "so I hope you forgive me. Let's be friends now. I hope you didn't suffer too much and hope you had a moment of peace before the end. If there is an afterlife, I don't want you to burn forever in Hell. You were a son-of-a-bitch, yes, but not a totally evil man—not even a little evil, for that matter—just another working-class stiff, a shanty clown, really, and I'll forever be grateful for your bequeathing each of us a sublime sense of the absurd. Take care and be well. See you around. Amen."

A Usable Past:
An Interview with Bharati Mukherjee

Bharati Mukherjee is the author of two books of short stories, *Darkness* and *The Middleman and Other Stories,* and the novels *Jasmine, Wife, The Tiger's Daughter,* and *The Holder of the World.* She also is the coauthor, with her husband, Clark Blaise, of *Days and Nights in Calcutta,* a book of nonfiction. Born in Calcutta, she attended college in India, earning two master's degrees at the University of Baroda, and then came to the United States to study creative writing at the University of Iowa. At Iowa, she received a master of fine arts degree in creative writing and, later, a double-doctorate in English and comparative literature. A winner of the National Book Critics Circle Award for Fiction, she is currently professor of English at the University of California at Berkeley. This interview took place at Whittier College on 26 September 1996.

SD Just yesterday I read the op-ed piece you wrote for the *New York Times.* I hadn't planned to discuss it here, but some of the questions that you raise really interest me. You say that your sister probably pities you because of the "erasure of your Indianness." I was wondering if you really feel that Indianness has been erased from your life, and if so, to what extent has that occurred?

BM Let me just preface whatever my answer might be by saying that the op-ed piece resulted from the *New York Times* asking me about my reaction to the current curtailment of rights of legal immigrants to the United States. My older sister, who is a child psychologist of some renown in Detroit and has been here for the last thirty-five years, has chosen to remain an Indian citizen but a green-card holder; whereas I became a u.s. citizen as soon as I was eligible.

Erasure of Indianness: I think that what my sister meant by that was not to accuse me so much as to say she felt sorry for me, because I no longer automatically wear—choose to wear—Indian saris. I find that Meera—we're wonderful friends; it's a very affectionate family and we call each other twice a week—that her accent has grown more and more Indian over the years because, I think, that gives her a kind of rootedness. She, who was one of the cool, stylish convent girls with short hair in Calcutta, now wears long sleeves and her hair in a bun. So she has that outward appearance of Indianness.

I don't think of myself in terms of being a Mukherjee daughter from such and such a family or such and such a caste—that's not my primary way of identifying myself. But certainly Indianness is a habit of mine now, which means that it's a cultural conditioning to certain things . . . the way that some Catholics—even if they've given up their religion—remain Catholics in habit. But I don't need, I guess, Indian clothes to feel Indian.

SD   So it's more of a surface Indianness that you are referring to, not—

BM   Well, no, I think it's much deeper than that. But if being Indian meant that you were typed, you were who you were because of where you had been born—soil, family, caste, religion, gender—then all of that has crumbled.

SD   You also wrote in the article that your sister's life in America sounds like "the description of a long-enduring, comfortable yet loveless marriage"—I really like that analogy—"without risk or recklessness." But you, on the other hand, have risked and have undergone what you refer to as "the trauma of self-transformation." What was it that led you to choose that path? Was it a conscious decision?

BM   Absolutely not. I'm afraid it was hormones! Coming to Iowa to co-educational classrooms was the first time, really, that I was in a co-educational situation. My father had made sure that we would never be in anything but girls' schools if he could help it. And so mine was a kind of whirlwind two-week courtship and a lunchtime wedding. I didn't have time to think, which is just as well.

That's the easy answer. The more honest answer, I think, is that somewhere at the gut level I must have wanted to turn my life around, or there was something that was freeing about being—and I'm talking about being in the heartland, you know, the heartland of Iowa City—a student in the States that wasn't possible for me in the very restricted, upper-class, patriarchal family that Calcutta provided me.

SD   When comparing your autobiography to your literature, especially the novel *The Tiger's Daughter* and "A Wife's Story," one of your short stories, I couldn't help but notice that there are parallels between your real-life stories and the fictional stories. I was wondering what role autobiography plays in your writing process.

BM I wasn't aware until I came to write *The Holder of the World* that there was any autobiographical impulse—let alone element—in my work. I thought I was writing about people who were totally outside of me. I realize now that each of the novels is sort of a way station in my personal Americanization. And so, even the sentence structures seem to have changed. I think that most writers, like actors, have to dig inside themselves for the passions of their characters. And that's for the good guys as well as the bad guys in any novel. So I feel that I am invested, metaphorically, in every single character in each of the books.

SD In a 1991 interview you talked about the frustration you had with the joint-family structure in Calcutta, and later about the "very traditional, hierarchical, caste society with overt oppression against women" in which you were raised. How has being a woman who lived in that society shaped your outlook on gender and gender issues?

BM Well, I didn't realize how traumatized I was by the sexism being practiced all around me. I didn't know while I was growing up that there was an alternate way of conducting life. Through age twenty, I was very much within solid, solidly rooted, comfortably financed, upper-middle-class family. And I saw all around me incredible physical as well as verbal abuse of women. My own mother—I owe everything that I may be today to my mother, who was not allowed to get an education—put her body quite literally on the line, so that her three daughters could be educated. I remember, to this day, my mother being told constantly, "You should kill yourself, you should die, you are unlucky because you don't have a son." And so that has fueled, I think, all three of us sisters' desire for an education. I'm sure I got a double Ph.D. only because of my mother's image in the back of my head. There are good sides to joint families—I'm not putting it down totally—but I was amazed at how much of the oppression of women is done by women themselves within these joint families. And how the women seemed to me to have only one way of exercising power and consolidating their own position, their own safety within the joint system: to be cruel to whoever is farther down the line.

SD In one of the articles, you mentioned your mother and how she had undergone physical and verbal abuse so that you could live alone once you returned from England. Yet you hesitated to call her a Gloria Steinem and a feminist. What are the differences you see between the kind of feminist your mother was and Western feminists? Was hers a type of Eastern feminism?

BM I don't even have a concept of something as big as "Eastern," and I don't think my mother ever thought of herself as feminist; yet she was fighting for the best life possible for her daughters. She would say continually—this was the refrain that my sisters and I grew up with—"I will not let my daughters be the chattel that I had been." She was furious. I don't know that my quarrel is with Western feminism as such, but with the mouthy American feminists of the early and midseventies. Particularly Gloria Steinem and the *Ms.* magazine group, who were doctrinaire and, we now know, often conducting intergender relationships and maneuvering for power when they had an overt but totally unacknowledged racist, colonialist attitude towards women of color. Particularly women of color who were not African American. And so the Kate Millets and the Gloria Steinems insisted on telling minority women, telling me, how I should conduct my life in order to be a feminist. It was all about talk, rhetoric, and self-examination—these were the times of consciousness-raising groups and examining yourself with mirrors—whereas my mother would have died if anyone had mentioned such things. But she was able to get things done without talking about it.

I don't see myself or my mother as anti-male, anti-men, but I do see myself as a champion of civil rights. Extending civil rights to all disadvantaged groups.

SD I see some of this expressed in the tension between your characters Ina Mullick and Dimple—and also Maya and her friend Fran. Were you thinking about these sorts of things . . .

BM Absolutely, yes. And even in *Jasmine,* Wylie is a version of those sorts of things, but by that time I had enough sympathy for the flaws of that particular kind of feminist, so I didn't have to hit as hard as I might have in the earlier novels. I'd taken a lot of flack in the seventies from exactly those doctrinaire feminists who resented me because I had actually gone ahead and gotten my Ph.D., gotten a job at McGill University while they were still finding themselves by throwing pots or drawing up domestic contracts for who would do the dishes on what day.

SD Maya, in "The Tenant," talks about this in her feminist class at Duke. She was criticized for being this feminine woman, but she couldn't make the others understand that this was how she was raised.

BM You know, when I was growing up, how you sat, how you talked to males older than you—all this was so ritualized that my big battle, personal battle as an American, has been to not be so polite.

SD In speaking about writing *The Middleman and Other Stories,* you said that you "can enter any gender and any culture, if the character and story excite" you. I was wondering if you feel that it is easier to work with your female characters than your male characters.

BM I don't know. Who knows down the line if the male will impact? I think the novel that I'm researching now, that I've been thinking about for a long time, will have a male protagonist. But I can never predict what minor character is going to take over and what major character is going to wind up on the cutting-room floor. I want to think that every character is a little—I guess like Flaubert saying, "Emma Bovary, c'est moi"—that I am the characters but the characters aren't me. So I can see myself being just as much at home if that male character is a metaphor for whatever is engaging my passions or my curiosity.

SD And you would probably say the same for the Indian immigrant, as opposed to the Asian immigrant?

BM Yes. It's having to know exactly how in culture-specific ways the character is going to show his or her emotion. The Indian community I know best, so a number of my major characters have been of Indian background. But when I was doing *The Holder of the World,* I knew what that particular Massachusetts family or young woman of a certain class and Anglo origin, graduate of Yale, how this one character would react. I have to know the thinking—all the details must surface on their own without my saying, Oh, let me look at my note cards and see.

SD Do you see a danger in putting the experiences of all Asian immigrants together, lumping them into one?

BM Absolutely. I've worked some with the Asia Society in Los Angeles to make sure that the dominant culture—the whites or the African Americans—doesn't lump all Asian groups together, because the histories, intra-Asian country histories, the immigration histories are so different. Every time I teach a contemporary Asian American literature course, the tensions that arise from the Chinese American students reacting to Japanese American novels or Japanese literature are so volatile still.

I want to see class introduced into the discourse to acknowledge that the young Vietnamese kid in the San Jose inner-city area experiencing the problems of inner-city kids has very little in common with, say, the Silicon Valley Asian family. That's where, I think, the intra-minority fights are very depressing to me. Race should be made a little less relevant in the 1990s and into the new century, and the disadvantaged-versus-advantaged situation emphasized.

SD Do you think that the immigrant experience of the Indian woman is fundamentally different from the Indian man's experience in North America?

BM I'm convinced it is, but I haven't seen enough research, academic research on this. With a Canadian government grant, I've done some of this research myself in Toronto's South Asian community. But perhaps because the women are trained to be adaptable, to accommodate themselves to the husbands' families, the husbands' lifestyles, etc., etc., the Indian immigrant women are so much more able to be bridges between the cultures. They can wear pants, drive a car, do their PTA meetings, bake cookies, do Halloween costumes and then come back to the home and be the more conventional Indian wife, who serves the right kind of Indian curried food and is non-belligerent, non-threatening to the Indian immigrant husband. Whereas the males—and I've seen some research on the males—seem with diaspora, with expatriation to . . . regress isn't the right verb . . . to become more and more reactionary, more and more so-called Indian because they feel threatened in terms of their status in the American work force.

You know, I feel that the Indian male who is very successful financially and who has his Mercedes-Benz and his BMW and kids in expensive private schools, etc., quite often has frozen the sense of his India and his Indianness in the year in which he left India and came as an immigrant to this country. So that it's an artificial homeland, artificial India that these guys have created.

SD So while the actual experience in India might have progressed twenty years . . .

BM Yes. I go to India every year, and urban Indians of that same class don't have a problem with westernization or consumerism. Even the rhetoric, the way English is used in newspapers like *The Statesman* or *Hindustan Times,* has become a weird mixture of Indian-English, British-English, and a lot of American-English. Whereas the group that immigrated from 1965 on . . . that first batch has, for self-protection—and I understand that totally—become very Indian in that sort of nervous way.

TB A lot of Asian American writers, particularly your colleague at Berkeley Maxine Hong Kingston, as well as Amy Tan, Chitra Divakaruni, and others, have tried to find in folk tales, or the history of their ancestral country what Van Wyck Brooks called a "usable past." Particularly a usable past with woman warriors, strong women, which could somehow be distinguished from an unusable past of patriarchy—in the case of Kingston and

Tan, of patriarchal Confucianism. Paradoxically, this unusable past is quite useful for providing conflict in their prose. What's your usable past? What aspects of your history can and can't you use in your fiction, and in your life?

BM   What an interesting, complicated question. I think that the reason that wonderful writers like Maxine Hong Kingston and Amy Tan use so much mythology, Chinese mythology, is that they are second-generation Americans. It's a kind of roots retrieval: "Who were my people?" Whereas I, being fresh off the jet, want to get away from a lot of the mythologies that were so genderist, that were created to reinforce patriarchy or the class system—not just caste system, but class system. When I grew up, I didn't have the bedtime tales of Hans Christian Andersen, but the Puranic tales, thousands of years B.C., and the Hindu epics. Which means that some of the stories, like that of Sita, the perfect wife who is self-sacrificing and self-effacing, are the ones that I want to attack, critique. Or I have rereadings of such legends in which I suddenly realize that the conventional interpretations were convenient to the male explicators, commentators. I would like to make up my own myths. As an immigrant I don't have models here in America.

TB   Have you come into criticism for that—in the way, for example, Frank Chin has criticized Kingston and Tan for changing Chinese mythology? Of course, Chin himself adapts the classic Chinese epic *Water Margin* to his own purposes in his novel *Donald Duk.*

BM   And Frank Chin is on record saying that Tan, Kingston, and so on are a kind of Christian women's whitening-of-myth conspiracy. Those are not his exact words.

TB   But that's essentially what he's saying.

BM   That they are appeasing, or satisfying—appeasing white guilt and satisfying white need for exoticism.
   The kind of criticism that I've gotten is from a very different source. It's the post-colonial theorists from South Asia—in fact, people I went to school with as a nursery-age student, who came from the same kind of upper-class background that I did, when our financial status was exactly equal—who despise fiction, or art, as being reactionary. I'm obviously thinking of Gayatri Spivak as one such critic. They want real life, meaning sociology, journalism; but a writer has to think of each character as an individual instead of representative of all South Asian immigrants. The theorists, in contrast, have to find a general principle. So I'm attacked because I married outside the community, because I'm fluent in English, because

I'm—their word is "privileged"—and therefore have no right to write. Because if I'm writing about people exactly like me—women from a certain background and with a certain status—then I'm immediately elitist and have nothing worthwhile to say.

TB   Does the writing of novels with didactic purpose invite this kind of criticism, the reduction of all the complexities of fiction to sociology, social policy? How can we separate the politics and the fiction?

BM   I think that all fiction, all speech, all act, in real life or fiction, is political—meaning that it is about power. Either being empowered or allowing someone to disempower you. Having said that, I'll add that the theoreticians right now—this is the Subaltern school of critics of South Asian origin who all have these fancy chairs that come with high salaries on u.s. or European campuses—need to see literature only in a Marxist context. So fiction is judged only by the biological, ethnic, and class status of the author and what they call the "field of production," which means that if your book is being published by an American mainstream press—even though it might be as small as Grove Press—rather than a basement press in Minneapolis, then you have "sold out." So the reasons for looking at work become non-literary. And I think it is also arrogance on their part that they need to see their criticism as more important than literature—they don't need the texts. Apparently, in Sri Lanka recently, for one of these commonwealth literature association meetings, someone did a statistical study that showed more papers had been done on "poor Mukherjee" than on anyone else. But so often the details, like the names of main characters, are wrong, or they think *Darkness* is a novel, which means that they're reading each other, not the texts.

SD   Do you think that since your novels and short stories put the women characters in the center, they offer a usable past for other Indian women?

BM   I don't know; I don't think of these things, and it would scare me if from now on I thought of any of this. And in fact I cringe when young Indo-Americans say, You're our role model; how come your characters have sex? I don't want to be anyone's role model. But one hopes that something will trigger in the reader the desire to question assumptions.

SD   What were your feelings on religion when you left India, and how have they since changed?

BM   I was a practicing, very observant Hindu—which doesn't mean that much because you don't really have to go to the temple once a week, as practicing Christians may have to. I had my little grotto of icons, and I still have them. I'm a very secular person, but I guess I still think of myself as Hindu. I'm a little hesitant to say this because nowadays if you say you're a Hindu, it immediately becomes identified with fundamentalism and particular political parties. I want to disassociate myself totally from that, but I do believe in the geophysical principle that Hinduism metaphorizes, that cosmic energy.

SD   And the idea of reincarnation?

BM   All of Indian religion, I've always felt, is a metaphor for physics and astrophysics, and that's why I'm so attracted to chaos theory or fractals. There are all these Puranic tales about millions of galaxies, millions of universes: there isn't just one god in this one little galaxy, and the moment you start thinking too much of yourself, Brahma is going to come from another galaxy and put you in your place.

TB   Can I read you a poem by Rabindranath Tagore that I happen to have in my backpack? This is a poem I always relate to a poem by William Carlos Williams in *Spring and All* called "The Rose." I was thinking about it when you were talking about physics and Hinduism. It's translated by William Radice.

THE SICKBED

When I woke up this morning
There was a rose in my flower-vase:
The question came to me—
The power that brought you through cyclic time
To final beauty,
Dodging at every turn
The torment of ugly incompleteness,
Is it blind, is it abstracted,
Does it, like a world-denying sannyasi,
Make no distinction between beauty and the opposite
    of beauty?
Is it merely rational,
Merely physical,
Lacking in sensibility?
There are some who argue
That grace and ugliness take equal seats
At the court of Creation,
That neither is refused entry
By the guards.
As a poet I cannot enter such arguments—
I can only gaze at the universe

In its full, true form,
At the millions of stars in the sky
Carrying their huge harmonious beauty—
Never breaking their rhythm
Or losing their tune,
Never deranged
And never stumbling—
I can only gaze and see, in the sky,
The spreading layers
Of a vast, radiant, petalled rose.

BM   That's beautiful.

TB   Very much what you're saying about physics, I think, and traditional Indian ways of seeing the complexity of the universe.

BM   And for a poet or fiction writer, if you're saying the goal is acquiring the perspective that makes you see you're really a speck in a giant design, then it affects the way you think of character: you dramatize character in a way that's the opposite of the way that protagonists or tragic heroes in European literature behave or should behave. It poses all sorts of narrative-strategy questions.

SD   In *Jasmine* the novel, "Jasmine" your short story, "The Tenant," "A Wife's Story," "The Management of Grief," and *Wife*, the female protagonists undergo transformations that touch on issues of Hindu reincarnation, immigration, and the American Dream—coupled with some sort of feminist realization. Would you describe your literature as being an intersection of these?

BM   I don't know. When I'm sitting in front of my computer screen, I'm not really thinking in those analytical ways. Things are happening in spite of me, and there's really a kind of physical change when the writing is going well: there's just so much adrenaline pumping that there's a physiological change, and I know I'm into the characters and they're doing things in spite of me. But in the sense of reincarnation, I'm saying reincarnation is right here on this earth for Jasmine. I believe in change and resilience, adaptability, that if you can't adapt to the situation, you're going to be totally broken. What were some of the other intersections?

SD   American Dream . . .

BM   Because I haven't worked through this myself, that's why Jasmine and so many of my other characters are really trying to find a comfort zone between belief and effort, and reward of effort, and destiny—which things are planned. And so it's always that tension that keeps the Jasmines going, and whatever morality they have is not the conventional morality. Instead they say, Let me treat every moment with reverence because I don't know the function, the purpose of my being here. The two of you coming into my life this afternoon, for example; how does this fit into the larger design?

So not American Dream in the sense of "Can I have a bigger car"—I don't even drive, never quite got the hang of it, and I've certainly gone through an incredible economic and social demotion by choosing to live as an American—but that sense of discovering for yourself what you believe and who you want to be.

SD   Would you say that Hinduism and feminism intersect? I'm thinking here of when your character Dimple envisions herself as Sita the ideal wife and—

BM   Which Dimple rejects. I think this is why I'm trying to be very careful about not being identified as a Hindu writer because this is not in the religion itself; but all the midrash, all the commentary surrounding it, is so sexist, is so patriarchal, that the legends are told and retold in such a way as to buttress patriarchy. My characters either reject Sita or reevaluate why Sita did what she did. And therefore, in *The Holder of the World,* I had an Indian woman character say that Sita is tempting the fates; she wants to step out of the safe chalk circle and see what the world out there is like. It's a misreading to see her as docile, passive.

SD   And we also see this when Jasmine is Kali?

BM   I needed that moment—it wrote itself—and then I realized that what had happened was that she had mythologized herself. I'll tell you an interesting story about the British reaction to that scene. Kali is the form that Bengali Hindus believe in: she's our patron; everyone has her icon in his or her bedroom. She is visualized as having a red tongue, a triangle hanging out, as she's doing a dance of destruction of evil. In this dance she's got all these bleeding weapons—scimitars and scythes—in her hand, and she's wearing a garland of bleeding, severed, mangled heads. So I needed for Jasmine to have a red tongue, right? Jasmine's got only one weapon at hand, so she cuts her tongue—a moment that's meant to be traumatic, motivating, and mythologizing: she turns into this goddess of destruction. In England, there was a year-long furor because *Jasmine* had been read week by week on a BBC women's program during the summer and one mother had written in saying, "This is mutilation, self-mutilation. It's like Oprah Winfrey!" [*Laughs*] I never even thought of it as self-mutilation!

TB   In one of his poems William Carlos Williams writes that "destruction and creation are simultaneous." Picasso said a very similar thing. For Williams, that's a way of mythologizing the avant-garde, the cutting edge: you have to destroy. Matisse once said, "In order to paint a rose you have to forget every painting of a rose that's ever been painted in order to paint it anew." It seems to me that Jasmine and other characters who go through the process of immigration—particularly to the United States, but also to Europe and elsewhere—have a capacity for destroying their past, for abandoning, for ceasing to be who they were, for living on the edge, for living on the frontier, kind of riding chaos perpetually. Is this for you in your personal symbol system also something about the process of creativity, or is it more about the process of movement from continent to continent?

BM   I think mainly a process of movement from continent to continent. I have a placid exterior, and a thrilling, crazy interior, so that I shouldn't have to leave a room in order to go through the chaos myself. I just try to hide it from people as much as I can. But I am convinced now that you can't straddle the fence—that if you're going to not remain an expatriate, then there has to be a traumatic, painful kind of break with the past. After that you might reclaim little bits and pieces of it and fit them into your new life in a different way, but there is no easy, painless way to make the change; otherwise, you're burrowing in nostalgia.

TB   I would assume then that it's also necessary for the culture to change, to acclimate itself to the new people who are making their home here.

BM   Yes, it is a two-way transformation. And whatever heritage I have come with is now collective, American heritage. Just as I have incorporated and absorbed so much American history—or trivia—so quickly. If I hadn't left India, or if I had married an Indian Silicon Valley tycoon, I would be a very different kind of writer because I wouldn't have been tested in what energized my material. I would have had safe, non-risk projects about conflictless, perfect, model immigrant families.

SD   Picking up on what Tony said about two-way transformations: you commented once in an interview that in America "diversity is accepted; the melting pot helps the newcomers to feel more welcome." So I was wondering if you see a melting pot where all cultures are dissolved into the dominant culture, or a melting pot in which each new ingredient changes and is changed by the others? And how does that play in your literature?

BM   I wish, at the time that I said this, there had been a phrase or I had been able to come up with a phrase more precise than *melting pot*—something like *stew pot*. The American mythology about the melting pot certainly helps others to come and say, Yes, I have a place here. The unfortunate part of the practice has been the nineteenth-century notion that you make yourself over following an Anglo or Puritan model. What I'm saying is that it's not like a salad, in which every bit of lettuce or radish or tomato or cucumber retains its original shape and taste and there's only the salad dressing as a kind of mild flavor that makes all these bits acceptable, but a stew in the sense that the stewing process has changed everything; the broth has become what it is because every bit has given some of its juices, some of its taste. I'm looking for every side to break down in some way and constantly create a new whole.

SD Would you say that in this broth, some degree of gain and loss is inevitable?

BM Yes, absolutely, and for everyone. That's what the whites have to understand and come to grips with if they are going to survive the new century, survive *into* the new century, for that matter. That's a very hard message to get across.

TB Your analogy reminded me of a moment in *Huckleberry Finn* when Finn is talking about the problem of "sivilized" eating, in which you keep everything separate on the plate and how he likes it better when everything swaps around in a big pot and all the flavors mix.

BM That's right. I hadn't made the connection; that's wonderful.

SD Why is it that the Vietnamese American character Du (in *Jasmine*) remains in the hyphen but Jasmine doesn't?

BM Because he chooses to. I wanted, through all of these minor characters—for me as a writer, the minor characters are really pivotal in the book—to build in many different kinds of immigrants, having many different reactions to the fact that they are suddenly in this culture. And so Du, because he's gone through such unspeakable horrors as a result of the Viet Nam War, may in junior high school, or high school, be able to act more American, get As in u.s. history, but he chooses not to give up some private part of himself. There's a resentment, and he goes off to Los Angeles to find his sister.

SD Is hyphenization insufficient? Does it make a person not whole?

BM For me, hyphenization is a very discomforting situation for two reasons. It makes you want a way out, a net. You say, All right, so this doesn't work: I am an Indian for the whites and I am an American for the Indians—a kind of fence straddling that is almost immoral. I am trying to get white Americans and African Americans to see how deliberately and cruelly or maliciously marginalizing it is to apply the hyphen only to Asian Americans, Chicanos, and so on—and to not routinely make European-Americans of the Updikes and the Joyce Carol Oateses. It's as though they're saying there is one kind of America, and the rest of you because you're hyphenated—whether you want to be or not, we are insisting that you be hyphenated—are not really like us. So that's why, in order to emphasize the two-way transformation, I'm saying either call everyone American or make everyone hyphenated. But I'm against the hyphen.

SD   And, instead, for this fluid notion of "American"?

BM   Which to me is about believing in certain social and civic ideals rather than blood and soil.

SD   Several of your Indian heroines have entered into what we call mixed marriages, which you refer to in the op-ed piece by saying that you were "prepared for (and even welcomed) the emotional strain that came with marrying outside my ethnic community." Do you have any comments to make on this point besides what you have already written?

BM   Yes, I believe that the answer to any problem in multicultural, multi-ethnic societies is—and I'm using this word very deliberately—mongrelization. I come from a society of "pure" culture, where any kind of hanky-panky with bloodline, caste line, is to be despised. That means you lose your caste altogether. And so to me there's an enormous amount of danger in the false retention of pride in bloodlines, purity of bloodlines. And I think that the babysitters, the caregivers like Jasmine, who then, like a Jane Eyre, marry their Mr. Rochesters, are in the vanguard of the new transformation of America.

SD   You infuse some Hindu notions of non-dualism in your literature, and I'm thinking specifically of Jasmine. When she's still called by her village name, Jyoti, she remarks about her father's death, "but that pitcher is not broken. It is the same air this side as that." I was wondering if the theme of non-dualism shapes your heroines in any way?

BM   Fusion, yes. Seeing that what seems opposite really is simply part of the same whole. Or it's the usual mythic journey where creatures who had seemed like enemies or monsters testing you turn out to be gatekeepers on your way to getting the golden fleece or the golden chalice, or whatever. Yes, I'm afraid that there I am reflecting the Hindu belief that it all boils down to God: *God is God, God is a man, God is an inanimate object, God is* *a snake.* There is no clear-cut, permanent division between good and evil but just different ways of looking at things.

SD How would you explain, then, why some of the Indian women in your stories—they're minor characters—avoid transformation or avoid the struggle against transformation? I'm thinking of Meena Sen in *Wife,* or Nirmila, the Professorji's wife who lives in Flushing, and probably that entire community in Flushing, or Santana, Dr. Chatterji's wife in "The Tenant."

BM I'm looking for people who test their fates and then either discard or reclaim them, as opposed to those women, like the Meena Sens, who never test the fates and who live according to rites and rituals. That's a very different kind of faith from saying, I really do believe or I no longer believe.

SD Would you hazard to comment on that lifestyle, on their chosen path?

BM No. Who am I to make judgments other than in fiction?

SD Do you know of any Indian males reacting to your literature in the same way that Amy Tan, Kingston, Toni Morrison, and Alice Walker have been accused of "betraying their culture"?

BM By male reactions, do you mean from the Frank Chins? Writers themselves, or the community?

SD Either.

BM I don't think people in India really read my novels or any other literary novels; they all read Shobha Day, who describes herself as the Jackie Collins of India. They loved me when I wrote my first novel and was in *Newsweek:* "Calcutta daughter makes good," you know. There was nothing I could do wrong. But years later, in 1990, I made a statement in some interview that "well actually I'm an American writer of Indian origin now because I'm writing about immigrant themes," and they saw that as betrayal. If you are Indian, then you can't ever want to lose any part of that.

I don't think our community in the States really is into reading. They're so busy doing other things, so they'll read nonfiction. They couldn't care less.

SD You illustrate women's oppression in Indian society quite often. Are your female characters—and if they are, to what extent—mouthpieces for

Indian women who are experiencing oppression at the hands of an Indian patriarchy?

BM I want to make it absolutely clear that I don't envision my characters as mouthpieces and I don't want them to be mouthpieces for anyone but themselves. Once you, as a writer, lose the eccentricity of character portrayal, then you're merely writing texts to be taught in college classrooms. That's a real, real danger to art. But I hope that my books make people think.

TB Do you find that there are ways in which Indian women—and this goes against the tenor of what we've said so far—are more liberated than their Western counterparts? Are there any particular sources of strength for women in India that aren't really present in Western culture?

BM Are we talking about Indian women still in India?

TB Well, yes, I think so.

BM In that case, the strengths are that you have a community of support. Especially in the 1990s, if the husband is beating up his wife, then the community will take a stand and give him a hard time. Whereas in a lot of the wife abuse, wife battering—which I'm afraid is not uncommon in the Indian immigrant community in the States—the battered wife doesn't have the same recourse to community support or community censure. That's the word I'm looking for: *censure.* I think that it's all about class in India, which means that the educated woman from the upper-middle class or upper class has such a support system of servants and a network; you're so well plugged in that it's far more liberated about jobs, careers. But the glass ceiling in the corporate world is even lower than it is here.

I'm trying to do more and more research into the Indian wives here— the most interesting group as far as I'm concerned, because suddenly they have been able to avoid the oppression, the ritualistic, traditional oppression by their mother-in-laws. They wait long enough for the wedding so that they can come right away, on green cards, and now they're the bosses in the household. There are more incidents now of abuse of aged in-laws by these young, hip wives. [*Laughs*] And they, even more than white American women, are able to use day-care facilities and have jobs set up, small businesses, and they're all reasonably well educated, you know. Many of them are coming with graduate degrees in biochemistry or are lab technicians, and so on. They're all economically independent in ways that the Indian wives in India are not.

TB   Do you think that there's been less of a—because of colonialism in India—decline in the status of Indian immigrants to the United States? Simply because of the language skills?

BM   Yes, yes. That's what distinguishes the u.s. Indo-American relationship from the Indo-Canadian relationship and certainly from the British and German situations, and separates the Indian immigrants from the other groups—the Filipinos and other Asians. We've been very lucky, but our luck has run out. And now with the new furor about scapegoating legal immigrants of color, especially in places like New York and California, you're going to see a new kind of discrimination.

TB   Let me ask you a few writing questions. Who are your American masters? I mean, writers who have influenced you, but even more, what passages from the novels you have read shine in your memory as passages you would like to be able to live up to or exceed, emulate?

BM   There are a number of American writers that I like. I can't say that any of them are masters. I mean, even though I admire the luminosity of, say, Updike's prose sentence by sentence, he's not someone that I want to emulate. So discarding the word master then, some of the writers whose sentences I just love are—this may seem totally amazing to you—Richard Ford, then Tom McGuane because of that energy in some of his earlier novels, like *Panama*. I like Lee Abbot, you know, who is small press but writes wonderful short stories. And I admire Joyce Carol Oates, because she takes on so many forms. I like Flannery O'Connor very much, but she's not living. When I grow up, can I be Flannery O'Connor? [*Laughs*] Some of Ann Beattie's passages are very moving to me, and I can still learn about structure from Hemingway.

TB   And a follow-up question to that. How about the early great Indian fiction writers: Saratchandra Chatterji, Premchand, others. Have they been influences?

BM   They haven't been influences simply because when I was growing up in Calcutta, even though India was independent at the time, my school was still a very Britishy spot in Calcutta and so we followed the syllabi for Cambridge University exams. As a very small child, I discovered Saratchandra and then again as a grown-up here in the United States. And he *speaks* to me.
    Bengali language doesn't translate well into English, I think, because it is such an emotional language. It's a very euphonic language—even Tagore in English translation sometimes sounds sentimental or flaky, so you have to

recite poems or recite sentences in Bengali. I like Saratchandra very much, but I see how much he also has been influenced by the alienation, marginalization of the individual from community, the desire to break away.

TB   So, in some ways, it's less useful.

BM   Ah, I love his work, but I can't say that it has had any influence.

SD   You've talked about transformation throughout this interview, and one thing that you said was that your characters, like yourself, have an intensity of spirit and especially of desire. Is there anything further that you can say to describe or illustrate what you mean by this phrase?

BM   Obsession. All good writing comes from obsessive passion and ambition to change the world. I'm afraid my characters and I suffer from those flaws.

A Man of Oonalashka. 1778.
*"Oonalashka," Russian settlement in
Unalaska, Aleutian Islands, in South-
west Alaska. Engraving by William
Sharp after drawing by John Webber.*
PL. 48

Passages Home

It's ninety-seven degrees out, and the late-July air is so dry that a deep breath might leave you choking. But we're bumping across a Pendant d'Oreille pasture, three hundred fifty kilometres southeast of Calgary, in the comfortably air-conditioned cab of Lee Finstad's green pickup truck. I can hear the truck's low belly being scratched by the tall grass that grows between the parallel grooves of the old, winding prairie trail we're following. Even if I knew where we were going, it would be difficult for me to gauge our progress. The meandering path curves and turns back, crossing itself at times.

The son of a rancher, Lee seems to have been born in boots, Wranglers, and a plaid shirt with mother-of-pearl snaps, and he walks with a sauntering gait that is unmistakably a horseman's. He is the fourth generation of a Norwegian family that was among the first settled in the area nearly a hundred years ago; he was raised just miles from the sod house that was his great-grandfather's homestead. Now a pilot with Canadian Airlines, Lee returns from Medicine Hat to the family ranch every chance he gets—most recently, because of a pilot's strike. When I ask how long it will be before he returns to the ranch for good, he grins and adjusts his cap. Flying from coast to coast, he's seen a lot of land, and he knows this place is special. "There's not much unbroken prairie left anymore," he explains, "though you wouldn't believe it from looking around here."

From our vantage point, prairie grassland is most of what you can see. As you drive north from this farming community towards Medicine Hat and Calgary, grain fields become predominant. And if you're driving at this time of year, the dusty, sage color of the landscape becomes more and more a patchwork of bleached-yellow fields, thick with nearly ripe wheat, and the dry, brown ridges of summer fallow. In a history book from my home town, Etzikom, a prairie hamlet seventy kilometres north of the U.S. border, some long-time residents claim the sky is so big that on a clear day you can see the Rocky Mountains on the western horizon.

We've driven down to the Finstad ranch to observe and photograph the native burrowing owl, a creature as "prairie" as anything. Lee's mother told me they often see the owls on the ranch. In fact, she said, a scientist from the Canadian Wildlife Service had recently flagged a few areas of their pasture as "protected." Lee has driven us to one of these places, but we haven't yet spotted a single owl. We spread out, stepping around sage and dragging our feet through clumps of short prairie grass, watching for any sign of movement. I'm looking for feathers, footprints, anything—but I sense Lee's patience wearing thin. As overwhelmingly gracious as he has been (our visit interrupted corral repairs), Lee is less than enthused about the owl quest. "We see them all the time," he shrugs, experience easily dismissing the government's theories and population statistics. "It's too hot for them to be out. Bad timing."

The burrowing owl, found throughout Canada's prairie provinces, makes its home by occupying abandoned gopher holes and digging them out for a better fit. The bird is cross-looking, even for an owl: its spotted forehead is marked by white eyebrows that draw down sharply to a point between its eyes, creating the impression of a deep frown. A white stripe at its neck looks like a collar, and its chest is barred—an effect rather like miniature stratus clouds drawn in brown against a white background. It has unusually long legs for an owl, and an erect, almost stately posture.

Returning to the truck, we discover that Lee has another plan: farther back on the Finstad land are Indian teepee rings he wants to show us. Before long we're standing on one of the highest rises in the area, near a few dozen stones, rounded with time and camouflaged among the grasses and sage by a covering of pale-green lichen. The circles mark where these stones once anchored the homes of people of the Blackfoot nation. Also nearby, Lee points out to us, is a roughly rectangular arrangement of other stones, overgrown by grass and weeds: the foundation of a pioneer's homestead.

Once you adjust to the mood of absence and the sheer *space* of things, the view is breathtaking: the Milk River basin lies to the south, several farms and ranches dot the patchwork of field and pasture to the north and east, and for miles around, small dips and rises like the one we're standing on ripple and crease this land we too easily call flat.

Lee has taken the binoculars from the truck and is scanning to the west. "Yup, I thought I saw antelope over there."

I follow his gaze, searching the land for signs of wildlife, but see nothing. Lee hands me the binoculars. "On the other side of the road," he says.

The Sweetgrass Hills in Montana loom into focus on the horizon; I lower my sights through the binoculars until I find fenceposts, then the gravel road. And there they are, fifteen or twenty of them, all turned broadside so their white rumps barely define their sandy-colored bodies against the landscape.

Lee is chuckling. "See the buck?"

I lower the binoculars further until I feel I must be looking at the ground in front of my feet. Then I see him: large and close, standing protectively in front of his herd, watching us, motionless.

In the summer of 1909, the Canadian government made the ranching country between the Medicine Hat railway line and the Montana border available for homesteading. Pressure from immigrants desperate for land prompted the decision: American ranchers were evicted, and as fast as the land was surveyed, it was advertised in land offices. On the final survey map of the region, a dense grid obscures place names, landmarks, and topographical features. The only areas that escaped the surveyor's pencil were Blood and Peigan Indian reserves, far to the west in the foothills of the Rocky Mountains, and Pakowki Lake, near the Cypress Hills, which spread across the Alberta-Saskatchewan border to the east. Perhaps to a farmer or rancher who refers to his fields by their township-section-quarter designations, such a grid isn't strange at all. But when I stood on the Finstad land looking out over that huge blanket of grassland, there appeared no homestead boundaries, no obvious divisions of ownership carved into the land. Although fences and roads probably follow some of the original survey lines, the scene appeared whole, intact—human life and its orders submerged beneath the surface.

It's hard to imagine very many people bothering now to break down the door of a land office to get a chunk of this territory. But that is exactly what hundreds did in Lethbridge in 1909, even though this strip of southern prairie was known, from the earliest surveys in the late nineteenth century, to have bleak prospects for farming. Described as sandy and "washed-out" in numerous government reports, the open plains primarily sustained short grasses, sage, and thistleweed; in the coulees there were saskatoon bushes and cottonwood trees. Though for centuries this land was grazed by roaming herds of buffalo, an uncle of mine who farms and ranches in Pendant d'Oreille tells me that today it would take fifty acres for him to graze a single free-range head of cattle for a year if he didn't also supplement the animal's diet with commercial feed and put it out to community pasture for the entire summer.

After the 1909 land rush, the Pendant d'Oreille area was homesteaded by one hundred forty families. But by disregarding the natural conditions of the land, the surveyor's grid had pinched the homesteaders too tightly, and before long most of those little square dreams disappeared entirely from the map. Now, fewer than ten families live modestly off the same land.

In this respect, Pendant d'Oreille's history is representative of the prairies as a whole. By 1920 the prairies were occupied by two million residents, almost one-quarter of the country's population at the time; of these, nearly one million were immigrants who had claimed free land in parcels of 160 acres each. Over the next seventy years, the population of the Canadian prairies increased more than twofold—but virtually all of this growth was in the cities, and the population of farmers plummeted. It simply became harder and harder to make a living off the land.

"Free land" is something of a misnomer. It was obtained through government treaties signed in the nineteenth century with the indigenous people, before much immigration had yet occurred. Once the homesteaders arrived, the transformation from wild grassland to cultivated field and fenced pasture was costly in more ways than one: to the original inhabitants, who lost their homeland; to the newcomers, whose dream of a simple agrarian life became a high-stakes game that only a few could win; and to the ecological balance of the land itself.

In September 1997, I traveled from my temporary home in Honolulu to these prairies to attend a conference of environmental writers in Waterton National Park, in the southwestern corner of Alberta. There I met several of the authors whose work would become part of this volume of *Mānoa*. I also met journalists, editors, park rangers, ecologists, farmers, and ranchers, brought together by a concern for Canada's environment and a commitment to writing about it for the general public.

To get to Waterton, I spent a sleepless night cruising 30,000 feet above the Pacific, glided into Vancouver International Airport at dawn, then soared over the Rockies the next morning. As the plane cleared the mountains and the heat-glazed prairies surrounding Calgary came into view, I was startled out of my exhaustion by something distinctly unfamiliar about the vista below. Having been raised in rural southern Alberta, I shouldn't have been surprised by this expansive view of the province's agriculture. But on this day the fields appeared to be something far different from what "field" means to me. The ground had become an intricate textile, as if the familiar surface had been pulled aside to reveal a hand-loomed carpet underneath. The image occupied my imagination for days, until I finally sorted out something of its meaning.

The textile effect came from the lines of fallow and harvest—not individual lines, but wide sets of parallel lines that are clearly visible from the air. They were a magnification of the tracks that would have been left years ago by the pioneer's horse-drawn, single-share plow and binder. Drawn now by monstrous cultivators and combines tracing a variety of bent spirals, the patterns in each field were determined by the particular lay of the land. Starting from the perimeter of a field, the machinery's tracks swerved around boggy lows, rock piles, and other obstacles and wound inward to merge, in places, with lines approaching from another direction. In many of the fields, the path of the combine's exit was undetectable—the execution was that graceful. The beauty of the scene, I began to realize, came from the choreography of several elements—the interplay of human activity and the earth's contours, and the suggestion of story, both past and present, in the patterns themselves.

Hidden behind these patterns was a story that predates by centuries the bounded fields on which they are drawn. Long before European immigrants arrived and began to coax a livelihood out of the prairies, this land provided home and sustenance to people of the Blackfoot, Cree, Ojibwa, and Assiniboine nations—but a very different kind of sustenance than that which marks the land now. As recently as the 1870s, Canada's plains were still populated primarily by Native peoples: at least three-quarters of the total population of the region in 1880 (only about 160,000) were indigenous. Echoes of this history are now faint, preserved in place-names (*Etzikom, Pakowki, Nemiskam*) and in landmarks that often don't carry much significance in the lives of the present inhabitants. Near Pakowki Lake, in the northern end of the Pendant d'Oreille coulee, lie stones and boulders in parallel lines eighty to three hundred feet in length, each ending at a cairn. These cairns are the burial places of great chiefs of the Blackfoot nation. Most of the time, we hardly notice them when we drive past; we are the descendants of other people.

In his opening comments at the Waterton conference, park ranger and author Kevin Van Tighem offered a poignant description of our moment in the history of this land: "We are a society of newcomers and, in a way, have orphaned ourselves from nature. We need to develop a native sense of belonging to the places we live in."

Paying rigorous attention to the land and to our relationship to it, finding new ways to see the places we call home—these are important aspects of the nature writer's project. And they are characteristics of the Western Canadian pieces gathered for this volume of *Mānoa*. Each writer's particular subject and orientation to *place* combine to produce forms that are sometimes surprising: a meditative poem about a common garden vegetable; an essay that includes favorite recipes; an arrangement of short prose sketches about the moods of March. Frequently there are moments of humour—sometimes wry, always self-conscious. In different ways, the forms and manners of these voices are reminiscent of our pioneer heritage, a legacy of pride and failure that lingers in the communities of Canada's west.

The stories, poems, and essays here are by no means a complete representation of Western Canada's literature, geography, or history. For example, missing is work from Manitoba, one of Canada's western provinces and an integral part of the prairie community. Nevertheless, the collection illustrates some of the directions writers here are taking as they turn a careful eye to the places where they live. Whether writing from a distinct sense of home or exploring the means to a "spiritual belonging," as one writer calls it, these authors give expression to some of the dynamics of life in this region that is still tied to a heritage of settlement.

On my final morning in Waterton, I found myself in an aspen grove with a dozen other writers, hiking in the foothills with author and grassland ecologist Don Gayton. We'd spent two full days sitting around tables discussing topics that ranged from the interpretation of scientific research to the educational goals of what the conferees called environment writing. So often an unpredictable component of life here, the weather had changed dramatically since we arrived: the first day was sunny and fifteen degrees Celsius, but now it was seven degrees, the sky was grey, and forty-mile-per-hour winds blasted us with icy rain off the mountain peaks.

For an hour we'd been meandering across a stretch of grassland a few miles out of the park, occasionally gathering around Gayton to watch him dissect blades of native and non-native grasses. As he told the story of how the different plant species came to be here and described what role each plays in this grassland ecosystem, we passed around samples of the vegetation, sniffing, touching, tasting. The wind whistled inside the hood of my jacket, and I hunched my shoulders against the cold. Others in the group were turning their backs to fend off gusts of mountain air. When Gayton's story was over, we spread out and trudged on. Sometime later I saw Gayton several yards away, lowering himself to the ground and leaning his side against a large boulder. With his feet he awkwardly propelled himself around the rock. Though I couldn't hear what he was saying to the group around him, I could see that he was depicting the back-scratching of a buffalo, the force that over hundreds of years wore a distinct groove around the base of the rock.

Partly to explore the two components of the foothills ecosystem—grassland and bush—but also to seek some reprieve from the wind and rain, we sauntered toward a stand of aspens. "Do you know what the largest living organism in the world is?" Gayton asked. Someone tentatively suggested the blue whale, but it was evident Gayton was after something else. "An aspen grove in Colorado," he said matter-of-factly. And suddenly I was no longer standing in the woods: I was on the back of a huge, terrestrial whale that had risen out of the land like a prairie mirage.

At last the group congregated in a small clearing. Stirred by our evolving perception of the foothills boundary zone, we began discussing the newest threat to this ecosystem in Alberta. The conversation was noticeably unlike our indoor meetings: it was more personal, more speculative. Someone described how a new breed of settler has been moving into the foothills region near Calgary: urban, white-collar commuters who are transforming the wilderness into what looks a lot like a suburb. For the majority of these new settlers the land is merely real estate. A somewhat self-implicating view of history began to mark the conversation. We were struggling to assess our own roles in all of this change, to understand how, in the midst of it, we could live with empathy and a value for our homeland that extended beyond our own species, and our own lifetimes. But the bottom line wasn't about an abstract environmentalism or public policy. It was about the question that to some degree concerned all the conference participants: *How can we live on the land without betraying it?*

The weather changed yet again. For brief moments, sunlight streamed through a break in the clouds, and the aspen leaves glowed and shuddered above our heads. We felt the warm rays on our shoulders, the land warming below our feet.

Bragg Creek, Alberta

Bragg Creek is a privileged part of Alberta, of the world for that matter. It lies in what ecologists call a zone of tension, where montane forest vegetation does pleasant battle with prairie. Fingers of each mesh together. The two armies of these Rocky Mountain wars have battled so long and honorably that they begin to look like each other: prairie is long and shaggy, and the open woods are full of grass.

This is also a kind of zone of human tension where the wealthy from nearby Calgary build monumental ranch homes, movie stars seek expensive refuge, and fourth-generation foothills cattlemen study the *I Ching*.

A group of us came to a lodge at Bragg Creek for a week to discuss grazing ecology, and our classroom meetings were surprisingly long and intense. The woods and fields outside the lodge were inviting, but they began to look more distant and inaccessible as our seminar hurried on with few breaks.

Midmorning on the third day I was finally able to slip out. I needed to distance myself from the coffee-laden, fluorescent press of the seminar for a while. Skulking across the lawn, I headed for the safety of the white spruce. As I got close, my steps slowed and my attention began to shift from escape to observation. I knew I was safe now. Even if someone called me, I could simply pretend I didn't hear. As soon as I was safely into the woods, I felt silly for being so furtive.

Rising modestly into the still winter air, the bodies of the spruce were intimate and enfolding. I had the strong sense they had been waiting for me.

I followed the small creek. Neruda was right: perhaps the highest duty of the poet and writer is to waste time while others work. Awareness is sharpened, and the nagging sense of guilt eggs one on to ever more daring and secret explorations.

It is surprising how much is green here, even in early March: the spruce, the labrador tea underneath, the aquatic plants in the creek itself. This forest still has a tenuous hold on the previous summer. I can see why this was a favored wintering area for the buffalo.

I walk along the creek, trying to read its cutbanks. The colors and textures of the raw earth are unexpected, like nakedness. Revelations abound in these exposures of soil and rock and root. Layers of meaning are tucked in between sand lenses, organic stains, and bits of old bone. Here in front of me, if I could only read it, is a tiny sedimentary history of the Rockies.

I often stop to study cutbanks, gravel pits, and roadcuts. I dig deep holes in fields and puzzle over the complex horizons below me. But I haven't looked long enough, and can't yet read the language.

Veering away at random from the creek, I stop to sit on a spruce stump. It is freshly cut, and honey-colored phloem sap still oozes from it. Off in the undergrowth, long strands of spider silk are shot through with random sunbeams. Wind riffles down the strands, and they become exotic neon. Ravens croak high overhead, and the creek talks to itself like a contented child. The moment holds, as if cast in amber, and I think I know why. Patterns again, patterns and high-angle March sun.

Some of our seminar discussions dealt with alternate realities, although few participants would have been prepared to admit to that. I am interested in alternate realities—not levitations, spoon bending, and things like that, but the very personal ones that can flit unexpectedly through our lives. I don't see great pinwheels of fire in the sky like Blake and Van Gogh did, and am probably not capable of the personal intensity behind that kind of alternate vision. But at just the right time of evening I can look at these shapely masses of spruce and see them neatly outlined in bright electric blue against the indigo of night sky. Fiery winter sundogs can sometimes multiply across the horizon for me. On bright winter days, black fenceposts against white snow can throw pale extensions of themselves into the air in the style of the German impressionist painter Lyonel Feininger.

I don't know whether these are purely optical phenomena, or whether the mind, and desire, are involved. Nor do I know if these experiences are unique to me. I guess I want them to be, since visions don't share well. But in any case, I am grateful for them. They are another kind of understanding, beyond data.

Our seminar leader argues that a truly holistic view of reality cannot coexist with the contemporary scientific and reductionist view. Holism, he says, is a thought model that considers all variables at once, but the scientific model of testing a single variable at a time destroys the essence of real-world systems. I don't know. We humans tend naturally to be rather woolly thinkers, forever bringing things in from left field and cobbling them on to the issue at hand. A meeting on aid to El Salvador will turn into a heated discussion on war toys. A committee looking into stocking rates will go off on an engrossing tangent of modifications to parliamentary procedure. And so on. It is our nature to be free-form, hot-dog, and eclectic; we live holism. So reductionist science, if nothing else, is probably a useful foil to lives full of multiplicity and concatenated events. A method to test things one at a time, as a check on ourselves.

The scientific method as a thought process has a splendid track record of progress. It is predictable then that an analytical tool this powerful would eventually be turned inward, on itself. Science tries to establish a relationship between cause and effect, but several scientists have taken the scientific method to hyperbole, and have begun to analyze our understanding of cause and effect themselves.

Subjects in an experiment are told to operate a simple electronic random number generator, to produce a normally distributed trend line of numbers. In a second trial, the subjects are asked to try to influence the generator as they operate it, to produce numbers either below or above the mean. After several thousand tries, sure enough, the trend line of the influenced trials begins to deviate from normal random expectations, and the deviations pass the test of statistical significance. The Princeton scientists who did this work call the effect "anomalous information transfer from an agent (the subject) to a percipient (the random number generator) who are separated geographically and not connected by any normal information channels." The subject's pushing of a button to activate a circuit is the obvious connection between cause and effect, but the scientists are telling us that there are other, less obvious connections as well.

This line of research is profoundly interesting. If corroborated and supported by other work, it could eventually lead to a wholesale rethinking of the scientific method as an objective tool.

The possibility of subtle information transfer from the perceived *back* to the perceiver could lay the foundation for our need for landscape. Rocks and grasses and mountains may have influence, something aboriginal cultures acknowledge and we have long suspected.

I came back to the lodge just in time for a noon meal and a volleyball game. The net was tied between two of several white spruce that some perceptive landscaper had left scattered about the large lawn. My context for volleyball had always been gymnasiums, and here was a pleasant contrast. As I went up for a spike, I looked up to see a white spruce like a sentinel, the ball descending perfectly to the net, and the brassy noonday sun. Often I mistime the spiking ritual, but this time I hammered the ball perfectly.

The seminar wore on relentlessly. After four days of theory, we finally broke away from our meeting room to actually visit nearby grassland to speculate on how grazing had affected it. An impressive collection of vans and pickups descended on a humble quarter-section, and some fifty of us jumped out. Many of the talismans of field biology began to appear: binoculars, bound floras, magnifying lenses, Swiss Army knives. The pasture was pleasant and shaggy, full of willow clumps and mole excavations. At some point there must have been abundant aspen growth on it, since many old sticks and stumps were visible. Now only two gnarled, dying specimens remained, their trunks rubbed smooth by cattle.

My comrade Barry Adams says that Peter Fidler rode through this country in 1792, and it was grassland then. Such a pure grassland, in fact, that Fidler complained in his journals about having to haul firewood along. So the recent evolution of this piece of ground would have been from grassland to aspen forest, and then back to the present hodgepodge cow-pasture grassland. These two trees were the last diehards of the most recent rout of the army of the woods.

On casual inspection, I count at least half a dozen grass species. Willow shrubs are everywhere in the pasture, and there is evidence that cattle are browsing on them. Shrubby cinquefoil is also here in abundance, but nothing is touching it. Silly and inappropriate plants like timothy and white clover are also present, two cultivated species that don't belong in native grassland. In this case cows must be acting as mechanisms of succession. They would have been moved to this pasture from some cultivated pasture somewhere, bringing seeds of the exotics in their rumens. The timothy and white clover seed would have come out in the manure, a moist, sheltered environment, and promptly added two new species to the general ecological confusion.

When all our individual inspections were finished, we gathered near one of the crippled aspens. The pasture soon became a battleground of ideologies, competing to explain its humble processes. Tense discussions were waged over soil compaction, stocking rate, selective grazing, nutrient recycling, and the herd effect. Bearded range managers fought with new-wave ecologists, and wildlifers clashed with cattlemen. No quarter was given. Fescue, pussytoes, and grasshopper eggs were trampled in the heat of discussion. The seminar leader had a comprehensive explanation for everything, which we all rejected as too simplistic, but then none of the competing explanations was strong enough to carry the day. At length we finally gave up and returned to our vehicles. Everyone was dissatisfied.

We left the rusty brown cinquefoil in silence, and returned to blackboards and flow charts, eventually to disperse. The motley collection of pasture flora got back to waiting for another turn at spring and the ongoing mystery of grazing.

I think about that shaggy pasture often, and wonder what might have helped us to truly understand it. We created our own kind of tension there, but it was mostly in the negative zone of professional ego. We based our theories on conventional (and hyperconventional) observation, and failed to reach any true understanding of the Bragg Creek landscape. Perhaps others trained in different modes of observation—poets, or painters— could have aided us, drawn out patterns or connections or contexts that we couldn't see. Or perhaps each of us should have stolen out to that pasture, individually and furtively, to explore fleeting visions of it that might not quite match reality.

13 Vignettes and an Ounce of Civet

One

A tight layer of granular snow and its beadwork of ice lay all over Saska-toon, and once more our backyard seemed to glow white in the dark. The wind moaned and sighed melodramatically all night long.

The blizzard continued, the snow piled up higher and higher, and the wind blew into yet another stormy day. After a very long time, the snow turned to flurries and the wind dropped to twenty miles an hour. Many times during the third and last day of the storm I found myself staring out the window.

Early on the third morning, huddled in bed, I caught sight of Gus, our tabby, staring out the window. Right next to me Kever was staring too. What a sight to behold: the three of us—man, woman, and cat—all staring out at the pure white world of wind and flurries, rendered immobile like people in a painting by Alex Colville. All waiting for the same thing. For winter to end.

Two

From February to March we move from blahs to yearning. This is not the first month of spring, but the last of winter. I always wander through March in a state of unarrested yearning. Already my mind is wandering and I'll just have to follow it.

Three

Yesterday I read an American commentary on the Bernardo-Homolka affair. Americans have been watching bits of the story down there on TV while we wait up here under a media blackout for the trial to get under-way. I suppose the blackout will serve to keep those lurid details out of some people's minds for a while. But they've entered my mind: the hor-rors those girls went through. What their families are going through.

I am reminded of my boastful claim that we in Saskatoon are not exactly up to our knees in corpses. Never wash your clean laundry in public. Now there is talk on local radio about the slaying of four women from Saskatoon. Shelley Napope. Eva Taysup. Calinda Waterhen. Janet Sylvestre. Murdered. Some sick troglodyte is out there wandering our streets. *Give me an ounce of civet; good apothecary, sweeten my imagination.*

Four

February in Saskatoon is so spectacularly dreary and April so dramatically melty that March suffers the fate of certain talented actors without star quality. What is the nature of March? Why do I respond to things differently in March from the way I do in the more welcoming months? I go to bed at night with gothic spectres of dread and wake up wondering where they came from, where they've gone.

No escaping it: they came from the newscasts, and they've gone looking for more atrocities, more victims.

Five

Wanuskewin is a Cree word meaning "seeking peace of mind." It's the name of a sacred place in a coulee a few miles north of Saskatoon. For thousands of years a refuge for Plains aboriginals to winter in, this lovely coulee is now dedicated to the cultural legacy of these people. It is indeed a good place to seek peace of mind.

Six

Yesterday I drove to Wanuskewin through a brownish-grey sorbet of slush, past dazzling fields of fresh melting snow. Over one field a large ominous dark bird was flying. At first I thought it was a crow. I'd already seen several that week, my first of the year. But this bird was much too big for a crow or even a raven. A golden eagle? No, the neck was too long. A greater Canada goose? No, too early.

At last I arrived in Wanuskewin. I went into the visitors' centre, walked up to the information desk, and stood face-to-face with three young Native women. They looked like university students.

"Who can I speak with about seasonal rituals among the Plains Cree?"

"Seasonal rituals, eh?"

"Yeah. Late-winter rituals, actually."

"Late-winter rituals, eh?"

"Yeah. Like March?"

"March!"

"Bummer of a month."

"Yeah."

"You should talk with Vance," one of them said. There was yearning in her voice.

"Vance McNab," said another.

"Yeah, he'll be around here sometime this morning."

"How would I recognize him?"

"Oh, he's this Cree guy and he's really tall and he's got this dark curly hair—"

"His eyes are the bluest blue—it's—no—it's like—it's like—"

"Royal blue."

"Yeah, royal blue. He's got these amazing eyes, they just look at you and it's like—"

"Thank you."

I went to the cafeteria and had coffee. A tall young man approached my table. As he came nearer, I squinted hard to see if his eyes were royal blue. He must have thought I was half-blind or barmy. The man was Vance McNab, the director of visitor services at Wanuskewin.

"Well," I said, trying to ease into the conversation, "here it is, March already."

"Yeah," said Vance, smiling. "Bummer of a month."

"Yeah."

Before I could ask him precisely how March was regarded among the Plains Cree—and I swear this all happened as I am telling it—a small wedge of Canada geese flew past the cafeteria window. Vance couldn't see the flock because he was facing away from the window. At that moment I realized that the large bird I had seen flying over the field had indeed been a Canada goose.

Just as the wedge of geese was passing out of sight, he said, "March is the Goose Moon."

"What?"

"March. It's the Goose Moon. The Moon of Returning Geese, as the elders like to say."

Seven

I must have always known. The first hopeful, haunting moment in March is when the first geese fly over your street. According to the Plains Cree, January is the Great Moon, February the Eagle Moon, and March the Goose Moon. One of Vance's March rituals is to watch the great flocks of returning geese circle the creek that drains the Wanuskewin coulee and runs into the South Saskatchewan River. Every March, well before the ice melts on the sloughs, a big stretch of river is open. Big flocks of greater and lesser Canadas use this open spot as a first landing strip and fly up through the coulee to feed in the fields. They use this coulee for the same reason people did hundreds and thousands of years ago. Refuge from winter.

Again and again I'm confronted by the elusive sense of creaturehood that unites people and animals. Yearning people and yearning animals. Yearning for winter to be done.

Eight

Catherine Macaulay and Laureen Marchand are visual artists. At their house in City Park, the walls are covered with paintings by their contemporaries. They are both former librarians, and they both quit their full-time jobs to become painters. A breakfast at their house is always a treat.

On this fine Sunday morning, a sort of hushed frenzy is radiating from their conversation with Kever. Even their cats seem to take an interest. Seed catalogues cover the breakfast table. The women have recently been to Gardenscape, Dutch Grower's annual garden show. In spirit they are already in their gardens, urging their shrubs along in the luxuriant warmth.

"When do you usually start your tomatoes?" Catherine asks Kever. "They were so incredible last year."

"I've already started mine," says Kever. "I started them two weeks ago."

To be accurate, I should place an exclamation mark at the end of each of the above utterances. I am not fond of these marks; they are too Pavlovian for my liking. But this is precisely what a bright day in March will do to human speech in Saskatoon. Conversations about the most ordinary things will be littered with exclamation marks. It must be the returning light.

"Lorna Russel gave me some leftover bulbs!"

"You mean for the jumbo crocuses?!"

"Yes!"

"No!"

"The ones she got from Cruikshank's?!"

"Yes!"

"No!"

"I kept them in the pantry!"

"In the pantry! That's where I keep my iris bulbs!"

"Can you believe how cold it was yesterday?!"

"Tell me about it!"

"Bummer of a month!"

Nine

I have my own favourite Theatre of Yearning, my equivalent of Gardenscape. It's the Annual Outdoors Sports and Leisure Show. Both shows arrive in March, about the time the first crows appear. At the Sports and Leisure Show you can get your fill of speedboats and luxury trailers and compound bows and wildlife sketches. You can talk with northern fishing guides and bear hunters, wild-crafters and trackers. You can drift through a forest of pamphlets on northern canoeing or learn how to get boneless fillets from a northern pike. You can fill up on sugared bannock, moose-burgers, thirty kinds of fudge. You can shoot rapids on video, shoot at targets with an air pistol, or just shoot the bull with one of the resort hucksters.

I usually start the day by heading for the Kilpatrick Flyfishers' display. There will always be a fly-tying guru surrounded by troutaholics. There will always be a healthy flow of information about good lakes to try and theories about big lunkers that just might fall for an olive hare's ear or a green woolly bugger. This information and the passionate talk about lunkers are every bit as intoxicating as garden talk.

The highlight of my day will be a visit to the Saskatchewan Environment and Resource Management booth. Not only will they have a glass tank filled with live brown trout, brookies, rainbows, and exotic trout hybrids . . . (pause for breath as prose becomes exclamatory) . . . but, best of all, they will be distributing the annual *Fish Facts.* This bulletin summarizes all the stocking, netting, and creel census stats—in other words, all the results of last year's fishing probes in the province. I read these stats with the obsessive attention one usually associates with aesthetes and poetry lovers. A sample from a recent issue of *Fish Facts:*

SANDS LAKE NORTHEAST OF MISTATIM
NETTED 36 BROOK TROUT
250 TO 1475 GRAMS
NETTED 4 BROWN TROUT
2000 TO 2200 GRAMS
STOCKED IN 1992 AND 1993 WITH BROWNS AND BROOKS
LIMITED ANGLING ACTIVITY TO DATE

Note the reference to *limited angling activity.* How could a poem vie with this list for hypnotic power?

Ten

March has cast a spell on our house. Kever answers with seedlings. On every available window ledge, any altar of sunlight, she has placed her trays and pots. Starters, we call them. In March we start things. Tiny seedlings no bigger than blades of grass. Kever's tomatoes are fragile hopes that someday will bloom in the backyard. Say *tomato salads,* and the word becomes flesh.

Eleven

I take home *Fish Facts* and read it in bed at night. Kever might say something perfectly reasonable like "This spring, let's rototill a week earlier."

I will look up from *Fish Facts* and see her face, but just as my response is forming, a large brown trout will casually drift between us and tail off into the deeper water.

"What?"

"I said, let's rototill a week earlier this year. In fact, let's rototill at the end of April. Susan D'Arcy does."

Another trout swims by, then flirches right above my head to grab an emerging caddis. A brook trout this time. Quite possibly it had been hiding in the folds of our blankets. You can tell it was a brook trout from its orange flanks and olive-green back. A plump, foot-long brookie just right for the pan.

"By the first week in April last year, the snow was gone—or at least most of it. Remember?"

"Oh. Yes. The snow. Yes."

"You don't remember, do you?"

We don't have communication problems; we have problems with trout swimming through our house in March.

Twelve

No sooner do the trout appear than they return to their lairs beneath the ice and venture out only in dreams: perfect, uncatchable, taunting like sirens. But the geese are as real as the cankered ice and grimy snow. They seem to precipitate the end of winter. All along our street, the word spreads: the geese are coming in. You can hear them over your house at night. Their frenzied falsetto barking comes closer and closer as they set their wings for a mass landing on the river.

Thirteen

It's seven o'clock in the morning and light out. Light in the early morning. I'm doing Saturday errands. The sky is clear, the wind a mere puff, the air willow-sweet and bracing.

Oh, yes. Must pick up a *Globe & Mail* at the newspaper box down the street from our house. CBC morning show on my car radio. George Shearing plays "Mack the Knife" on the piano. Reflectively he plays, tenderly, as though picking out just the right chords as consolation for a hangover. It sounds like that unguarded, winding-down session just *after* a jazz concert. I cannot get out of the car to buy my newspaper. I just sit there hypnotized, and listen.

Shearing plays very slowly. Perhaps he is demonstrating each chord to aspiring pianists. A song I knew eons before Bobby Darin did it in the early sixties. But has Mack the Knife ever been so alive and meditative as he is right now? Could you add anything to this moment to make it more perfect? Is this what the mystics describe as that instant before the onset of prophecy? If so, where will the prophetic words come from?

I roll down my window, open the car door. Coins in hand, I take three or four steps in the direction of the newspaper box. Shearing's languid notes follow me out my car window, bop across the street, and bounce in slow motion off the windows of the Soul Kitchen. I watch the notes as they wobble back to me, a little discordant but still on course. Because of the frost on the glass, even when I squint at the little window on the newspaper box, I can't make out the headlines. So I slip in my coins and yank open the little window. BERNARDO TRIAL ON HOLD—get the hell out of my life!

It's not in the headlines, so just when I've abandoned the search for my epiphany in the *Globe & Mail,* it comes to me without words: a clamour in the sky, louder and louder, the ultimate expression of yearning.

Honk-a-honk!

Seventeen Canadas, calling low and musical into the jazzy morning, seventeen saxophones with laryngitis, holding a perfect V, one at the apex and eight on either wing, and not there for me alone. More likely dropping by to jam with George Shearing: who knows that the shark has pearly teeth, Babe, and that he swims among us, so why not just stick the little predator into a song and forget the headlines for one perfect moment?

Peace, brothers and sisters. Honk on by.

Brief Biography: A Prose Poem for Leon

SASKATCHEWAN

After supper he rode his bike up and down the streets of the town in
the gray dusk of the prairie, wind blowing past his ears. He pedalled
faster and faster feeling a small fire tingling in his body, a fire hidden
from the vast sky which in winter flamed with the borealis, and in hot
summer flaked yellow at midday.

MONTREAL

At the university he found his friends talking of poetry and fiction
in rooms where he wanted to be, to listen. He was part of the journal
they founded, destined to be historic. They pursued new voices,
new rhythms, new forms. They questioned, they declared, they
discovered.

A professor told him of the man whose life and words would feed
his fire.

PARIS

Twenty-one and in Paris at a desk, or a lecture, or drinking coffee in
a café on the street. He went to concerts, to the theatre, he wandered
beautiful old boulevards. And he continued to work on the biography
of the man whose life and words were the shape of his future.

When the night streets moved in the rain, he could see a bit of the
flame in himself—safe from the confusion of the shadowed dark, his
body trembled. He leaned against a pillar of the Théâtre Française. As
years went on he kept coming back and back to that reality, Paris.

NEW YORK

There in the great city the flame burst its way out like a huge string of firecrackers held up before the red mouth and bulging eyes of the dancing Lion. The Lion, of course, was himself: throbbing with form and rhythm, with the discovery of mysterious living in the labyrinth, the fragile human skull. The Lion with his head held high to seize the flow of firecrackers which were his own—the Lion in his golden glory.

HONOLULU

The fire is still in him just as fire lives on in the belly of these volcanic islands. It bursts out in red lava and muted roars. The sea stretches in blue calmly to the horizon; valleys lie deep in green and purple air. He walks the hill where he lives, the trades blustering in his ears, singing, flaming.

from *The Strasbourg Incident and Other Recollections*

I was suddenly brought out of these shocked feelings by the calm voice of our driver: "Where to, Sergeant?" We were moving away from the milling crowd and turning into the rue de Rennes. In my mind I still saw the fat face of terror sinking into the crowd. I told the driver to continue down the street, named for the city we had so recently liberated. We passed here from turbulence to claustrophobia. Storefronts were covered with metal fretwork. Many windows had old-fashioned shutters of another age. The heavy double doors that opened into the courtyards were tightly sealed. We were in a street of emptiness and silence. As we drove down that closed avenue, I asked myself, Why was I prepared to shoot German soldiers and accept their being shot at or killed by Molotov cocktails, and yet nauseated by the violence I had witnessed? War was something else. Bad enough, planned murder. This was lynching. I kept being aroused from this intermittent reflection by the way the shut-in walls on either side of the rue de Rennes seemed to press against us. After the terror and disgust of the Gare Montparnasse, we were moving in sinister solitude, very like the woods through which we had passed to avoid ambush.

Again the driver asked, "Where to now?" We had completed our descent, crossed the Boulevard Raspail near the Hotel Lutétia. The driver apparently wasn't sharing my mood of lostness or bewilderment—signs, I came to realize, of how dependent I had become on the great war machine of which I was a part, its gregarious network of vehicles, weapons, humans, its moving mass. I was staring at the Café des Deux Magots, its glass front cluttered with its furniture. Before us was the Romanesque church of St. Germain de Prés and the plain wide façade of its ancient tower. To the left of the Deux Magots, chairs and tables were piled up around the Café Flore, Sartre and de Beauvoir's hangout. In the midthirties, during the time of the Spanish Civil War, I used to spend evenings there playing bridge or poker with fellow correspondents. Ahead, looking down past the church, I saw the familiar narrow little street that seemed aptly named for war: the rue Bonaparte. In the twenties I used to window-shop in it, looking at paintings I could have bought for a few francs, the work of the avant-garde that Gertrude Stein collected.

I think now of this late-afternoon scene, the deserted streets into which we had wandered, bathed in soft, faded yellow, the sunset of the late summer hour. For some minutes we remained in the very center of a trafficless Boulevard St. Germain. Then suddenly there was a sign of life. Swinging into the boulevard from a side street, a group of firemen marched, wearing their brass casques. In the old days I had seen such groups marching around the Opéra to their various evening safety stations: a dozen men, in proper formation, with a neat, precise swing of their arms. They were preceded now by a young black-haired girl dressed in white, her breasts bouncing. She held high a white flag with a red cross. They marched by twos in rhythm and unity with the assurance of a clock. Our driver swung beside them. I called out that we were Americans looking for directions. The leader shouted, *"Halte!"* They stopped. Impulse suddenly triumphed over discipline. They broke ranks, clambered over our recon, embraced and kissed us. We were the first Americans they had encountered. Cheerful, friendly, excited, they dissipated my brooding sense of isolation. Politely and resolutely they then fell back into formation.

"Is it safe to go by way of Concorde to the Opéra?" The leader looked at me. He had no answer. "What's the best way?"

"There is no best way. There's a lot of shooting. It'll be dark soon."

"Could we go down rue Bonaparte to the Seine?"

"Dangerous. One never knows where the shooting will start!"

He said many Nazis were in civilian clothes; there were also French collaborators who knew they were now outlaws. They were shooting too. I asked about Boul' Mich. Negative. No telling what things were like. Would our best choice be to go to the insurrection headquarters, the Préfecture of Police? The leader thought that might be a good idea. We shook hands. He wished us luck. We wished them luck. They sprang back into rhythm; they were precise, neat, professional, and humane. In front, keeping the good pace, was the dark-eyed, dark-haired young woman, bouncing, carrying her flag of mercy. It was she who told me as we talked that they were the medics of the insurrection.

Books' Survival

When I was a teenager, there were two rooms in my home in Shanghai full of books and various kinds of printed materials. Among these were many kinds of local chronicles and pictures my father had collected for decades, and also a great many hard-cover English books my mother had enjoyed reading in her youth. In order to prevent the loss of these valuable materials, my father put a sign on the wall of the rooms that said, THESE BOOKS ARE NOT FOR BORROWING, BUT YOU ARE WELCOME TO READ THEM HERE.

At the beginning of the disastrous Cultural Revolution, which lasted from 1966 to 1976, books such as these were being destroyed. The Red Guards, many of whom were my mother's students, ransacked our house in August 1966. Claiming that the books were part of the "four olds" (old culture, old ideology, old habits, and old customs), the Red Guards began to take them away in a three-wheel cart. As there were many books and only one cart, they had to go back and forth many times. Finally, they got so tired that they stopped coming back. Thus, many of the local chronicles and English books remained in our house. Not long after that, the local authorities forced us to give up the use of some of the rooms in our house, on the pretext that "no place is allowed for the 'four olds.'" My parents had no choice, so they tried to move all the remaining books and printed materials into their bedroom. Soon their room became an overcrowded storage place, but there was just not enough space for all the books.

While my father moved books, he said to my mother sadly, "These local chronicles are valuable national relics, and many of them are the only existing copies. The pictorial documents are of great historical value too. They should be kept safe and passed down for generations to come. Since we don't have space for everything, it seems we will now have to discard these English books." Upon hearing this, my mother was greatly saddened, and I knew that she felt a lot of pain deep in her heart. However, she nodded her agreement. So the next day, she and I carried the English books on a bicycle to a salvage store. On the way my mother told me how she had gotten these books. In her school days she and her brother had bought them one by one, with the little pocket money they had painstakingly saved from their lunch money. Their signatures and the purchase dates were written on the title pages of all the books. They had always been very special to my mother and my uncle. Even when they were fleeing from the Japanese during World War II, they carried the books with them. Now that it was too dangerous to keep them, she had to reluctantly give them up. At the salvage store, before my mother and I put every book on the scale, she would look at the title page affectionately, as if she were bidding farewell to a dear friend. In the end, my mother decided to keep some of these books at any cost and to take them back home. All that left a lasting impression on my mind.

On the way home I promised my mother that I would begin to study English diligently, starting with the alphabet, so that someday I would be able to read the books that had survived these disasters. With this my mother held me in her arms, and I saw the tears in her eyes. At that moment, I felt the whole world was icy cold and only her tears were warm.

When we got home, we saw that my father was as worried and restless as before. We still had no idea how to deal with the remaining books and printed materials. What would we do if the Red Guards came again to take them? We thought and thought, and finally we figured a way out. We classified all the books and made two identical lists of them. My father submitted one copy to his work unit, the Shanghai Foreign Trade Bureau, and we displayed the other copy in front of one of our bookcases. This solution proved effective. Later on, another group of Red Guards came to loot our home. We showed them the list and told them that these books had been turned in to the government and would be picked up by my father's work unit sometime soon. We also told them they could check this out with the Foreign Trade Bureau if they wanted. My father outwitted those Red Guards by acting as a solemn "protector of state property."

Thirty years have passed since then, and many relatives and friends have dropped in to see our books and chronicles, all wondering how they survived the destruction of the "four olds" during the disastrous Cultural Revolution. Meanwhile, I have become more and more appreciative of my parents' determination, wisdom, and brave efforts to protect these valuable materials from destruction. I kept my promise to my mother and embarked on English studies and read these surviving English books. Now, I even have a career as an English-speaking guide. I owe much to the survival of these books.

Three Poems

IN SAIGON

Nobody at the wharf,
no one to welcome our ship.
The French town I'd dreamed of
floated on the nameless sea of an Eastern colony,
the young paramilitary man's corpse
covered with white cloth,
was carried unsteadily out of the hatch—
a suicide by the blade.
This was our Saigon.
Though the worries of France were
the worries of her people,
were our soldier's sufferings
the sufferings of our homeland?
There, over the huge ship that raised three tricolored flags
was the defeated country's
transparent blue sky.
When many friends died,
and many more friends prepared to die,
the sick soldiers
talked without speaking of the newly dead,
of how the black maggots crept
beneath the skin of the living.
In the bright breeze,
pressing against our thin throats
the razor blade that released the young soul,
the boat carrying the stretcher
slowly departed,
pushing the green waves aside.

(July 1953)

THE DEAD MAN

From out of the mist, for example,
or the sound of a footstep on each stair,
the executor of the will's vague figure appears.
—This is the beginning of everything.

Faraway yesterday—
sitting on the stools of the dark bar,
we sometimes didn't know
what to do with our wry faces,
turning envelopes inside out.
"Is there really neither shadow nor shape there?"
—After I failed to die, this is how it was.

Dear M, yesterday's chilly blue sky
remains on the razor blade, doesn't it?
But I forget when and where I lost you.
The short golden age—
we exchanged printing type or pretended to be God,
murmuring, "That was our old prescription."

Always the season was autumn,
yesterday and today.
"Autumn leaves fall through loneliness."
The voice drifted toward the shapes of people, the city,
walking on the leaden black road.

On your burial day,
there were no words,
no one in attendance,
not rage, grief,
or the fragile chair of complaint.
Your eyes turned toward the sky,
your feet in heavy boots,
you lay your body gently down.
"Goodbye. Neither the sun nor the sea can be believed in."
Dear M, M sleeping beneath the earth,
does the wound in your chest hurt even now?

(January 1947)

VANISHED HORIZON

I won't go
anywhere.

In this world,
what ruins me has vanished.

There is no place to go
nor return to,
neither war nor homeland.
Having sold his life to the machine,
a man's world is finished.

A shadow hanging over his head,
the miserable actor is lost in thought backstage.

Even if you disappear
from all the places you belong,
nothing changes in this world.

Existence is as nothing
nothing is as existence.
You have lived life on the margin.

Even the road of living and suffering,
slouching towards the earth,
will finally reach the heaven of lost souls.

Like a forgotten seed,
he lives in the clouds of a city without substance.

Sweating Coca-Cola,
coughing smog,
dropping mercury tears,
forty-seven floors of aching vertebrae, swaying.

(September 1973)

Translations by Shogo Oketani and Leza Lowitz

How Far Away the Ground

Shigatse, home of the Panchen Lama and the fifteenth-century Tashil-hunpo Monastery, is a dogcatcher's dream. The dogs seem to outnumber the people. They meet on the dry ridges and smell each other, tails wagging with their newfound knowledge. At dusk, we watched canine shadows along the ridges where an old fort is crumbling, and then we heard them, the night through, barking from the darkness of their bodies. The peak that supports the fort's remains, we discovered in daylight, is covered with droppings—it's dog territory, where they grow up, playing and fighting. During the day, the dogs descend on the city and dodge the traffic to dig through piles of garbage. The dogs and the people coexist, but they keep their distance from each other.

At the monasteries, whole populations are fed by monks who believe the dogs are reincarnated monks who failed to live nobly in previous lives. The dogs lap up thin *tsampa,* laid out in great stone bowls along the *kora* where the pilgrims follow their prayers. They sleep in the sun until it swells and its heat is too intense, then curl into the crevices of stones carved with the long fingers of Tibetan script, the smoke of incense clouding over them.

Tourists are warned to stay away, to wield pockets full of stones to ward off savage dogs on the pilgrimage paths. But the dogs we saw were always wary, disinterested, or sleeping. They turned their eyes down and away and avoided crossing our path, more timid than Tibetan children, who grabbed our arms and walked with us, pleading for a pen or a half-empty water bottle. At Samye Monastery, a remote temple whose surrounding hills are studded with hermitage caves not visible from the ground, we witnessed an all-night circle of Tibetan stomping and singing. On the edge of daylight, I heard the last of the singing and emerged from the guesthouse to find only dogs where the pilgrims had been: alert, sitting upright, as if in wait for scraps from their master.

In our country, obedient dogs guide the blind and we're not inclined, as the pilgrims are, to carry a clump of ground meat to toss to the fallen monks who, in their latest incarnations, are reduced to a life of sleep, sex, and begging outside the monastery walls. But see what we saw outside of Lhasa, behind Sera Monastery's southernmost wall: whining as a dog will when its leash is tangled around a tree, a dog crawled out onto a dry drainage pipe jutting from one of the monastery buildings, wrestled his hind legs free from where they anchored him to the building, pawed at the air with his front legs, and stumbled from the pipe. We didn't hear his bones break when he hit the bottom of the shallow ditch.

But he began to cry, and all of us witnesses—two travelers and three pilgrims—watched as he dragged his body back along the deepest part of the ditch, panting, howling. He got himself upright and shook as if from massive cold before he collapsed again, facing the whitewashed monastery wall.

Gradually, the pilgrims wandered away, perhaps used to such suicides: monks who throw themselves from the roofs rather than be denied the ability to pray. To interfere, to try to save him, was out of the question. He had had a look in his eye that only a dog with a monk's heart could. He knew how far away the ground was. He was catching up to his soul, or so his cries said—cries that weren't of protest, but of an intimate and infinite sorrow. So we left him. From a rocky peak behind the monastery, I saw a man and his child circling the cairn where the dog had fallen. I could hear the dog's cries until we were far above the fires and had crossed a spring where a young monk poured water onto a man's bald head and gave him two mouthfuls to drink, where an old pilgrim and his wife approached us, pointing to their throats, and we gave them our last two lozenges.

A Woman of Oonalashka. 1778.
*"Oonalashka," Russian settlement
in Unalaska, Aleutian Islands, in
Southwest Alaska. Engraving by
Jean Marie Delattre after drawing
by John Webber.*
PL. 49

Two Poems

ASPEN IN WIND

Little tree, tree of slopes and coulees
and wolf-willow scrub, tree of seven
months of winter and a two-week spring,
of childhood and the endless

sky of loss, I've come
for the light in your leaves,
those brief mosaics of starched silk, the rill
and sifting of the August air against

the speechless blue, for this light like light
off water gurgling past the snowbank in the first
real thaw, for shade, for the rest
of weightlessness, I've come

to close my eyes
under the bright wind of summer,
the light-in-water of the wind in your leaves,
the starched silk of their rushing, that quilt

of sorrow and of light.
What is the light for but
to lie down in? What is sorrow for
but to lie down in.

HIGHWAY 879

North out of the Sweetgrass Hills, their mass
fixed and improbable in my rearview mirror
the better part of an hour. Sunday,
near-record heat in April, he is asleep
beside me in the front seat.
The air is hazy with evaporating ice, still
you can see for thirty miles:
sheds, dugouts, the gridlock
of stubble and summer fallow, windbreaks
paralleling the section lines, and the road
like some edict of connection,
empty.

       Until
that coulee—the highway
dipping for a moment into olive-velvet shadow
and emerging
changed: the way two people
exhausted by a hard winter can make love
in the late afternoon and wake
to find the clutter of their lives no more than
a few already-leaning fenceposts under wind.
It is that easy to be happy.
Or unhappy. Vastness itself
a singularity.

The Good Shopkeeper

Radhika was making the evening meal when Pramod gave her the news. The steam rising off the *roti*s she was making on the pan burnt his nostrils, so he backed off into the narrow hallway next to the kitchen. She turned off the gas and joined him. He put his arms behind his back and leaned against the wall.

"What should we do?" she whispered, although there was no one nearby except the baby, who was asleep in the bedroom.

"I don't know," he said. "Who could have foreseen that this would happen?"

"Hare Shiva," she said, and opened the bedroom door to check on the baby. "How are we going to give the next month's rent to the landlady?" Her eyes turned watery.

"What is the use of crying now? That's why I don't like to tell you anything. Instead of thinking with a cool mind, you start crying."

"What should I do other than cry? You worked there for three years, and they let you go just like that? These people don't have any heart."

"It is not their fault." He tried to sound reasonable. "The company doesn't have money."

"So only you should suffer? Why couldn't it be one of the new accountants? What about Madan?"

"He knows computers," Pramod said.

"He also knows many influential people."

"All right, don't cry now. We will think of something. I will go and see Shambhuda tomorrow. Something or other is bound to happen. We will find a solution."

Despite the assurances he had given his wife, Pramod couldn't sleep well that night.

The next morning while it was still dark, he went to the Pashupatinath temple. He made a slow round of the temple complex, and even stood in line to obtain *tika* from the priest in the main shrine. By the time he had finished, the sky was tinged with a gray light. He became aware that he would not need to go home to eat and change and then go to work.

Yesterday afternoon, the director had called him into his office and said, "Pramodji, what can I say? Not everything is in my power." Power, thought Pramod. Of course he had the power! But he was a coward and didn't want to stand up for a man who had worked hard for his company.

Walking away from the temple, Pramod saw pilgrims on their way to pay homage to Lord Shiva. The beggars who slept around the temple complex were lined up on the side of the street, clanking their tin containers. When people threw money and food in their direction, the beggars eyed each other to see who got the better deal. Monkeys that roamed the area were also alert now, ready to snatch bags and packets from timid people they could take advantage of. The smell of deep-fried *jalebie,* vegetable curry, and hot tea wafted out from stalls.

Pramod saw Ram Mohan slowly walking toward the temple, his cane hanging from his arm. A few years ago Pramod had worked with Ram Mohan in the accounts department of the education ministry.

Pramod looked away from him, but Ram Mohan had sharp eyes. "Pramodji, I didn't know you were such a religious man!" he shouted. Then, coming closer, he added, "What is the matter, Pramodji? Is everything well?"

Pramod hesitated, then remembered that Ram Mohan was a kind man and told him about the loss of his job.

"Tch, tch," said Ram Mohan, slowly shaking his head. "I had heard that the profits of your finance company were not so good these days, but I didn't imagine it would come to this: letting go of a diligent worker like you."

The ringing of the temple bells sounded in the background as they stood in the middle of the street, contemplating this strange twist of fate. Then Pramod remembered that he had to catch Shambhuda before he left for his office, so he excused himself.

At Shambhuda's house, there were two other people waiting in the living room. The old servant told Pramod that Shambhuda was still in *puja* and would be out in the next half-hour. Pramod sat down on the sofa and gazed at the pictures of the religious figures on the wall. The other two men eyed him suspiciously. He ignored them and stared at the framed picture of Lord Shiva with the snake god, Nag, around his blue neck. After a few minutes, one of the men asked him, "Aren't you Prakashji?"

Pramod gave him an irritated look and said, "No, my name is Pramod."

"Oh, yes, yes, Pramod. Why did I say Prakash? I know you, you are Shambhuda's brother-in-law, aren't you?" He was a small, ill-dressed man with a pointed nose and a small mouth.

Pramod nodded.

"I met you here a year ago—don't you remember me?" the man asked. Pramod shook his head.

"Kamalkanth, that's my name," said the man and looked at him expectantly. The other man, who had a broad, dull face, nodded.

"So what brings you here this morning?" the ill-dressed man asked.

"Oh, nothing," Pramod said. He wanted to slap the man.

"You work for Better Finance, don't you?" the man asked. Pramod was about to say something when the servant came in with three glasses of tea and announced that Shambhuda was coming out. The other men forgot about Pramod and concentrated on the door, from which Shambhuda emerged shortly.

Shambhuda was wearing only a *dhoti* around his waist, unashamed of his hairy, bulging stomach and his ample breasts. He was singing a hymn from the *puja* he performed every morning. He unsmilingly distributed the *prasad* to his guests and asked the servant to bring him his juice, which the old man promptly did.

"What brings you here today, Brother-in-law?" Shambhuda asked Pramod.

"Oh, it had been quite a few days, so I just came to inquire about your health. Radhika sends her regards." Shambhuda nodded. He turned toward the other men.

The ill-dressed man extracted a sheaf of papers from his briefcase and said, "I have arranged everything here in order, Shambhuda. All the figures are accurate—I checked them again and again myself."

"All right," said Shambhuda. "Why don't you two come back again after a week? Then we can sit down and talk about your commission." Shambhuda was involved in construction contracts throughout the city, which entailed numerous under-the-table handouts.

The two men left, smiling obsequiously. Shambhuda turned his attention again to Pramod.

"Everything is finished, Shambhuda," Pramod said. "I am finished."

Shambhuda took a sip of his juice.

"I have lost my job."

"Why?" Shambhuda didn't look the least bit perturbed.

"They say the company doesn't have any money."

"Do they have other accountants?"

"Yes, a young man who knows computers."

"Ah, yes, computers. They are very fashionable these days, aren't they?" Shambhuda smiled, then became serious again. "This is not good. Not good. Hmmm. How is my sister taking all of this? How is the new baby?" Shambhuda was fond of Radhika, even though she was a distant sister.

They talked for a little while, and then Shambhuda said, "I will see what I can do. Not to worry." He asked Pramod about the director of his former company and jotted the name down. Then he stretched and yawned. The telephone rang, and he became engrossed in a conversation that brought forth only "hmmm" and "eh" from his mouth. Pramod looked at all the religious figures adorning the living room and wondered if they had anything to do with Shambhuda's prosperity and quiet confidence in life.

When he saw that the telephone conversation was not going to end soon, Pramod got up to leave. Shambhuda covered the mouthpiece with his palm and said, "I will see what I can do."

Everyone came to know about Pramod's loss of his job, and everywhere he went, friends and relatives gave him sympathetic looks. He was sure some of them—those who saw his work at the finance company as having been lucrative and prestigious—sneered inwardly, gloating over his misery. He tried to maintain a cheerful attitude, telling his friends and relatives that these things happened to everyone and that he would ultimately find a job that was even better than the one he had lost. After all, his years of experience as an accountant had to count for something.

But he hated his voice when he said this. He hated his smile, which seemed to stretch the skin around his mouth painfully, he hated having to explain to everyone why he had lost his job, he hated their commiseration, and he hated the forlorn look on Radhika's face, especially when they were around her relatives, who were better off than his side of the family.

He took walks to the Pashupatinath temple every morning before sunrise. The fresh early-morning air cleared his mind, and he found solace in the temple lights, which stayed lit until dawn. A couple of times, he came across Ram Mohan, who always asked anxiously, "Anything yet?" Eventually Pramod timed the walks so that he would not run into Ram Mohan again.

After his morning walk to the temple, he made his rounds to people of influence, people who could maneuver him into a job without the rigors of an examination or an interview. He tried to keep his faith that something would turn up, that one day he would find himself in a room of his own, seated behind a desk and served tea by a peon every couple of hours. He missed the ritual of going to the office in the morning, greeting his colleagues, and then settling down for the day's work, even though he had been doing the same kind of work for a number of years. He delighted in working with numbers, juggling them, working out percentages, making entries in his neat handwriting. He loved doing mental calculations, and saw it as a challenge to refrain from using calculators till the last moment, or only as a means of verification. He loved the midday lull, when everyone in the office ordered snacks and tea and a general feeling of camaraderie came over the workplace: people laughing and eating, talking about mundane things that had happened at home, teasing each other, commenting on politics.

Pramod maintained a frequent attendance at Shambhuda's residence, showing his face every week or so, asking if anything had come up, reminding Shambhuda of his predicament, reinforcing Shambhuda's sense of family by reminding him that Radhika was his favorite sister. On every visit, Shambhuda sounded positive, assuring Pramod that a job prospect appeared really good and that it would be finalized in a few days. But even though Shambhuda nodded his head gravely when Pramod told him about his strained financial situation, it took him longer and longer to give Pramod an audience. The ill-dressed man snickered whenever they happened to be in Shambhuda's house together. Sometimes, when he and his companion would look at Pramod and start murmuring, Pramod felt like getting up and leaving Shambhu-da's house once and for all.

When a month passed with no job in sight, Pramod started to feel a burning in his stomach. He and Radhika managed to pay the month's rent from their savings, but the problem of next month's rent loomed in his mind. Radhika borrowed some money from her parents, but Pramod did not like that at all: it made him appear small in their eyes. "Don't worry," Radhika said. "We will pay this back as soon as you get your first salary." She was still trying to maintain an optimistic attitude, he knew, but it was an optimism he no longer shared.

A few nights later she brought up the idea of selling their land in the south to finance some sort of shop of their own, perhaps a general store or a stationery outlet. Pramod killed the idea instantly. "I am not going to become a shopkeeper at this stage in my life," he said. "I am an accountant, do you understand? I have worked for many big people." Later, when she slept, he regretted having snapped at her. He doubted very much whether the land in the south would fetch much money, as it was getting swampier every year and was far from any major roads. He didn't want to go to the village now to try to get a real-estate agent. Moreover, he could never imagine himself as a shopkeeper. How humiliated he would feel if he opened a shop and someone like Ram Mohan came in looking for something. What would he say? Or would he even be able to say anything? What if someone like the ill-dressed man came in? Could Pramod refuse to sell him goods and ask him never to enter his shop again? No! If he did, what kind of reputation would his shop gain?

Staying up late engrossed in such thoughts became a habit for Pramod. He slunk into bed, faced the wall, and let his imagination run wild. Radhika put the baby to sleep and got into bed beside him. He could feel her vibrations coming towards him, but he did not turn. After some time, she muttered something, turned off the light, and went to sleep.

Often Pramod imagined how it would be if he were a feudal landlord, like those who used to run the farmlands of the country only twenty years before. He imagined himself with a big, royal mustache that curved at the end and pointed toward the sky, the kind that he could oil and caress as a show of power. He saw himself walking through a small village, a servant shielding him from the incessant southern sun with a big, black umbrella while all the villagers greeted him deferentially. He saw himself plump and well cared for. Then he would imagine himself as an executive officer in a multinational company where Shambhuda worked as an office boy. Shambhuda was knocking on the door of Pramod's spacious, air-conditioned office, where he sat behind a large desk in a clean white shirt and tie, his glasses hanging from his neck, a cigarette smoldering in the ashtray. He saw Shambhuda walk in, his cheeks hollow, wearing clothes that were clearly secondhand. Shambhuda started pleading for an advance, which Pramod refused. Shambhuda started crying, and Pramod, irritated, told him that the company didn't have a place for such whiners.

Pramod giggled at this little scene. Then when he realized what he was doing, a moan escaped his lips. Radhika woke up, turned on the light, and asked, "What is the matter? Having a bad dream?"

One morning Pramod was sitting on a bench in the city park and smoking a cigarette after having made his usual futile, humiliating morning round, when a young woman came and sat next to him. She started shelling peanuts that she had brought bundled at the end of her *dhoti*. The cracking of the peanut shells was beginning to get on Pramod's nerves, and he was thinking of leaving when the woman asked him, "Do you want some peanuts?"

Pramod shook his head.

"They are very good. Nicely roasted and salty," she said. She was a small, plump woman. She looked like a laborer of some sort, or perhaps a villager who was working as a servant in the city.

"I can't eat peanuts in the morning," said Pramod.

"Oh, really? I can eat peanuts all day long," she said. "Morning, day, night."

Pramod did not answer and watched a couple of men in suits and ties walk into an office across the street, carrying briefcases.

"The mornings here are so beautiful, no?" he heard the woman say. "I come here every day." She watched him as she popped more peanuts into her mouth. "Where do you work?" she asked.

The gall of this woman, who was clearly in a class much below his own! "In an office," he said.

"It's nearly ten o'clock. Don't you have to go to the office? It is not a holiday today, is it?"

"No, it's not a holiday."

"I just came back from work. Holiday or no holiday, I have to work."

"Where?" asked Pramod.

"In Putalisadak," she said. "I wash clothes, clean the house. But only in the mornings. They have another servant who goes to school in the morning. My mistress is very generous, you know, she works in a hotel."

"Where is your husband?" asked Pramod. He felt a wry smile appear on his face. Talking to a servant girl in the park was an indication, he thought, of how low he had fallen.

"He is back in the village, near Pokhara. He works as a carpenter, building this and that. But, you know, the money is never enough. That's why I had to come here."

"You don't have any children?"

She shook her head and blushed.

They sat in silence, but Pramod felt her eyes on him in between the cracking of her peanuts. "You know, my husband says one shouldn't think too much." There was a note of pity in her voice.

"Why does he say that? Does he say that to you?"

"Not me. I don't think that much. What is there to think about? For us poor people, life is what God gives us. My husband says that when one of our relatives becomes unhappy and comes to him for advice. In this city I see so many worried people. They walk around not looking at anyone, always thinking, always worrying. This problem, that problem. Sometimes I think if I stay here too long, I will become like them."

Pramod felt like laughing at her simple ways.

By now the streets were getting crowded. People were on their way to work. The park where they sat provided a good view of the surrounding office buildings, many of which were major government complexes.

The woman got up, stretched, and said, "Well, I should be going home now. Make some tea and cook some rice for myself." She looked at him sweetly. "I can make some tea for you in my room."

Pramod was startled by her suggestion.

"It is all right," she said. "You don't have to come if you don't want to. Here you are sitting, worrying, and thinking I don't know about what. So I thought you might want some tea. My house is not that far, right here in Asan." She pointed in the direction of the large marketplace.

Pramod stared at her. "All right," he said.

They walked out of the park with her leading the way. He felt embarrassed, walking along with this servant girl, and afraid that someone would see him. He also felt a slow excitement starting in his abdomen and moving up towards his chest. He walked a few steps behind her, and she seemed to understand his predicament, for she didn't turn around to engage him in a conversation.

When they entered the neighborhood of Asan, they were swept into the crowd, but he maintained his distance behind her, using the bright color of her *dhoti* to keep her in sight. A pleasant buzz started in his ears. He sensed that whatever was happening to him was unreal, but then so were the events of the last two months. His worrying appeared to vanish as a lightheadedness came into him. He floated behind her, and the office-going and vegetable-buying crowd in the marketplace helped him move forward. He didn't feel constricted, as he normally did in such places. In fact, his chest seemed to have expanded and his heart to have grown larger.

They reached an old house in a narrow alley, and she turned around at the doorway. "I have a room on the third floor, the other side," she said. She led him into a dirty courtyard where snotty children were playing marbles. They went through another door, and Pramod found himself in the dark. He could smell garlic and onions on her and hear the swish of her *dhoti*. "The stairs are here," he heard her say. "Be careful, they are quite narrow. Watch your head." He reached out for her, and she held his hand as she led him up the wooden stairs. Now Pramod could see the faint outline of a door. "One floor more," she said, and he thought she looked quite pretty in that semidarkness. On the next landing she unlocked the door, and they entered a small room.

In one corner were a stove and some pots and pans, and in the other corner a cot. A poster of Lord Krishna, his chubby blue face smiling at no one in particular, was above the bed. A grayish light filtering through the one small wooden window illuminated her face and objects in the room. She was smiling at him.

He was drawn to the window, where he was startled to find a partial view of the center of the marketplace. In the distance the vegetable sellers squatted languidly next to their baskets, smoking and laughing. A faint din from the market lifted itself up into the room, like the hum of a bee, and he stood by the window and gazed at the rooftops and windows of other houses that crammed this part of the city.

"You can sit on the bed," she said.

He promptly obliged. She proceeded to boil water for tea. He wondered how she, with the meager income of a housemaid, could afford a place like this. Then a curious thought entered his head: he wondered if she was a prostitute, though he knew she wasn't. Without turning, she said, "The owner of this house is from our village. He knew my father, and he treats me like a daughter. Very kind man. Not many like him these days, you know."

He smiled to himself. He knew a lot more than she did, but he didn't say anything.

When she brought the tea, she sat down next to him. They sipped in silence. Later he felt drowsy and lay on the bed. She lay down with him, took his hand, and placed it on her breast. He turned toward her and ran his forefinger across her plump face. Her eyes were closed. He didn't know what he thought of her, except that there was an inevitability to all of this— something he had sensed the moment he first talked to her in the park.

When he made love to her, it was not with any hunger or passion. The act had an inevitability that he could not control. He was not the one who lifted her *dhoti*, fumbled with her petticoat, smelled the ooze of her privacy. She didn't demand anything; she just lay under his body, matching his moves only as far as the act made it necessary.

He stayed with her till the evening. They ate, and slept, and then he got up to watch the marketplace again. The crowd had swelled. Strident voices of women haggling with vendors rose up to the window. He felt removed from all of this, a distant observer who had to do nothing, fulfill no obligations, meet no responsibilities, perform no tasks.

When he reached home that evening, he felt uncharacteristically talkative. He even played with the baby, cooing to her and swinging her in his arms. Radhika's face brightened, and she asked him if there was good news about a job. But he said, "What job? There are no jobs," and her face turned dark again.

During the afternoons, Pramod still pursued his acquaintances, thinking something might come along, but the late mornings he reserved for the housemaid. They often met in the park after she finished her work, and then walked to her house in Asan. On Saturdays and holidays he stayed at home, sometimes playing with the baby and sometimes listening to the radio.

Once while he and Radhika were preparing to sleep, she looked at the baby and said, "We have to think of her future."

Pramod caressed the baby's face and said, "I am sure something will happen," though he didn't know what he meant by that.

Putting her hand on his, Radhika said, "I know you are trying. But maybe you should see more people. I went to see Shambhuda yesterday. He says he will find something soon."

"Shambhuda," said Pramod, suppressing a laugh.

"He is the only one who can help us."

"I don't need any help," said Pramod.

"Don't say that. If you say that, then nothing will happen."

Pramod jumped out of the bed and said, trembling, "What do you mean nothing will happen? What is happening now, huh? Is anything happening now?" His hands were shaking.

One cloudy morning as Pramod and the housemaid left the park and entered the marketplace, Pramod saw Ram Mohan coming toward them, swinging an umbrella in the crook of his arm.

"Oh, Pramodji, have you come here to buy vegetables?" Ram Mohan asked, looking at the housemaid curiously. Pramod did not know what to say, so he swallowed and nodded. "Nothing yet, huh?" Ram Mohan asked. "My nephew is also not finding a job. But his situation is different from yours."

Pramod became very conscious of the housemaid by his side and wished she would move on. He put his hands in his pockets and said, "Looks like rain, so I will take my leave," and he walked away, leaving her standing with Ram Mohan. Later, when she caught up with him, she said, "Why were you afraid? What is there to be afraid of?"

Pramod kept walking with a grim face, and when they reached her room, he threw himself on her cot and turned his face away from her. His chest was so tight that he had to concentrate to breathe properly. She didn't say anything more. After setting the water to boil for tea, she came and sat down beside him.

Pramod stopped looking for jobs altogether and was absent from the house most of the time. One night he even stayed over at the housemaid's place. When he reached home in the morning, Radhika was in tears. "Where were you?" She brought her face close to his to see if he had been drinking. "What has happened to you? Don't you know that you are a father? A husband?"

Now when he went to family gatherings, he didn't feel surprised if relatives looked at him curiously. The bold ones even started mocking him, "Pramodji, a man should not give up so easily. Otherwise he is not a man." Some sought to counsel him. "Radhika is very worried about you. These things happen to everyone, but one shouldn't let everything go just like that." He didn't feel the need to respond to them. He sat silently, abstractedly nodding his head. His father-in-law stopped talking to him, and his mother-in-law's face became strained when she spoke to him.

At a family feast one bright afternoon, Pramod was sitting on a chair and watching a game of flush. The men sat on the floor in a circle and threw money at the center while the women hovered around their husbands. The children were barred from the room. Shambhuda was immaculately dressed in a safari suit, and his ruddy face glowed with pleasure as he took out carefully folded *rupee* notes from his pockets. Radhika was sitting beside Shambhuda, peering at his cards and making faces.

"Pramodji, aren't you going to play?" asked a relative.

Pramod shook his head and smiled.

"Why would Pramodji want to play?" said another relative, a bearded man who had been Pramod's childhood friend. "He has better things to do in life." This was followed by a loud guffaw from everyone. Radhika looked at Pramod.

"After all, we are the ones who are fools. Working at a job and then—*poof!*—everything gone in an afternoon of flush." The bearded relative threw some money at the jackpot in a dramatic gesture.

"No job, no worries. Every day is the same day," someone else said.

Radhika got up and left the room. Pramod sat with his chin resting on his palms, not looking up.

Shambhuda looked at the bearded man scornfully and said, "Who are you to talk, eh, Pitambar? A bull without horns can never call itself sharp. What about you, then, who drives a car bought by his in-laws and walks around as if he earned it?"

At this, some men nodded their heads and remarked, "Well said" and

"That's the truth." The bearded relative gave Shambhuda an embarrassed smile and said, "I was only joking, Shambhuda. After all, it is a time of festivities."

"You don't joke about such matters," said Shambhuda with a sharpness that was not in his character. "Why should you be joking about this thing anyway, eh? What about the time when you embezzled five *lakh rupees* from your office? Who rescued you then?"

The room became quiet. Shambhuda himself looked surprised that he had said such a thing.

Pitambar threw his cards down on the floor and stood up. "What did I say, huh, what did I say? I didn't say anything to you. Just because you are older than me, does that mean you can say anything?" His right hand started gesticulating wildly while his left hand rapidly stroked his beard, and his voice got louder. "What about you? Everyone knows that you had that police inspector killed. We are not fools. How do you make all your money, donkey?"

The use of the word "donkey" prompted the other men to get up and try to restrain Pitambar, who seemed to be almost frothing at the mouth. "Enough, enough!" cried one woman. Radhika came back into the room, asking, "What happened?"

A shadow came over Shambhuda's face, and he got up. "What do you think, huh, what do you think? Say that again, you motherfucker, just say that again. I can buy people like you with my left hand."

Radhika came up to Pramod. "See what you have started," she said.

Bitterness rose inside his chest, and he could no longer stay in the room. "You are a fool," he told her as he walked out.

A feeling of numbness engulfed him, and things disappeared into a haze. Words and phrases floated through his mind, and he thought of suicide. He had heard stories of how people jumped into the Ranipokhari pond at the center of the city and were sucked underwater to their death by a demon. Could he do it?

Pramod walked the two miles to Asan, towards the end jostling with the marketplace crowd. He moved through the darkness of the stairwell to the housemaid's room, his body becoming heavier with each step.

She was pleased to see him.

"I want to lie down," he told her.

"Shall I make tea for you?"

He shook his head and lay down on her cot. Its smell was usually intimate to him, but today he felt like a patient, ready to be anesthetized so that his insides could be removed.

"Are you all right?" She put her palm on his forehead.

He nodded and fell asleep. It was a short sleep filled with jerky images that he couldn't remember clearly when his eyes opened.

The housemaid was cooking rice. "You'll eat here?" she asked.

He gazed at her for a while, not saying anything. "Aren't you afraid your husband will come here? Unannounced?"

She laughed, stirring the rice. "Then he'll catch us, won't he?"

"What will you do then?"

"I don't know," she said. "I never think about it."

"Why?"

"It's not in my nature," she said as she took off the rice pot and put on another pot into which she poured *ghee.* She put some cut spinach in the burning oil. It made a *swoosh* sound, and smoke rose from it in a gust. Pramod pulled out a cigarette and put it between his lips without lighting it.

"You know," she said, "if this bothers you, you should go back to your wife."

"It doesn't bother me."

"Sometimes you look worried. As if someone is waiting to attack you."

"Really?" He leaned against the pillow. "My face?"

"Your face, your body," she said. She stirred the spinach and sprinkled on some salt. "What will you do?"

"I will never find a job," he said, sucking on the unlit cigarette. He made an O with his lips and blew imaginary circles of smoke to the ceiling.

"No, I mean if my husband comes here."

He waved away the imaginary smoke in the air above him. "I will kill him," he said, then laughed.

She also laughed. "My husband is a big man. With big hands."

"I will give him one karate kick," Pramod said and stood up. He kicked his right leg vaguely in her direction. Then he struck some of the poses he had seen in kung-fu movies. "I will hit Pitambar on the chin like this." He jabbed his fist hard against his palm. "I will kick Shambhuda in the groin." He lifted his leg high and threw it in the air. His legs and arms moved about him, jabbing, punching, kicking, flailing. He kept it up until he became tired, then sat down next to her, breathing hard, an embarrassed smile on his face.

"What good will it do," she said, "to beat up the whole world?"

He raised a finger as if to say, Wait. But when his breathing became normal, he merely smiled at her. Then he leaned over and kissed her on the cheek. "I think I should go now."

"But I made dinner."

"Radhika will be waiting," he said.

It was already twilight when he left the housemaid's room. The air had a fresh, tangible quality to it. He took a deep breath and started walking through the marketplace, passing rows of meat shops and sweets vendors.

At the large temple complex of Hanuman Dhoka, he climbed the steps to the three-storied temple dedicated to Lord Shiva. There were a few foreigners taking pictures. He sat down and watched the courtyard, which was emptying as the sky grew dark.

When he reached home, Radhika didn't say anything to him. She silently placed rice, *dal,* and vegetables in front of him. He ate with gusto, his fingers darting from one dish to another. When he asked for more, she said, "How come you have an appetite like this?" His mouth bulging with food, he couldn't respond. After dinner he went to get the baby, who stared at him as if he were a stranger. He picked her up by the feet and raised his arms to the ceiling, so that her tiny, bald head was upside down above his face. The baby smiled. Rocking her, Pramod sang a song popular on the radio: *The only thing I know how to do is chase after young girls, / then put them in a wedding* doli *and take them home.*

When Radhika finished in the kitchen, she came into the room and stood in the doorway, watching him sing to the baby. Without turning, he said, "Maybe we should start a shop, eh, what do you think?"

Radhika looked at him suspiciously at first, then realized he meant what he was saying. She became excited as they made plans. Later, when they were in bed and he was about to turn off the lights, he said, "Can you imagine me as a shopkeeper? Who would have thought of it?"

"I think you will make a very good shopkeeper," Radhika assured him.

"I will have to grow a mustache."

In the darkness, he started to think. Perhaps he would become such a good shopkeeper that even if the ill-dressed man came in to buy something, he would be very polite and say, "Thank you" and "Please." Pramod smiled inwardly. If Shambhuda came in, he would talk loudly with other customers and pretend Shambhuda was not there. And if the housemaid came in, he would invite her to sit on a stool and perhaps Radhika would make tea for her.

This last thought appealed to him tremendously.

Reviews

■ FICTION

Noli Me Tangere by José Rizal. Translated by Ma. Soledad Lacson-Locsin. Honolulu: University of Hawai'i Press, 1997. 426 pages, cloth $47, paper $27.95.

On December 30, 1896, just after dawn on a greensward overlooking Manila Bay, José Rizal, a short, handsome Filipino of Malay and Chinese heritage, was marched from his prison cell and shot in the back by a firing squad. According to legend, at the instant of death Rizal raised himself on his toes and contorted his body so that when he fell, he would face the sky, thereby foiling his executioners' desire that he fall ignominiously, facedown in the dirt.

Rizal's offense was lobbying for a change in the Philippine colonial power structure. For centuries, Spanish friars had dominated the colonial government, holding the Philippine natives in thrall. They refused to allow them full education and, hence, access to power and influence, and generally dismissed any desire for political and social change.

When Rizal was born in 1861, the Philippines were ready to explode. Early in his life, Rizal's genius, and an essential strength of will, became obvious. A scrawny child, he had taken up physical exercise by the age of seven to build himself into a robust youth. His early writings far surpassed anything produced in his native town of Calamba.

Rizal's elder brother, Paciano, had aligned himself with the incipient colonial revolution. When in 1872 Spanish authorities garroted three local clergymen charged with having taken part in what became known as the Cavite Mutiny, Paciano Rizal, a twenty-year-old witness to these events, was radicalized, and, through him, his younger, more accomplished brother. José Rizal went on to advocate Philippine autonomy in several works of fiction, poetry, and nonfiction—many of which were considered highly subversive.

By 1882, it had become apparent to Rizal and his family that the young man would have to leave the Philippines in order to achieve a broader education and a larger perspective, so he sailed for Europe. There he grew even more convinced that the Philippines needed autonomy and self-government, and though he went so far as to advocate that they become an independent province of Spain, he never supported a complete break with the mother country.

In 1887, after five years in Europe, Rizal published his first novel, *Noli Me Tangere* (Latin for "touch me not," a reference to the New Testament), written in Spanish but published in Germany. The *Noli* opens at a party at the home of Don Santiago de los Santos, a Filipino landowner and widower whose beautiful daughter, Maria Clara, is betrothed to the story's hero, Crisóstomo Ibarra. As Rizal introduces us to the partygoers—priests, soldiers, upper-class men and women—he also suggests the conflicts that simmer below the Philippine surface: racism, political and social repression, corruption.

Partway through the evening, Ibarra appears. He has just returned from a long sojourn in Spain and learned that his father, once a highly respected townsman, has been the victim of injustice and died in jail. Newly radicalized by his stay in the mother country, Ibarra formulates a plan of social and political action, only to be broken by the iron hand of the Spanish friars.

The power of the *Noli* comes from Rizal's genius at creating startlingly memorable characters who represent various social and economic classes. Rizal weaves these characters and their settings into a lifelike Philippine tapestry, making them appear and disappear into the woof until their threads comprise the whole cloth of the novel. A political melodrama, the *Noli* has been compared to Dumas père's *The Count of Monte Cristo,* though the comparison is more apt if one takes the *Noli* and Rizal's other novel, *El Filibusterismo* (The Subversive), together as two parts of one text. The comparison is even more understandable when one realizes that *The Count* was an extraordinary literary phenomenon in Europe (and America), both in its original prose and in dramatic productions, which were performed in the last quarter of the nineteenth century around the time Rizal lived in Spain.

Rizal's works were wildly popular during his lifetime despite their interdiction, and in the hundred years since his death, his literary influence has remained powerful (for example, in contemporary Filipino writers like Linda Ty-Casper and Ninotchka Rosca) while his political reputation has wandered in and out of Philippine mythology. A reluctant revolutionary who never preached independence from Spain, he was nevertheless appropriated, in the years after his execution, as the spiritual head of the Philippine Revolution. According to one story, William Howard Taft, then the governor of a newly colonized Philippines under American control, proposed Rizal as the national hero in 1901: unlike the anti-American freedom fighter Emilio Aguinaldo, Rizal was nonviolent, nonrevolutionary, and dead —precisely what the new colonial power needed to serve as the guiding light for the natives. With the coming of age of each new generation, Rizal's reputation undergoes a change as political and literary movements take him up or drop him to suit their purposes. Ultimately, his reputation may rest on the fact that he was the most compelling figure of the Spanish colonial era, and the first Asian to openly defy Western rule. His image presages not only those of other Philippine patriots, but of such Asian political activists as Rabindranath Tagore, Sun Yat-sen, and Mohandas Gandhi.

I am aware of four previous translations of the *Noli* for u.s. readers. The first, titled *An Eagle Flight,* was published in 1900 by McClure, Phillips & Co., without a translator listed. Despite a readable style, *An Eagle Flight* is missing sections of the original text, especially the satirical parts in which the Filipino bourgeoisie is made to appear ridiculous, and thus much of Rizal's humor is also absent. In 1902, Lewis, Scribner published *Friars and Filipinos,* translated by Frank Ernest Garnett, another abridgment. Finally, in 1912, the World Book Company published a very good, almost complete translation by Charles Derbyshire called *The Social Cancer*—the title is derived from a phrase in Rizal's own foreword and is perhaps the worst title of any of these translations—which omitted only minor passages from the manuscript and which was the standard translation for many years.

Fifty years passed until León Guerrero, a Filipino consular officer in London, published *The Lost Eden,* brought out in the United States by Indiana University Press. The title was derived from a phrase in Rizal's untitled prison poem, which after his death was dubbed "The Last Goodbye." Guerrero's translation was stylistically first-rate, arguably the most readable of the four. However, Guerrero also omitted passages that made fun of the Filipino bourgeoisie, which exposed him to criticism, most notably by Benedict Anderson in *Imagined Communities,* a superb book on ethnicity and nationalism.

For the past thirty years, the *Noli* has been unavailable in the United States except in a few libraries—an extraordinary gap in America's understanding of Filipino history and culture, and an odd situation given the major role the Philippines played in America's Pacific strategy during the Cold War.

In her eighties when she translated both the *Noli* and *El Filibusterismo,* Ma. Soledad Lacson-Locsin died before Bookmark, Inc., of Manila, published her rendering of the *Noli* in a handsome hard-cover edition in 1995. She obviously approached the work with great seriousness. Taken from facsimiles of the original manuscript, her text appears to be the most complete translation yet available in English and is accompanied by helpful explanatory notes. She also wisely retained the original, though less commercial, title.

Unfortunately, her ability to translate the novel into English is sorely lacking and her *Noli* is, stylistically, the most unreadable of the five translations that have appeared in the United States to date—a great disappointment to Rizal devotees who have waited three decades for the work to become available again in the States. Lacson-Locsin opens with an *apologia,* an explanation of her approach to translating (she cites Hemingway's style), in which she declares an intention to retain the flavor of Rizal's nineteenth-century Spanish.

But though the text is supposed to be in an English that reflects Rizal's wonderful, often formal Spanish, its syntax is muddled, its grammar questionable, and its style wooden. Ironically, as Guerrero noted in his introduction to *The Lost Eden,* "when the *Noli* was essayed by Filipinos [these translations] suffer from an, it seems to me, exaggerated reverence for the original text, which makes for tortured constructions." In Lacson-Locsin's *Noli,* not only does this attempt to be faithful result in many passages of twisted English, but the text ends up riddled with mistakes and confusion. For example, in the original, Ibarra's great-grandfather goes to a small town and asks for the owners of a plot of land in which a stream flows. Several men appear, pretending to be the owners, and he buys the land from them. In Lacson-Locsin's translation, when the men appear, Ibarra's great-grandfather himself pretends to be the owner and buys the land, which makes no sense whatsoever. In another passage, the phrase *precedido por* ("preceded by") is translated as "preceding," with the result that Rizal—who, as an eye surgeon, received rigorous scientific training—declares that peals of thunder come before flashes of lightning.

If these were isolated incidents, one could forgive them, but the book has many such problems. Lacson-Locsin's English omits the attributive apostrophe, overuses definite articles before classes of objects, and misplaces modifying phrases. In the end, the text is barely readable and does no justice at all to Rizal's work.

What a shame. A century after his death, Rizal is still without a complete, high-quality translation of his *Noli.* And American readers are much the poorer for it.

HAROLD AUGENBRAUM

The Fruit 'n' Food by Leonard Chang. Seattle: Black Heron Press, 1996. 226 pages, cloth $21.95.

Leonard Chang's prescient first novel, *The Fruit 'n' Food*—one of several in a richly diverse outpouring of Korean American fiction that includes Chang-rae Lee's *Native Speaker,* Heinz Insu Fenkl's *Memories of My Ghost Brother,* and Nora Ok-ja Keller's *Comfort Woman*—captures the tensions of operating a mom-and-pop store in a racially mixed neighborhood. The setting is Queens, but the events mirror the ethnic violence that shattered the Korean community in Los Angeles a few summers ago. Remarkably, Leonard Chang finished this book just months before the eruption in Los Angeles.

The Fruit 'n' Food is the story of Tom Pak, an artless, confused man in his mid-twenties. His parents are dead, and his only blood relative is an aunt who may be in California or back in Korea—he isn't sure which. Tom is painfully inarticulate, at first by temperament and then through injury, for in the course of the novel he is shot and blinded. The book begins as, after months in a coma, he starts to recover his memory.

The Fruit 'n' Food is also the story of Mr. and Mrs. Rhee, Korean immigrants whose mom-and-pop store, The Fruit 'n' Food, is all they have. It is an investment in the future of their only child, sixteen-year-old Jung-Me, who will use the proceeds from the store for her college education. Mr. and Mrs. Rhee speak to Jung-Me, who prefers to be called June, in Korean; she answers in English.

Into their lives walks Tom, needing a job but wanting only to buy a grapefruit at their store. Tom discovers he has lost his wallet, and Mr. Rhee gives him three grapefruits free. June is occupied with summer school, leaving her parents short on help, so the next day, Tom begins working at the store. Soon June is sleeping with him. It seems Tom has regained a family. But then things go very wrong: a confrontation with a suspected shoplifter turns violent, causing a neighborhood boycott of the store, protests, and then looting and rioting.

The Fruit 'n' Food is a total loss. The Rhees carried no insurance and are bankrupt. Tom knows that the tragedy shouldn't have happened, but somehow did. The rush of events and the somnolent midsummer heat discourage him from making sense of the turns in his life. Only later, when he is blind, apathetic, and institutionalized, does he have a revelation: "There were many things he could have done differently, things he should have done to avoid what wasn't an inevitable conclusion of violence, but what does it matter now? He can't care anymore." For Tom there remains only a distant, beatific memory: blue skies and blue water—a visit to the beach with his mother when he was a small child.

The Fruit 'n' Food is a compelling account of ordinary people who are traumatized, maimed, and killed—an account that lacks villains or heroes. Chang's prose is visceral, and it is a triumph of the book that the climax, though inevitable, is stunning. This is not a novel that is easily forgotten.

BRUCE FULTON

■ **POETRY AND POETICS**

Questions for Ecclesiastes by Mark Jarman. Brownsville, OR: Story Line Press, 1997. 100 pages, paper $10.

"To everything there is a season, and a time for every purpose under heaven." In his time, the author of Ecclesiastes considered the paradoxes of belief, listing them for future study. Mark Jarman's *Questions for Ecclesiastes* is fraught, too, with the contradictions of its historical moment. Jarman's work interests us partly for its range: a kid from California, Jarman moves easily between surfing, with its rock soundtrack, and the biblical texts his father would have explicated from his pulpit. Jarman's previous collection, *The Black Riviera,* had a secular focus, taking the urgencies of sixties rock for its emotional center; *Questions for Ecclesiastes,* almost exclusively religious, takes the urgencies of prayer as its theme and main form of discourse. As with the ancient biblical book, the central theme of *Questions for Ecclesiastes* is belief—and the difficulty of belief. The book is often successful as prayer, but not so often successful as poetry. Though related, the two genres are divided by profound ontological differences, perhaps especially pronounced at the end of the second millennium after Christ.

Let me state at the outset that, insofar as it is possible to judge contemporaries, Mark Jarman appears to be a poet of major importance. His long poem *Iris* effectively reinvents the technique and spirit of Robinson Jeffers's bleak narratives; and *The Black Riviera* is nearly flawless in execution. Though masterful in parts, *Questions for Ecclesiastes,* however, strikes me as not merely uneven, but deeply divided in its obligations.

Questions for Ecclesiastes presents itself as theogeny, but its deepest concerns, as well as its rhetoric, are the stuff of developmental psychology. Taken as a whole, *Questions for Ecclesiastes* is not so much about God, as the jacket copy claims, as about the distance between children and parents and the ways in which one inevitably turns into the other. Jarman is a poet of family remembrance: his great theme is the memory of childhood. *The Black Riviera* is filled with achingly precise recollections of youth; it is a Wordsworthian tour de force. *Questions for Ecclesi-*

astes gives us the older Wordsworth, remembering his memories instead of his experiences.

The book falls under the twin influences of liberal Christianity and the New Formalism's subdenomination the New Narrative, a religious and poetic—or cultural—doctrine. The New Formalism is not about whether one uses meter or not, and the New Narrative is not about telling stories in verse; both movements are essentially cultural reactions to postmodern doubt. As such, both are evangelical in their intentions. Christianity, too, offers refuge from the cynical play of signifiers in which poets live and breathe at the end of the century. Jarman is not so naive as to accept Christianity as unproblematic. The powerful title poem effectively dramatizes the impossibility of faith when confronted with what feels like God's personal animosity, a theme given a comic turn in the twelfth of the "Unholy Sonnets." The sonnet begins "There was a pious man upright as Job" and concludes with the man discovering his ruin and asking, "Why?" to which God replies, "I can't say. / Just something about you pisses me off."

Jarman concludes his 1991 essay "Poetry and Religion" by drawing a distinction between poems that merely take religion as a subject for poetry-making and those that are intrinsically religious, by which he means Christian. Quoting Philip Wheelwright, Jarman writes that a religious poem takes as a fundamental assumption "belief . . . in . . . 'a reality transcending and potentially sanctifying . . . experience.'" This seems a deeply problematic position, not so much for religion as for poetry, which has since the Romantic movement tended to subvert transcendent belief. There may not be any deep linkage between religious belief and conservative poetics, but in our recent literary history such a linkage has been established and maintained by some neo-formalist poets and critics. In a recent *American Poetry Review* essay, Edward Hirsch quotes Roland Barthes on "the asocial character of bliss." Hirsch comments, "I am suggesting that lyric poetry especially moves beyond speculation to give us the particulars of asocial bliss, asocial despair."

For better or worse, *Questions for Ecclesiastes* will be read and reviewed on the basis of what may be taken as its central sequence, "Unholy Sonnets." The jacket copy suggests that readers ought to see the poems in this, Jarman's fifth collection, as planets orbiting the sun of the central sequence. Though there are several strong poems, the sonnets do not hold up as a sequence. I am suggesting that Jarman's real gift is lyric, but that his beliefs about poetry, religion, and culture lead him to deny this gift, replacing it with a formulaic poetics that too often produces a free verse that is almost formal, and formal verse that too often lacks metrical conviction. It is salutary in this context to review *The Reaper Essays* (recently reissued by Story Line Press), the polemical salvos coauthored by Jarman and Robert McDowell when they edited *The Reaper,* a magazine devoted to narrative poetry and to slamming the slack habits of contemporary American verse. Sadly, half the poems in *Questions for Ecclesiastes* would have been eviscerated by *The Reaper,* which would have found them loosely structured and self-involved. John Donne was probably the last poet—coming before Eliot's famous "dissociation of sensibility"—who could write with an almost sexual passion about God.

Prayer is the most harrowing form of human discourse, for it consists of language flung at silence. And prayer has often drawn on the resources of poetry to make its case more forcefully; perhaps God was the first audience for poetry, and only later did the supplicant think to use the same tools of rhythm and sound to address a human audience.

A better entrance than "Unholy Sonnets" to *Questions for Ecclesiastes* is the book's least formalist major poem, "Last Suppers." While the "Unholy Sonnets" proclaim their formalist and religious credentials, "Last Suppers" serves as an alternative center of gravity and a means to understanding the complex flaws of this book. The poem appears in section IV, which contains four poems. The first two are short lyrics that do not use a particular meter, though the ghost of meter flutters at the edges of the poems, which are written in a relaxed blank verse. The next two are long poems, "The Past from the Air" and "Last Suppers," which offer two approaches to the writing of metrical verse in the late twentieth century, when it is obviously no longer possible to trip along in Tennyson's meters. "Last Suppers" represents Jarman at his rhythmic best, "The Past from the Air" at his weakest. Jarman's rhythms suffer when he moves too close to traditional meters, and also when he moves into the looser sort of free verse. "Last Suppers" is thematically convincing at least in part because it is rhythmically convincing.

Reading *Questions for Ecclesiastes* leaves me facing a contradiction. How can the poet of *The Black Riviera* have written this book, which, with the exception of the title poem and the long "Last Suppers," seems not so much a book of poems as an exercise in ideological purity? What has compelled that fine poet to contort his lines with rhymes in this rhyme-poor American language? What compels him to bind himself with meters not natural to his genius? There is a sort of literary ideology at work here, and Mark Jarman wants so badly to practice it that he is willing to ruin himself as a poet. In many of these poems Jarman seems to be trying to live up to his own prescriptive formulas for verse; in others, he seems to have lost heart, falling back on the stale formulas of the contemporary lyric, which *The Reaper* rightly consigned to the dustbin of moribund genres.

JOSEPH DUEMER

Flower & Hand by W. S. Merwin. Port Townsend: Copper Canyon Press, 1997. 172 pages, paper $15.

With sixteen books of poetry, seven books of translations, and four books of prose, W. S. Merwin has demonstrated his prodigious talent and secured himself top billing in the poetry hall of fame. Yet, the preoccupations of his middle period, from 1977 to 1983, now gathered in a collection called *Flower & Hand,* don't reveal Merwin at his best. The three books that compose this collection—*Compass Flower, Feathers from the Hill,* and *Opening the Hand*—painstakingly pursue meaning and permanence, only to find that, despite the often lovely textures and images they share, resolution appears nowhere in sight.

Merwin's thorough banishment of punctuation from this collection strikes me as somewhat didactic, though around this technique pivots a kind of syntactical house of mirrors. Sentences merge and reemerge with new meanings that entice because they are circumstantial. Series of prepositional phrases add to the surprise —or confusion, depending on how you prefer to read them. Take these lines from "The Helmsmen," for example:

> increasingly they imagine echoes
> year after year they
> try to meet
> thinking of each other constantly
> and of the rumors of resemblances between them

As the lines progress, the gist changes. Prepositions blur the meaning and give an edge to the otherwise innocent plot. And if you add terminal punctuation after "echoes," the duration of the couple's longing—and the nature of their relationship—changes.

Sentiment, above all, styles *Flower & Hand,* but the people in Merwin's poems feel generic, exchangeable. He thus fools us into thinking we can be intimate with him. In "Kore," a love poem with flowing, paragraph-length stanzas, the woman whom the speaker has loved "in the four capitals of four worlds before this one" seems disturbingly placid. In this poem, Merwin's tenderness gets syrupy and long-winded, and the woman—or muse—he celebrates with Whitmanesque fervor might as well be Helen of Troy for all we understand about her. Merwin loves this woman the way he thinks she wants to be loved: protectively, exhaustively. He confesses: "What I thought I knew falls aside a thought at a time / until I see you naked." Unable to find anything, including punctuation, to hold on to, Merwin roots himself in sensation.

"Coming Back in the Spring," a poem about returning home to Manhattan's West Village, also associates words with terror and loss:

> many travelling behind the same headline
> saying second
> IRA hunger striker dies
> in British hands in Ireland
> and some ingesting the latest
> smiling sentencing
> from the face in the White House
> whose syllables wither species and places
> into deaths going on before us
> as the print turns to the day's killings
>
> around the planet
> the words flowing under the place on the Avenue
> where the truck ran over
> two small boys at the intersection

In contrast to Merwin's flexible, recombinant diction, fact-based words—printed in newspapers, spoken to the public, or written on street signs—express finite dangers. Though ineffective against death, words remain the imaginative means by which Merwin comes to terms with it and tries to understand the world. His deeply ironic disappointment in the words that have made him famous increases the weight of his doggedly passionate, determined tone, and he uses moist, eroticized landscapes—like the Athenian woods in *A Midsummer Night's Dream*—to provide a temporary corrective to unreliable or painfully ineffectual words. Merwin realizes that imagination is our foremost coping mechanism; in "The Snow," for example, facing death is easier with beautiful metaphors to allay its fierce aspect:

> You with no fear of dying
> how you dreaded winter
> the cataract forming on the green wheated hill
> ice on sundial and steps and calendar
> it is snowing

Yet unlike Shakespeare, Merwin offers no comic foil to counteract his verbal and romantic excessiveness. He offers instead a rugged, Old Testament–flavored spiritualism that centers on four obsessively repeated words: *light, mountain, house,* and *stone,* used 100, 51, 40, and 29 times, respectively. By overstating the point, Merwin tells us something useful, which two poems from the 1983 volume, *Opening the Hand,* help to elucidate. "One Night" is short enough to quote in full: "I ride a great horse climbing / out of a rose cloud / onto a black cinder mountain // long ago and a horn is blowing / and far ahead the light / answers." Echoes of a shepherd, Mount Horeb, a shofar, and a burning bush aside, Merwin's universe is about believing. Similarly, "The Houses" is about believing: twice a son tells his father that he has discovered a house in the woods; the father denies the existence of any such houses, and of course, when he accompanies his insistent son to the woods, he finds nothing. After the father dies, the son sees these houses again. With their different rooms and window angles and shifting occupants, houses resemble Merwin's flexible poetic structures. For Merwin in this collection, believing is about perspective, not about seeing: like Elizabeth Bishop's roosters, "each one [is] an active displacement in perspective; each screaming 'This is where I live!'"

It's *Feathers from the Hill,* Merwin's 1978 book, that turns out to be the most rock solid in the collection. Each of the book's ten poems contains a sequence of haiku-like Polaroid photos: for example, "Birds on the roof / if I went up to see / they would be gone" and "Where the cliff / splits / later the dove nests." A kind of unshakable tenacity characterizes these simple, efficient frameworks. Each poem creates an atmosphere rather than a narrative; some sections offer insights while others describe or entice. However, certain ones, in their zeal to sound meaningful, come across as awkward: "Living it up / in the afternoon / at the shopping center." Yet overall, it's here that Merwin is at his most concise, lucid, and lyrical, engaging us in the way we want to be engaged.

DIANE MEHTA

Forbidden Family: A Wartime Memoir of the Philippines 1941–1945 by Margaret Sams. Edited by Lynn Z. Bloom. Madison: University of Wisconsin Press, 1997. 316 pages, paper $12.95.

In 1936, Margaret Coalson, aged twenty-five, left her small southern California hometown for the Philippines, where she was to marry her college beau, Bob Sherk. Up to this point, Margaret's ambition in life was "to grow up and be a nice wife for someone, have a nice home, nice children, and a nice husband. I also wanted to see things." Expecting to live in Baguio, a mountain resort 155 miles north of Manila, Margaret and her husband instead went to live in a remote gold-mining camp, where Margaret was the only white woman. The Sherks were thus encamped in what she called "the boondocks" on the day Pearl Harbor was bombed.

These are the opening events of Margaret Sams's memoir, *Forbidden Family*. She goes on to relate the story of her imprisonment by the Japanese in the Santo Tomás and Los Baños concentration camps in the Philippines during World War II. And, as if imprisonment wasn't an extraordinary enough event, Margaret also tells of being separated from her husband, meeting the love of her life in fellow internee Jerry Sams (whom she later married), and having Sams's child while still a prisoner.

Two days before Japanese troops landed to the north of Baguio, on December 20, the U.S. Army evacuated most of the area's residents south to Manila, itself under attack by air. The Sherks found themselves in Manila with no friends, no place to stay, and only twenty dollars and two suitcases to their name. Margaret had what she calls "the beginning of many rude awakenings life had in store for me" during an air raid:

> I shall never forget, when we heard the first bomb hit, the sight of a man (whom I knew) pushing his wife down on the floor out of his way so that he could get under the nearest safe-looking object. Granted, it's a terrifying feeling to be shaken around by falling bombs, but we are brought up to expect something better than that under duress. Or maybe I'd just read too many stories of bravery and valor, and hadn't really awakened to the fact that fear can do terrible things to the human animal.

On Christmas night, Margaret and Bob Sherk sat on the roof of their hotel watching fires burning all over Manila—oil and gasoline being destroyed so that the Japanese couldn't use them—and trying to believe that "Americans couldn't be taken over by the Japanese, no matter how many of them there were and how few of us there were. They simply *couldn't,* for we were Americans!" Bob enlisted as an engineer and left to join the troops at Bataan on New Year's Eve—the last time Margaret ever saw him. The Japanese entered the city two days later and began to round up all Allied civilians. Margaret, along with 5,000 other civilians, was interned in a camp on the grounds of Santo Tomás University, which had been founded in 1601 by four Dominicans and was the oldest Western university in Asia.

Margaret describes vividly the turmoil of life at Santo Tomás: the lack of space, the lack of food, the strange social hierarchy that developed, separating rich and poor, "Manila people" and Americans. Santo Tomás was a place where the simplest things became luxuries:

> A straight pin, a safety pin, a needle, a piece of thread, a piece of string, a shoe lace, a bobby pin, a bottle, a can, a piece of Kleenex, a cup, a spoon, a plate, a washboard, toilet tissue, toothpaste, a toothbrush, a fingernail file, a piece of paper on which to write, a pencil, a bar of soap, a razor blade. If one has them, one is wealthy beyond measure; if one does not have them, one is a pauper. Food, clothing, a roof over one's head, a bed—these are the essentials, but the others are the luxury items. If one has the last four items, one is blessed, but one is only an animal. If one has the luxuries, one is a human being.

But most of Margaret's bitterness about the conditions of camp life seems to be directed not at the Japanese but at fellow internees. Within the cramped, hungry, fear-ridden confines of Santo Tomás, she stood out because of her transgressions—having an affair, and then becoming pregnant, while her husband was imprisoned in a POW camp at Cabanatuan—and she seems to remember every slight she received. Margaret writes that when she discovered she was pregnant, she

> decided to tell two more women because I saw them frequently. I wanted to give them a chance not to be seen with me before the news broke. I do not believe I overemphasize this event, though I realize I have dwelt too much upon it. We had been interned for almost two years, everyone recognized every face. . . . There I was, for the whole five thousand of them to look at and talk about and discuss the pros and cons of the affair. "Who was it?" "What will he do about it?" "Surely he won't *marry* her?" "What will her husband do about it?" "What will the central committee do about it?" "What will the Japanese do about it?"

At times it does seem, as Margaret admits, that she dwells a little too much on the disapproval she imagined coming from the other prisoners. After all, it was a *war,* you want to say to her; surely everyone was too busy trying to survive to worry about her. But, nevertheless, it is her sensitivity to the relationships within the camp and to her own conscience that makes this such a fascinating account. And though this is a story that takes place during the war, it isn't really a war story. It is a story about making peace with one's past. Margaret writes:

> For two specific reasons I have wanted to write Jerry's and my story. First, we think, it is a love story deserving the name. Second, it may help our children judge us a little more dispassionately when the time comes. Until then, we can only show them by word and deed that our love has been good; therefore we

should not be judged in haste. . . . I want to make it very clear that we offer no apologies or excuses for our actions during the years we spent in Japanese internment camps.

More striking than the events in *Forbidden Family*, though, is the way in which it is told, in a voice from another time. Written seven years after the war's end for the daughter Margaret gave birth to in camp and then left unpublished for forty-odd years, *Forbidden Family* captures Margaret's bitterness frozen in time. Despite being happily married, in her memoir she is still grappling with the most salient event of her life: not the war, but her adultery, her betrayal of her deeply held values, and her guilt over the fact that she survived the war and remarried while her first husband died in 1944, one month before the American liberation of the Philippines.

The book is accompanied by photos taken in Santo Tomás by Jerry Sams with a contraband camera (Sams managed to hide this camera throughout his internment, despite regular room searches by the Japanese and the threat of severe punishment if it had been found) and extensive footnotes based on other internees' recollections and historical accounts. *Forbidden Family* is also, less fortunately, accompanied by a self-conscious and patronizing preface, introduction, and afterword, written by editor Lynn Z. Bloom of the University of Connecticut. Don't bother with the irritating editorial commentary: get right to the memoir.

LISA OTTIGER

From My Grandmother's Bedside: Sketches of Postwar Tokyo by Norma Field. Berkeley: University of California Press, 1997. 219 pages, cloth $24.95.

From My Grandmother's Bedside is Norma Field's tribute to her grandmother and a reflection on twentieth-century Japan. In a series of sketches, Field juxtaposes intimate details of her grandmother's illness against broad events of the summer of 1995: French nuclear testing in Tahiti, the release of Aung San Suu Kyi in Burma, the fiftieth anniversary of the end of World War II, among others. Field also ponders Japanese language and culture—and, to a lesser extent, American—while exploring Japanese aggression during World War II, the atomic bombing of Hiroshima and Nagasaki by the United States, and postwar accountability. The sketches are given titles like "Homecoming," "Garbage," and "Reason and Dementia," and they vary in length from one paragraph to several pages. The cumulative effect is photographic: snapshots of thought and remembrance mixed with newspaper clippings and images of Field's much-loved, dying grandmother. *From My Grandmother's Bedside* is a thoughtful work in which important themes build on each other and patterns gradually emerge. Conclusions, however, remain elusive.

The daughter of a Japanese mother and an American "soldier-father," Field grew up in Japan and now lives in the United States. She knows both countries well, and with great care, she raises the "slow, hard questions" that are too often ignored by these nations: How does Japan's failure to fully acknowledge and apologize for its actions in World War II affect the recovery of its victims and its own people? Was the use of the atomic bomb justified "for having ended, or at least speeded the ending of, Japanese colonialism"? Is it possible to sort out "victims and victimizers, between and within nations"?

Throughout the book, Field considers various interactions among art, language, and politics. She discusses Domon Ken's postwar photographs of ancient Buddhist temples and his earlier, 1930s photographs of Japanese military recruits; Ishigaki Rin's poems about "life" and "livelihood," one of which Field has translated and placed at the beginning of the book; and language and its use—what is "sayable" or "translatable."

The heart of the book, however, concerns her grandmother, whom she calls Obaachama and who, she tells us, has moved "beyond language." Field recalls the quiet force of her grandmother in health and laments the disability and speechlessness caused by illness. This is not the old age that Field imagined for her:

> Since the second stroke, it's hard to tell if my grandmother's body has in fact been turned. Neither leg will straighten, and however she's positioned she ends up facing her right. If you tuck her pillow in deeper just to reassure yourself that you've done the job, her face is drawn in pain from having all the weight rest on one shoulder. So you have to tilt that shoulder back and redistribute the weight to her back.
>   Her face relaxes.

Field tells us that her "grandmother's terror before death and our horror before her incapacity merge without producing a common courage." Readers, however, can't help but see courage in the women's actions, past and present. Field's mother, who is the elderly woman's primary caretaker, has grown thin, and Field writes: "I have given up weighing my grandmother's life against my mother's in years, but I still do it in kilos." Field has two aunts, one of whom lives next door; neither provides practical assistance with caretaking. Rivalry between Field's mother and aunts complicates family relationships, and an ongoing property dispute erupts intermittently. In the section "Flower Talk" she writes:

> My aunt next door brings over potted flowers . . . nearly every day. . . . She replenishes the water in the plastic container. . . . Because the whole affair is done up in lacy cellophane and ribbons, she cannot tell how much water to add. Later, my mother removes the soaked doily underneath. If she doesn't catch it, the Home Helper will, with much muttering.
>   . . . My aunt has also tried planting some of the potted plants in the ground. After nightfall, my mother pulls each stem from the ground.

Field brings the larger world into the personal, reminding us of the common elements in all experience and of the pervasiveness of politics. In "Apology and Forgiveness" she thinks about the words of a friend:

> Wouldn't it be funny . . . if nothing really gets exchanged after terrible wrongs are committed?

An apology is offered, forgiveness is granted. We do it for ourselves so that we can go on living with others.

It wouldn't happen in my family . . .

With candor and clarity, Field writes about problems stemming from the events of World War II, among them the plight of Asian women used as sex slaves by the Imperial Army, the pain of Japanese citizens whose family members died from "unchosen suicides, the result not only of terror but of the ideology of honor," and the long-term effects of radiation poisoning. Field "want[s] to draw together the parts of the history we live more and more disjunctively," and she succeeds in an unusual and discerning way made possible by her knowledge and understanding of Japan and the United States and of the history of World War II shared by the two countries.

Through Field's diverse images, her readers are made to see Japan and the United States differently. The strongest images, however, are of Field herself, her mother, and her grandmother, whose brave constancy in facing life, illness, and death inspires us and gives us hope that we, individually and collectively, can do the same.

PHYLLIS YOUNG

In the Ring of Fire: A Pacific Basin Journey by James D. Houston.
San Francisco: Mercury House, 1997. 221 pages, paper $14.95.

For those who want to understand deeper truths about the people and places of the world's largest ocean, titles are vital in James D. Houston's *In the Ring of Fire: A Pacific Basin Journey.* "Ring of Fire" refers to the volcanoes that both fringe the Pacific and have built many of its islands. Houston's journey introduces us to a variety of people who see much that is mystical and unifying about these living mountains.

I'm glad he didn't use the unfortunately fashionable term "Pacific Rim." Too often that evokes a doughnut image, excluding thousands of islands and the millions who inhabit them. In fact, the one time Houston does use it, he gives the term a positive spin: "Pacific Rim turns our seemingly boundless ocean into an enormous wheel, a mandala of interconnected places."

While one doubts the term "Pacific Mandala" will catch on, it overlays this imaginative book. Houston draws arresting pictures of place, but he is at his best linking what he finds in Japan, Hawai'i, Indonesia, the Marianas Islands, and his native California.

He makes his point early on:

Melody lines. Memory lines. Dream lines. Fracture lines. Battle lines and air lines and blood lines. I have tried to follow a few of them here, journeys both outward and inward, forward and backward, always returning home again, as most journeys do. It was the poet T. S. Eliot who said,

We shall not cease from our exploration
And the end of our exploring
Will be to arrive where we started
And know the place for the first time.

In this process, the author delves into his Texas heritage and the heritage of his Japanese American wife, writer Jeanne Wakatsuki Houston. We see how their families' cultures came together in California and now echo in their travels. Not only does he evoke World War II, he describes the ironic situation of present-day Japanese tourism on Saipan (the scene of much bloodshed in the Pacific campaign), and the continuing controversy over U.S. military bases on Okinawa. Along with the seismic and tectonic lines of the Ring of Fire, we see links among Koreans, Balinese, Native Americans, and Hawaiians, who all label special volcanoes "the navel of the world." Various songs lead Houston to connections, starting with Hawaiian music—loved by his father, who was stationed in the islands while in the navy— and its effect on Houston as he was growing up in San Francisco.

Houston presents a broad cast of characters, historic and current. He gets a lot from simple slices of life, notably in Japan. He presents exotic adventures, such as his hike with a geologist who helps him scoop a sample of flowing lava on Hawai'i's Big Island. He's unafraid to take seriously the story of an elderly Hawaiian woman, a respected *kupuna* (elder), who talks to rocks and is called in to advise a troubled construction project. His editorial comments encompass the novel *Rising Sun,* the hot topic of Hawaiian sovereignty, and the lingering issues of war, American bases, and nuclear testing in the Pacific.

On the down side, some of Houston's links and lines seem strained. His itinerary is limited considering the Pacific's boundless possibilities. At times I wished for more (which is better than wanting less). He went to the Marianas to visit a daughter working on Saipan, so I wondered why he didn't hop over to nearby Tinian to see where the B-29 *Enola Gay* loaded the atomic bomb that devastated Hiroshima. Reading about his Japan travels, I thought the section would have been stronger had he also visited Hiroshima, where the immigrant father of his wife lost many relatives to that bomb.

But that's to quibble with a book in which the blood and battle lines are vivid and many scenes are memorable. I especially liked Houston's treatment of Hawai'i, in which he centers on the Big Island and Hawaiian culture and spiritualism. It reminds us that Hawai'i, like many islands, has a dual history: one colonial and political, linked to the West; the other, underlying and continuing, as a Pacific place. It's a reason many of us live here. Although a longtime resident of Hawai'i, I have not been a volcano person, rushing off to see the latest eruption or hiking endless old lava flows. After a while, some of us find the moonlike landscape limited. But Houston adds poetic perspective. So before long, I may revisit volcano country to meditate in an old crater, listening for the kind of silence he finds unique yet evocative of that of a Zen-temple rock garden in Japan.

Bali, the Hindu island in Muslim Indonesia, provides Houston with another epiphany and a theme he carries to the end of his journey: the idea of a culture where people live in and move between interconnected material and mystical worlds.

Before that ending, however, he makes a more secular yet increasingly important point: the American West Coast, long pictured as the last frontier and end of the line for hardy Caucasian pioneers, has also been the starting point for immigrants coming from Asia, the Pacific islands, and Latin America—a flow that is still growing. The thought is drawn in several ways, from the story of Hawaiians who helped John Sutter build his fort in pre–Gold Rush Sacramento to the California Zen master from Japan who had his ashes buried in both countries, joining Asia and America. Houston sums it up this way:

> Land of Promise.
> Continent's End, and shipwreck beach.
> The last stop.
> The first stop.
> Shoreline on a wheel of shores.

James D. Houston is best known as a California author of fiction and non-fiction. This book underscores the fact that he is also what our changing world needs: a writer of the new, yet timeless Pacific.

JOHN GRIFFIN

Nā Mamo: Hawaiian People Today by Jay Hartwell. Photographs by Anne Kapulani Landgraf. Honolulu: ʻAi Pōhaku Press, 1996. 248 pages, paper $22.95.

As with other books created by well-known Hawaiʻi book designer Barbara Pope, Jay Hartwell's *Nā Mamo: Hawaiian People Today* is an eye-catcher. On the cover, a farmer stands knee-deep in mud and water, placing recently cut *kalo* (taro) into a skiff loaded with stalks and buckets of corms. To the left, almost out of view, more *kalo* wait to be harvested. On the bank behind the farmer, several large, bulging sacks stand upright, not far from a simple wooden house. Behind the house, two lines of smoke rise in the breeze carried down from the mountains in the distance. The scene is reproduced in a hazy green, as if it were a kind of dream.

For most of us in Hawaiʻi, such a scene is a dream, a dream of a past that no longer exists. Rapid urbanization and a Western way of life have all but smothered such a lifestyle. But for people like Clarence Eli Kaona, the farmer on the cover, the ancient *kalo* farming tradition still lives. Places like Nāmolokama, the mountains in the distance, still carry water down to *kalo* terraces.

Nā Mamo presents about a dozen Hawaiian practitioners of some aspect of their traditional culture: *mahi ʻai* (farming), *mele* (music), *hula* (dance), *ʻōlelo Hawaiʻi* (language), *hoe waʻa* (canoe paddling), *heʻe nalu* (surfing), *kapa* (tapa), *lapaʻau* (healing), *pono* (righteousness), and *hoʻomana* (religion). Hartwell is explicit about having chosen individuals who are "optimistic, independent, hard-working," and who have forsaken the mainstream American dream for "a lifestyle that combines the foreign and native cultures." He is also explicit about his purpose: to increase the understanding and sympathy of non-Hawaiians for the growing Hawaiian movement. Many people, he says in his introduction, care in an abstract way about preserving Hawaiian culture, but they don't really know or appreciate the Hawaiian experience.

Hartwell himself is non-Hawaiian, and he approaches his subject with a humility born of an awareness of the long history of *haole* (foreign) exploitation and misrepresentation of Hawaiians. The text is based on interviews as well as extensive documentary research. Songs and chants are used liberally, drawing on Hawai'i's rich oral tradition. On the cover and throughout the book, the photographs of Anne Kapulani Landgraf, a rising star in the Hawaiian community, beautifully complement Hartwell's text. Hartwell's strategy of combining personal histories with larger historical narratives and analysis makes the abstract more real. We come close to experiencing for ourselves what it feels like "pressing, yanking, stacking, weeding, and shoving" *kalo* for hours—all while maintaining a second job as a bus driver. We understand more deeply the attempt to keep Hawaiian music and dance alive while doing National Guard duty or teaching high school. We are reminded that Hawaiian roots extend beyond these islands, to the canoe clubs of California and into the South Pacific, roots that penetrate the legal profession, guard the surfing tradition, confront the prejudices of Western medicine, restore desecrated land.

The book's tone is summarized best at its close. Hartwell quotes "E Mau Ana ka Ha'aheo" (The Pride Endures), a *mele* by songwriter S. Haunani Apoliona, who serves as a trustee for the State's Office of Hawaiian Affairs:

> [HUI]
> E mau ana ka ha'aheo, ka ha'aheo o ka nohona
> E ola kamaēhu o ka lāhui, o ka lāhui Hawai'i
> E mau ana ka ha'aheo, ka ha'aheo o ka nohona
> Ka lāhui pono'ī o nā kai, o nā kai 'ewalu.
>
> Me nā mea 'oi loa mai nā wā mamua, o holomua kākou i kēia au
> Ua hiki mai ka wana'ao no ka ho'ōla a me ka ho'āla hou.
>
> [HUI]
> E mau ana ka ha'aheo. . . .
>
> E hō'ā kākou i ka lama kūpono no nā hulu Hawai'i
> E kūkulu a'e kākou no ke ea o ka 'āina me ke aloha a me ke ahonui.
>
> [HUI]
> E mau ana ka ha'aheo. . . .

[CHORUS]

The pride endures, the pride in our lifestyle and values.
The lifestyle that is firm in resolution and fixed in purpose.
The pride endures, the pride in our lifestyle and values.
The lifestyle that has been nurtured by Hawaiians of all the islands.

Let us move forward to the future carrying with us the best from the past.
The time has arrived for the revitalizing and reawakening of our
community.

[CHORUS]
The pride endures. . . .

Let us set aglow the light of justice and positive improvement for all our
Hawaiians.
Let us build the forward momentum for the good of our land and people
moving as one in the spirit of love and patience.

[CHORUS]
The pride endures. . . .

The message of *Nā Mamo* is decidedly proud and upbeat. The more negative aspects of Hawaiian life have not been totally ignored here, but have instead been presented as challenges to be overcome. By concentrating on cultural practitioners, the book steers away from directly examining Hawaiian political activism, and thus from the problems arising out of the different rhetorical positions current in the Hawaiian movement. At the moment, Hawaiian national harmony is still a dream. However, as Hartwell's book shows us, for some that dream is already very close to becoming reality.

D. MĀHEALANI DUDOIT

The Road to Mexico by Lawrence J. Taylor. Photographs by Maeve Hickey. Tucson: University of Arizona Press, 1997. 178 pages, cloth $45, paper $17.95.

The Road to Mexico twists and turns through a vast imagined wasteland of scrub brush and creosote and hardscrabble, past rickety tarpaper-and-cardboard shacks flung against the demons of night and the phony corporate smile of an exclusive American ideal, crossing through a flimsy peripheral cobweb of moral deceit and drug deals gone bad and lurid paintings on black velvet of Elvis or Marilyn or Satan —or, I suppose by now, Princess Diana—riding a Harley, and somehow crosses the Rio Grande, or the border between New Mexico, Arizona, and California, to emerge into the country that improbably borders the American dream like a distant relative who's just been released from prison and is crashing the family reunion: drunk, loud, flashy, obnoxious, in-your-face.

This is one of the low-brow versions of Mexico that persist in the American mind, thanks to the many myths of popularization that we create to keep ourselves entertained—and to keep Mexico in its place. And there's some small truth to it, as there is to any myth. But most American visitors to Mexico—other than curious daytrippers to the border—fly over all this riffraff and check into their resort of choice, or join one of the umpteen tour groups that bounce along pot-holed highways to *oooh* and *aaah* at yet another pyramid rising from the mists of some bloodthirsty ancient civilization. The border is generally reserved for the peculiar American yahoos who cross over to get crazy on the streets of Tijuana or rip up the deserts of Baja in their off-road vehicles.

That's why we can be immensely pleased, blessed really, to have *The Road to Mexico,* written by Lawrence Taylor and illustrated with photographs by Maeve Hickey. The book functions as a bridge between cultures so that those who honestly wish to travel can do so in their own way, at their own pace, taking their time. It is a means to the compassion and understanding that form one true way into Mexico.

The Road to Mexico has a well-crafted, brightly lit design that is immediately engaging: the square format, the friendly colors that reflect *paletas* (Mexican popsicles) or the storefronts and simple homes seen throughout the country. The road of the book's title runs between Tucson, Arizona, and Santa Ana, in the northern Mexican state of Sonora. But the road is many roads, weaving in and out of the ubiquitous interstate highway and sometimes ending up as a dirt track leading into an Indian reservation or a tiny village on the outskirts. The text is permeated by the motion of pilgrimage, not only in the religious sense, but in a cultural and psychological one as well: a move toward a personal and transpersonal destiny, the symbols and epiphanies of transformation, the journey of the soul in tattered cloth or the raiments of a richly textured fiesta or church celebration along the beaten path:

> We came here as strangers and, I suppose, pilgrims like everybody else.
>
> [This] pilgrimage has always been, not toward the center, but toward the edge, seeking salvation in movement as well as in destination. For Americans the road, like so much else, is about the individual, evoking a free self disconnected from constraints of place. . . . But each of us is a latter-day Ulysses, whose journey is also about self-transformation. The restless western pilgrimage has deep roots: a voyage in which one learns to see oneself by moving through places. The question is, Can one also learn to see others, people like those who voyage along this road or have settled on its edge, momentarily or for generations, raising monuments to their passing and their presence? And in making such a journey, can one find Mexico?

I've undertaken this journey many times myself, both as a writer and photographer, and oftentimes not with paper and pen and camera, but as a supplicant, arriving in a certain place at a certain time in a state of surrender; so I can answer the question with an unrestrained, emphatic, and even jubilant *yes.*

But can one gain *enough* insight into Mexico in the intertidal zone—the border between the two countries? This is a question that naturally arises from an investigation into any resource such as *The Road to Mexico,* but in a very important sense, it is the wrong question to ask. It is necessary to go beyond borders to seek the essence of any cultural identity, to dissolve borders, do away with them, for a moment to forgive and forget the imposition of government and bureaucracy and only be with the people who live and travel the country as the coyote moves like smoke across the desert or birds fly without passports through the air.

The Road to Mexico would benefit from a slightly less academic text and more photographs, and also from more detailed maps than the general one presented at the beginning, but Lawrence Taylor and Maeve Hickey have provided us with a useful beginner's guide to the border crossing, and borderless crossing, between the United States and Mexico. Their book gives the reader an introduction in the formal sense, like a letter that presents the traveler to a stranger's house and allows him or her safe passage, and in the informal sense of allowing the reader to wander at will down streets of Mexican twilight, drifting through old customs and new transmutations of the constantly shifting cultural identity that is Indian and Anglo and drifter and temporary entrepreneur along the road to Mexico.

MICHAEL SYKES

About the Contributors _____

Harold Augenbraum is director of The Mercantile Library of New York and the library's Center for World Literature. Among his books are *Growing Up Latino* (coedited with Ilan Stavans), *The Latino Reader* (coedited with Margarite Fernández Olmos), and *The Norton Anthology of Latino Literature* (forthcoming).

Ayukawa Nobuo (1920–1986) was born in Tokyo. He attended Waseda University and was a founding member of the *Arechi* (Wasteland) group of poets. Drafted into the Japanese Imperial Army in 1942, he was sent to Sumatra, where he contracted malaria, and then home to recuperate. With the 1947 publication of his first major poems, "The Dead Man" and "America," Ayukawa emerged as Japan's preeminent war-protest poet, an important literary critic, and the conscience of the postwar generation.

Dorie Bargmann worked in Central America for five years. She lives in Austin, Texas.

Tony Barnstone is the translator of two books of Chinese poetry, *Out of the Howling Storm: The New Chinese Poetry* and *Laughing Lost in the Mountains: Poems of Wang Wei,* and a book of classical Chinese literary criticism, *The Art of Writing: Teachings of the Chinese Masters.* His articles have been widely published, and his poems have appeared in *Seattle Review, Agni,* and *Berkeley Poetry Review.* His book in progress is an anthology of Chinese poetry from ancient times to the present.

 Dave Carpenter is from Saskatoon, Saskatchewan. His latest book is a novel, *Banjo Lessons.* He writes in a monastery in Muenster, Saskatchewan, and fishes in a secret location northeast of there.

Shefali Desai is the author of "American Nirvana: Immigration as Hindu Transformation in the Fiction of Bharati Mukherjee," an article published in *McNair Scholars Journal.* She is currently working on a biography of her mother, which explores the lives of Indian immigrant women and their American-born daughters.

D. Māhealani Dudoit is a graduate student in creative writing at the University of Hawai'i–Mānoa and is an active member of the Hawaiian sovereignty movement. She has had poetry and prose published in *Puerto del Sol, Southwest Review, Sister Stew: Fiction and Poetry by Women,* and various Hawai'i journals.

Joseph Duemer has published two books of poetry, *Customs* and *Static.* With Jim Simmerman, he is the coeditor of *Dog Music.*

Leon Edel (1907–1997) was born in Pittsburgh and grew up on the prairies of Saskatchewan. He studied in Paris from 1928 to 1932, then returned to Canada during the Great Depression. During World War II, he fought in northern Europe, seeing combat in the Battle of the Bulge, and rose from private to lieutenant. His decorations include the Bronze Star. After the war, Edel began a life of letters. In 1963, he received the Pulitzer Prize and the National Book Award for the second and third volumes of his classic five-volume biography of Henry James. He retired from New York University in 1973, then taught at the University of Hawai'i until 1978, dying in Honolulu four days short of his ninetieth birthday. The piece in this issue is from his unpublished memoirs.

Bruce Fulton is the cotranslator of the anthologies *Words of Farewell: Stories by Korean Women Writers, Land of Exile: Contemporary Korean Fiction, Wayfarer: New Fiction by Korean Women,* and *A Ready-Made Life: Early Masters of Modern Korean Fiction.* He was the guest editor of *Mānoa*'s winter 1996 issue, *Seeing the Invisible.* In 1995, he and his wife, Ju-Chan Fulton, received a National Endowment for the Arts translation fellowship.

Gao Da was born in Shanghai in 1950. He worked in a cotton-textile mill before attending Shanghai Foreign Language Institute. He now works as a senior English-speaking guide for Shanghai China International Travel Service. He wrote and published a bilingual pictorial, in English and Chinese, on Shanghai's Bund entitled *The Bund Then and Now.*

 Don Gayton lives in Nelson, in southeastern British Columbia, and works as a rangeland ecologist for the Canadian Forest Service. He is the author of two books of creative nonfiction, *The Wheatgrass Mechanism* and *Landscapes of the Interior,* which recently won a U.S. National Outdoor Book Award.

 Charlene Gilmore has been the associate editor of *Mānoa* since 1995. Originally from Etzikom, a small town in the southeast corner of Alberta, she now lives in Honolulu with her husband and daughter. Parts of her essay in this issue are from "Breaking Ground," which appeared in *American Nature Writing 1997.*

John Griffin is a former editor of the *Honolulu Advertiser.*

Kimiko Hahn is the recipient of a 1998 Lila Wallace–Reader's Digest Writer's Award. Her most recent book of poetry, *The Unbearable Heart,* received a 1996 American Book Award, and her new collection, *Volatile,* is forthcoming from Hanging Loose Press.

 Alan Haig-Brown has been a commercial fisherman, schoolteacher, magazine editor, and author and has published four books. He is a regular contributor to *Pacific Fishing* and *Professional Mariner* magazines. His essay in this issue originally appeared in *Wild Steelhead & Salmon.* His father was renowned conservationist and writer Roderick Haig-Brown, author of the children's classic *Saltwater Summer,* which won the Governor General's Award, and the definitive book on Western fly-fishing, *The Western Angler.*

Susan Haley taught philosophy at the Universities of Calgary and Saskatchewan before moving north to Fort Norman, Northwest Territories, where she ran a charter airline for fifteen years. She now lives in Black River, Nova Scotia, with her partner and two daughters. She has published several novels, the most recent of which is *Blame It on the Spruce Budworm.* Her story in this issue is from a novel in progress.

Anatoly Kim was born in 1939 on a collective farm in Kazakhstan, two years after Stalin relocated ethnic Koreans from eastern Russia to Soviet Central Asia. Kim has been a highly regarded author in Russia since the publication of his first novel, *The Squirrel,* in 1984, and won the Moscow Prize in 1994 for *Settlement of Centaurs.* His works have been translated into twenty-five languages. He lives in Moscow, where he is an assistant editor at *Nozyi mir* (New world).

 Theresa Kishkan lives with her family on the Sechelt Peninsula, north of Vancouver, British Columbia. She has published five collections of poetry and a collection of essays, *Red Laredo Boots,* and has recently finished a novel. She and her husband, John Pass, run High Ground, a private press specializing in letterpress books and broadsides.

Ken Lamberton has had work in *Oasis, Northern Lights,* and *South Dakota Review.* His essay in this issue is part of *Wilderness and Razor Wire* (Mercury House, forthcoming), a book about his encounters with nature in an unnatural place: prison.

Edward Bok Lee has studied at the University of Minnesota, Kazakh State University, and University of California–Berkeley. He is a graduate student in Brown University's master of fine arts writing program.

 Tim Lilburn lives in Saskatchewan. His most recent book is *Moosewood Sandhills.* His fifth book of poems, *To the River,* will appear early in 1999.

 Charles Lillard was the author of more than thirty-five books, including nine collections of poetry, the last of which, *Shadow/Weather: Selected & New,* was short-listed for the Governor General's Award. Born in California, he grew up in Alaska and later worked there and in British Columbia as a roustabout, faller, rigger, machine operator, truck driver, and boom man in the logging industry. Later, he became one of British Columbia's most important scholars of Northwest Coast history and mythology, working outside of university sponsorship. He was also an editor, reviewer, publisher, teacher, linguist, and arts supporter. He died in March 1997 at age fifty-three.

Leza Lowitz is a writer, translator, and editor. She is working with Shogo Oketani on a book of poems by Ayukawa Nobuo, a project for which they received a 1997 National Endowment for the Arts translation fellowship. Her most recent book is a collection of her own poems, *Old Ways to Fold New Paper.* She co-wrote the experimental film *Milk,* which was shown at the Berlin International Film Festival.

 Sid Marty is an Albertan writer and poet and a former national park warden. His first prose work, *Men for the Mountains,* is still in print. He writes mainly on western and natural history topics.

Diane Mehta lives in New York.

Carol Moldaw has recently published poems in *Triquarterly, Colorado Review, Southwest Review,* and other journals. Her latest book of poems is *Chalkmarks on Stone.* She lives in Pojoaque, New Mexico.

Colleen Morton has published poetry and nonfiction in the *American Voice, Willow Springs, Sycamore Review,* and other magazines. She recently spent one and a half years teaching in Beijing, China.

Shogo Oketani is a writer and translator. He lives on the Northern California coast and is working with his wife, Leza Lowitz, on a book of poems by Ayukawa Nobuo, a project for which they received a 1997 National Endowment for the Arts translation fellowship.

Lisa Ottiger was born in the Philippines and grew up in Indonesia and Hong Kong. She is a graduate student in creative writing at the University of Hawai'i–Mānoa.

 Joe Peters Jr. was Kwakiutl. Born in 1960 in Alert Bay, British Columbia, he came from a long line of master carvers and hereditary chiefs and started carving at the age of ten. He painted and carved masks, rattles, bowls, and other pieces of significance to his culture.

 Elizabeth Philips is a poet, editor, and journalist. Her two poetry collections are *Time in a Green Country* and *Beyond My Keeping.*

 Monty Reid is the assistant director of the Royal Tyrrell Museum of Palaeontology. A poet and essayist, he has published twelve books, including *The Life of Ryley* and *Dog Sleeps.* Twice winner of the Stephansson Award for Poetry from the Writers Guild of Alberta and a silver medallist in the National Magazine Awards, Reid is also a three-time nominee for the Governor General's Award. His poem "The Migration of the Zucchini" is part of *Flat Side,* a collection forthcoming from Red Deer College Press.

Maximilian Schlaks moved to America from Guadeloupe, French West Indies, in 1989, when he was eighteen. He has also been published in *Missouri Review.*

Marjorie Sinclair is a poet, novelist, and biographer who lives and works in Honolulu. Her books include a volume of poetry, *The Place Your Body Is,* the biography *Nahi'ena'ena: Sacred Daughter of Hawai'i,* and the novel *Kona Wind.* The poem in this issue was written for the ninetieth birthday of her husband, Leon Edel.

Edward Smallfield has had poems and stories in *Caliban, Mānoa, Seven Hundred Kisses,* and other journals.

Hans Jorg Stahlschmidt is a German writer who moved to Berkeley, California, fifteen years ago. He works as a building contractor and is finishing his doctoral work in clinical psychology. His poetry and essays have appeared in many journals and anthologies, among them *Madison Review, Atlanta Review,* and *Texas Poetry Review.*

M. G. Stephens has published two novels, *Season at Coole* and *The Brooklyn Book of the Dead,* and a memoir about living in Korea, *Lost in Seoul.* His book of essays, *Green Dreams: Essays Under the Influence of the Irish,* won the Associated Writing Programs award in creative nonfiction.

Virgil Suarez was born in Havana, Cuba, in 1962 and grew up in Madrid and Los Angeles. His books include *Latin Jazz, The Cutter, Havana Thursdays, Going Under: A Cuban American Fable,* and *Welcome to the Oasis.* He has coedited several anthologies, among them *Iguana Dreams: New Latino Fiction, Paper Dance: 55 Latino Poets,* and *Little Havana Blues.*

Michael Sykes is the editor and publisher of Floating Island Publications and the proprietor of a bookshop, Great Basin Books, in Cedarville, California. His collection of poems is *From an Island in Time.*

Kyoko Uchida has had poems in *Phoebe, Prose Poem, Quarterly West,* and other journals. New work by her is forthcoming in *Shenandoah.* A translator, she lives in Brooklyn.

Samrat Upadhyay is from Kathmandu, Nepal. His work has appeared or is forthcoming in *Indiana Review, Chelsea,* and *North Dakota Quarterly.*

 Kevin Van Tighem is a native of Alberta who lives in Waterton Lakes National Park with his wife and three children. He has worked for more than two decades as a biologist and naturalist and is the author of six books and more than two hundred articles. His story in this issue is reprinted from his latest book, *Coming West: A Natural History of Home.*

Cedric Yamanaka has published short stories in local and national publications. His screenplay, *The Lemon Tree Billiards House,* won a Hawai'i International Film Festival award for best Hawai'i film. For over a decade, he has worked as a radio and television journalist.

Phyllis Young lives and works on O'ahu. In 1952 she spent six months in Japan, where her father was stationed in the u.s. Army.

 Jan Zwicky has published several books, including *Wittgenstein Elegies, The New Room,* and *Lyric Philosophy.* Her most recent collection is *Songs for Relinquishing the Earth.* A native of west central Alberta, she lives and works in Victoria, British Columbia. Her poem "Aspen in Wind" originally appeared in *Malahat Review.*

Fresh Tracks
Writing the Western Landscape

Pamela Banting, editor

A diverse gathering of over 40 writers, **Fresh Tracks** *is an entertaining and thoughtful exploration of how the western landscape influences all aspects of human life and creativity...* **Fresh Tracks** *offers an insightful exploration of our relationship to the natural world, an exploration whose importance continues to grow as we face the ecological and social concerns of the next century.* — QUILL & QUIRE

In words that are at once profound, humourous, earthy and sublime, some of Canada's finest writers use a variety of genres — creative non-fiction, essays, memoirs, short stories, poetry, song lyrics — to investigate landscape, animals and birds, ecology, and the human connection to place in the west.

Contributors include: Rudy Wiebe, Lorna Crozier, Di Brandt, Sharron Proulx-Turner, Guy Vanderhaeghe, Slim Davis, Sharon Butala, Karen Connolly and Gregory Scofield.

Pamela Banting teaches at the University of Calgary. She has previously published *Body, Inc.* (Turnstone, 1995) about translation poetics.

ISBN: 1-896095-42-9 • 320 pages • $21.95 CAN / $18.95 USA pb

POLESTAR
BOOK PUBLISHERS

Polestar Book Publishers
P.O. Box 5238, Station B, Victoria, BC V8R 6N4
email: polestar@direct.ca

Treat yourself. Treat a friend.

NEW LETTERS

"One of the best literary journals in this country."
Charles Simic, Pulitzer Prize for Poetry

New Letters quarterly has, for more than 60 years, published fiction, art, poetry and essays by the world's finest new and established writers, including Pulitzer Prize winners, National Book Award winners and Nobel Laureates.

"*New Letters* is one of the very few indispensable
literary magazines."
— Susan Fromberg Schaeffer, novelist

Often selected for *The Best American Poetry, The Best American Essays, Prize Stories: The O. Henry Awards, The Pushcart Prize Anthology* and many other honors. Join our family of subscribers.

Magazine subscription rates

Individuals:	$17 one year	Libraries:	$20 one year
	$28 two years		$34 two years
	$55 five years		$65 five years

New Letters, University of Missouri-Kansas City, Kansas City, MO 64110